Mathematics Education

Mathematics Education: exploring the culture of learning identifies some of the most significant issues in mathematics education today. Pulling together relevant articles from authors well known in their fields of study, the book addresses topical issues such as:

- Gender
- Equity
- Attitude
- Teacher belief and knowledge
- Community of practice
- Autonomy and agency
- Assessment
- Technology

The subject is dealt with in three parts: culture of the mathematics classroom; communication in mathematics classrooms; and pupils' and teachers' perceptions.

Students on postgraduate courses in mathematics education will find this book a valuable resource. Students on BEd and PGCE courses will also find this a useful source of reference as will teachers of mathematics, mentors and advisers.

Barbara Allen is Director of the Centre for Mathematics Education at The Open University and has written extensively on the subject of mathematics teaching.

Sue Johnston-Wilder is a Senior Lecturer at The Open University and has worked for many years developing materials to promote interest in mathematics teaching and learning.

Companion Volumes

The companion volumes in this series are:

Fundamental Constructs in Mathematics Education
Edited by: John Mason and Sue Johnston-Wilder

Researching Your Own Practice: the discipline of noticing
Author: John Mason

All of these books are part of a course: *Researching Mathematics Learning*, that is itself part of The Open University MA programme and part of the *Postgraduate Diploma in Mathematics Education* programme.

The Open University MA in Education

The Open University MA in Education is now firmly established as the most popular postgraduate degree for education professionals in Europe, with over 3,500 students registering each year. The MA in Education is designed particularly for those with experience of teaching, the advisory service, educational administration or allied fields.

Structure of the MA

The MA is a modular degree and students are therefore free to select from a range of options in the programme which best fits in with their interests and professional goals. Specialist lines in management and primary education and lifelong learning are also available. Study in The Open University's Advanced Diploma can also be counted towards the MA and successful study in the MA programme entitles students to apply for entry into The Open University Doctorate in Education programme.

OU Supported Open Learning

The MA in Education programme provides great flexibility. Students study at their own pace, in their own time, anywhere in the European Union. They receive specially prepared study materials supported by tutorials, thus offering the chance to work with other students.

The Graduate Diploma in Mathematics Education

The Graduate Diploma is a new modular diploma designed to meet the needs of graduates who wish to develop their understanding of teaching and learning mathematics. It is aimed at professionals in education who have an interest in mathematics including primary and secondary teachers, classroom assistants and parents who are providing home education.

The aims of the Graduate Diploma are to:

- develop the mathematical thinking of students;
- raise students' awareness of ways people learn mathematics;
- provide experience of different teaching approaches and the learning opportunities they afford;
- develop students' awareness of, and facility with, ICT in the learning and teaching of mathematics; and
- develop students' knowledge and understanding of the mathematics which underpins school mathematics.

How to apply

If you would like to register for one of these programmes, or simply to find out more information about available courses, please request the *Professional Development in Education* prospectus by writing to the Course Reservations Centre, PO Box 724, The Open University, Walton Hall, Milton Keynes MK7 6ZW, UK or, by phoning 0870 900 0304 (from the UK) or +44 870 900 0304 (from outside the UK). Details can also be viewed on our web page www.open.ac.uk.

Mathematics Education

Exploring the culture of learning

Edited by Barbara Allen and
Sue Johnston-Wilder

 RoutledgeFalmer
Taylor & Francis Group

LONDON AND NEW YORK

The Open
University

First published 2004 by RoutledgeFalmer
11 New Fetter Lane, London EC4P 4EE

Simultaneously published in the USA and Canada
by RoutledgeFalmer
29 West 35th Street, New York, NY 10001

RoutledgeFalmer is an imprint of the Taylor & Francis Group

©2004 The Open University

Typeset in Garamond by
Bookcraft Ltd, Stroud, Gloucestershire
Printed and bound in Great Britain by
MPG Books Ltd, Bodmin, Cornwall

British Library Cataloguing in Publication Data
A catalogue record for this book is available from the British Library

Libraty of Congress Cataloging in Publication Data
A catalog record has been requested

ISBN 0–415–32699–0 (hbk)
ISBN 0–415–32700–8 (pbk)

Contents

Figures

Tables

Sources

Chapter 1 Reproduced, with kind permission of the author, from a chapter originally published in Keitel, C. (ed.), *Social Justice and Mathematics Education*, pp. 45–58, Taylor & Francis (1998).

Chapter 2 Reproduced from an article originally published in *British Journal of Sociology of Education*, 11(3) pp. 241–56, Taylor & Francis (1990).

Chapter 3 Reproduced from a chapter originally published in Burton, L. (ed.), *Learning Mathematics: from hierarchies to networks*, pp. 232–45, Falmer Press (1999).

Chapter 4 Reproduced from an article originally published in *Educational Review*, 52(2) pp. 105–15, Taylor & Francis (1999).

Chapter 5 Reproduced from a chapter originally published in Filer, A. (ed.), *Assessment – Social Practice and Social Product*, pp. 87–109, RoutledgeFalmer (2000).

Chapter 6 Reproduced from a chapter originally published in Burton, L. (ed.), *Learning Mathematics: from hierarchies to networks*, pp. 36–61, Falmer Press (1999).

Chapter 7 Reproduced from a chapter originally published in Atweh, B. and Forgasz, H. (eds), *Socio-cultural Aspects of Mathematics Education: An International Perspective*, pp. 201–15, Lawrence Erlbaum (2000).

Chapter 8 Reproduced from an article originally published in *Proceedings of the British Society for Research in Mathematics Learning*, pp. 80–92, Institute of Education (1994).

Chapter 9 Reproduced from an article originally published in *For the Learning of Mathematics*, 21(3) pp. 2–8, FLM Publishing Association (2001).

Chapter 10 Reproduced from an article originally published in *For the Learning of Mathematics*, 21(1) pp. 33–9, FLM Publishing Association (2001).

Chapter 11 Reproduced from an article originally published in *Educational Studies in Mathematics*, 15(2) pp. 105–27, Taylor and Francis (1984).

Chapter 12 Reproduced from an article originally published in *British Educational Research Journal*, 23(5) pp. 575–95, Taylor & Francis (1997).

Chapter 13 Reproduced from an article originally published in *British Educational Research Journal*, 25(3) pp. 343–54, Taylor & Francis (1999).

Introduction

Issues in researching mathematics learning

Barbara Allen and Sue Johnston-Wilder

> Culture [...] shapes the minds of individuals [...]. Its individual expression inheres in *meaning making,* assigning meanings to things in different settings on particular occasions.
>
> (Bruner, 1996)

The purpose of this book is to bring together readings which explore the culture of learning in a mathematics classroom. These readings show how knowledge of this culture assists teachers and learners to improve the teaching and learning of mathematics and to address concerns of social justice and the need for equity.

Most educators and researchers assume that there are relationships between teachers' experience of and beliefs about mathematics, the classroom atmosphere they develop, the experience of learners in those classrooms and the resulting attainment in and attitude to mathematics. These are relationships that researchers try to demonstrate, and it is not easy. In recent years many researchers have become interested in the culture in mathematics classrooms. This is not purely a sociological stance as can be seen in the work of researchers such as Lave. In Lave's view the type of learning that occurs is significantly affected by the learning environment. The notion of *community of practice* (Lave and Wenger, 1991) has been very influential over recent years alongside the recognition of learning as being socially constructed and mediated through language (Vygotsky, 1978). In order for learners to take control over their own learning they need to be part of a community of practice in which the discourses and practices of that community are negotiated by all the participants. Within a community of practice, the main focus is on the negotiation of meaning rather than the acquisition and transmission of information (Wenger, 1998). The features of such a community include collaborative and cooperative working and the development of a shared discourse. This view of the classroom as a community of practice is very different from that of the panoptic space (Paechter, 2001) displayed in many English mathematics classrooms where pupils are under constant surveillance in terms of behaviour and learning.

The publication of this book comes at a time when schools in England and in many other countries are facing a critical shortage of mathematics teachers. In England this shortage is due to a failure to recruit and retain sufficient teachers of mathematics to meet the increased demands made by a 10 per cent increase in the school population from 1996 to 2002. A survey of teachers of secondary mathematics estimated that England was short of over 3,500 qualified mathematics teachers in 2002 (Johnston-Wilder *et al.*, 2003). It is worth noting that there are about 4100 new mathematics graduates per year in the UK (HESA, 2003). In this context, relying on new mathematics graduates as the source of people to fill training places is not an appropriate strategy.

Many researchers believe that the shortage of mathematics teachers will become worse before it becomes better. Since the introduction of AS level examinations, in England, in Year 12 there has been a reduction in both females and males studying mathematics at A level. This will inevitably lead to a reduction in the numbers going forward to study mathematics in higher education and a concomitant change in the numbers training specifically to be teachers of mathematics.

The problem of negative attitude towards mathematics continues in the population as a whole. Although it was researched heavily in the 1990s, and some solutions were found in the form of intervention studies, the disaffection of pupils with mathematics continues and some researchers (Pollard *et al.*, 2000) argue that the age at which pupils get turned off mathematics is falling. Pollard *et al.* (2000) found that primary school pupils had an instrumental view of mathematics and were unlikely to be intrinsically motivated. They suggested that:

> ... the structured pursuit of higher standards in English and Mathematics may be reducing the ability of many children to see themselves as self-motivating, independent problem solvers taking an intrinsic pleasure in learning and capable of reflecting on how and why they learn.
>
> (Pollard *et al.*, 2000, p. xiii)

This work of Pollard *et al.* was based in primary classrooms where the National Numeracy Strategy had been introduced and the format of the mathematics lesson in three parts had taken hold.

Initiatives such as the National Numeracy Strategy have had some impact on teachers' practice and have led to improved National Test results in some schools. But it seems that these changes are not necessarily having a positive impact on pupils' attitudes to mathematics. Some mathematics educators (Zevenbergen, Chapter 7) suggest that the changes instigated may have a deleterious effect on how some pupils view themselves as learners of mathematics.

Many researchers have moved away from a concern about how people learn mathematics and are more concerned with the conditions under which each individual can best learn. This generally involves recognition of the social nature of learning and the importance of collaborative and cooperative learning.

The research included in this book is indicative of a change from looking at teachers' perspectives to looking at those of pupils. The underlying reason for much of the research has remained the same: how can the learning environment be improved for pupils and their teachers? Some recent educational developments, that were thought to be productive, now appear to be inequitable and do not support the learning of all pupils. Many researchers are now looking at the inequities that exist in the education system, some of which have occurred as a result of changes in the curriculum and assessment. In order to do this there has been some shift from working with only teacher, to working with teacher and pupils and finally to working with pupils alone. This change is evidenced by the chapters in this book which show the various ways that researchers have tried to find out about teacher and pupil perspectives and how these can be used to improve the education system.

In the 1980s, there was a general interest in the effectiveness of teachers when researchers like Wragg and Wood (1984) wanted to know how pupils identified the characteristics of 'good' or 'bad' teachers. In these classrooms teachers were seen as central figures where changes in their behaviour and practice could have a positive impact on pupils' learning. However there were some like Meighan (1978) who viewed classrooms as places where the teacher was not the central figure. These researchers also felt that the views of pupils should be sought because the information they could give about their learning environment was generally untapped. There were some large-scale quantitative studies carried out, for example by Ruddock, Chaplain and Wallace (1996) who wanted to find out more about pupils' views of schooling. For some researchers there was still some caution about findings based only on the views of some of the participants in a learning environment.

> Most of the conclusions of this study have been based on students' perceptions of their schools and their teachers, which may not, of course, always accurately reflect life in school.
>
> (Keys and Fernandes, 1993, pp. 1–63)

Cooper and McIntyre's (1995) research found that a key issue for effective learning by pupils was the extent to which teachers shared control with the pupils on issues relating to lesson content and learning objectives. The move towards gaining pupil perspectives was supported by Ruddock, Chaplain and Wallace (1996) when they wrote that what pupils tell us:

> provides an important – perhaps the most important – foundation for thinking about ways of improving schools.
>
> (Ruddock, Chaplain and Wallace, 1996, p. 1)

Research by McCullum, Hargreaves and Gipps (2000) into pupils' view of learning found that pupils wanted a classroom that had a relaxed and happy atmosphere where they could ask the teacher for help without fear of ridicule. They also preferred mixed ability grouping because this gave them a range of people with whom they could discuss their work. It appears that these pupils were suggesting that they could like to be working in a collaborative community – a community of practice.

This book then is about the culture of the mathematics classroom and the research that has been done in that area over recent years. An underlying assumption is that classroom culture is mediated largely through communication and individual perception. Hence the book is structured in three sections:

- Section 1: Culture of the mathematics classroom
- Section 2: Communication in mathematics classrooms
- Section 3: Pupils' and teachers' perceptions

This book has been produced primarily for students studying the Open University course ME825 Researching Mathematics Learning and as such it contains articles that would be relevant to the work of practising teachers and advisers of mathematics at all phases. However, when selecting the articles the editors had a wider audience in mind, to include teacher educators, mathematics education researchers and those planning to become mathematics teachers. With this in mind the book can be used in a variety of ways. It is not envisaged that any reader would work their way through the book from start to finish. It is more likely that the reader will dip into the chapters that are of initial interest and then read more widely round the subject.

Before each section is a brief introduction to the chapters in that section. All the chapters except that by Barbara Allen have previously been published elsewhere. There is suggested further reading for each section. In addition you may wish to consider the following questions:

- What resonates with your own practice?
- Can you think of an example in your own experience that contradicts some of the findings?

References

Bruner, J. (1996). *The Culture of Education,* Harvard University Press, Cambridge, MA.

Cooper, P. and McIntyre, D. (1995). The crafts of the classroom: teachers' and students' accounts of the knowledge underpinning effective teaching and learning in classrooms. *Research Papers in Education,* 10(2), 181–216.

HESA. (2003). Qualifications obtained by and examination results of higher education students at higher education institutions in the United Kingdom for the academic year 2001/02, http://www.hesa.ac.uk/press/sfr61/sfr61.htm.

Johnston-Wilder, S., Thumpston, G., Brown, M., Allen, B., Burton, L. and Cooke, H. (2003). *Teachers of Mathematics: Their qualifications, training and recruitment,* The Open University, Milton Keynes.

Keys, W. and Fernandez, C. (1993). *What do students think about school?* A report for the National Commission on Education, NFER, Slough.

Lave, J. and Wenger, E. (1991). *Situated Learning: Legitimate Peripheral Participation,* Cambridge University Press.

McCullum, B., Hargreaves, E. and Gipps, C. (2000). Learning: The pupil's voice. *Cambridge Journal of Education,* 30(2), pp. 275–289.

Meighan, R. (1978). A pupils' eye view of teaching performance. *Educational Review,* 30, 125–137.

Paechter, C. (2001). Power, gender and curriculum. In C. Paechter, M. Preedy, D. Scott and J. Soler (eds) *Knowledge, Power and Learning,* Paul Chapman Publishing in association with The Open University.

Pollard, A. and Triggs, P. with Broadfoot, P., McNess, E. and Osborn, M. (2000). *Changing Policy and Practice in Primary Education,* Continuum, London.

Rudduck, J., Chaplain, R. and Wallace, G. (1996). *School Improvement: What Can Pupils Tell Us?* David Fulton Publishers Ltd, London.

Vygotsky, L. S. (1978). *Mind in Society*, Harvard University Press, Cambridge, MA.

Wenger, E. (1998). *Communities of Practice Learning Meaning and Identity*, Cambridge University Press.

Wragg, E. C. and Wood, E. K. (1984). Pupil appraisals of teaching. In E.C. Wragg (ed.) *Classroom Teaching Skills,* Croom Helm, London, pp. 79–96.

Section 1

Culture of the mathematics classroom – including equity and social justice

Each of the authors included in Section 1 is arguing about the importance of the creation of a classroom culture that supports effective learning. Underlying their work is the recognition that the values of the teacher impact upon the classroom but they do not assume that this is a simple system of cause and effect. The authors all see mathematics as a personal construction but are not necessarily agreed on the nature of mathematics.

If a classroom has a culture that values learners creating their own mathematics and becoming authors of mathematics, then the learners are more likely to become positioned as successful learners of mathematics. For this to happen you need a community of learners working together collaboratively and creatively. There needs to be a shift in the way some teachers view the nature of mathematics and an examination of the value they place on assessment and target setting. For a community of practice to flourish learners need to develop personal autonomy and be able to recognise for themselves that they are creating and understanding mathematics.

The first chapter by Paul Ernest focuses on the public image of mathematics. He is concerned that the public image of mathematics as cold, abstract and inhuman has an impact on the recruitment of students into higher mathematics.

Ernest highlights the importance of changing the negative public image of mathematics and challenges the general acceptance of an 'I can't do maths' culture. He looks at teacher philosophy and values and argues that it is the values that have most impact on the image of mathematics in the classroom. This image of mathematics also impacts on the way learners position themselves as successful or unsuccessful. In a classroom where a learner is expected to develop techniques and skills with single correct answers to questions it is not unusual for them to see themselves as an unsuccessful learner of mathematics or indeed to become mathephobic (Buxton, 1981).

He argues that school mathematics is not a subset of the discipline of mathematics but a different subject made up of number, algebra, measure and geometry and not studied for its own sake. But, even so, he believes mathematics should be humanised, for utilitarian and social reasons.

Andrew Pollard's research (Chapter 2) was not carried out in mathematics classrooms but has been included here because the findings are relevant for mathematics teachers. It is common for research about pupils' views to be carried out across subjects rather than in a particular subject. Pollard argues that researchers should cooperate across the disciplinary boundaries of psychology and sociology, in a joint effort to look at learning in schools. One of his concerns, like many others in this book, is that little attention has been given to the effect that the new curriculum in the UK has had on learners.

Pollard looks at the changes in research into effective teaching practice over 30 years. That interest has gone from looking at teaching styles, to examining opportunities to learn, to considering the quality of tasks. He is also interested in pupils' coping strategies and looks at those in subsequent articles – the focus here being on identity and learning. He looks at the relationship between self and others and the importance of social context in the formation of meaning – that is all part of developing a model of learning and identity. The identity of the learner is formed when they have a view of themselves as able to do mathematics or not. He demonstrates the importance of the social context in which learning takes place.

The article by Hilary Povey and colleagues (Chapter 3) takes the reader beyond Pollard to look at people in terms of identity and their responses to the classroom situation. The writers explore the idea of learners author/ing their own learning and how they come to know mathematics.

The article builds on Povey's work with mathematics teachers with the main thrust being about discursive practices and how they can liberate a learner. The authors argue that when thinking of mathematics as a narrative rather than a fixed form, a learner can create their own narrative in the same way you would a story. Thinking of mathematics in this way enables the learner to have ownership and author/ship over their own learning thus giving greater autonomy to the learners. But both teacher and learners need to create a supportive and collaborative classroom environment in order for this to happen. Many current classrooms do not encourage autonomy because pupils are required to produce responses that are authored by another and not themselves.

Anne Watson's article (Chapter 4) is concerned with a particular aspect of classroom culture, that of teachers' informal assessment of students' mathematics. She believes that the sort of assessment used by teachers reflects their values and, like Ernest, believes this has an impact on the classroom culture. Watson's research with 30 UK mathematics teachers resulted in the identification of some differences in their practices that could lead to inequity in the classroom. She concludes that the teachers' practices showed six contrasting beliefs and perceptions about assessment and that teachers could be positioned differently within each of these. It is these different forms of assessment that Watson believes could result in social inequity and contribute to a discriminatory curriculum.

Cooper and Dunne (Chapter 5) are particularly interested in the effects of social class on pupils' learning. In this article they are concerned with those tasks in the National Curriculum tests that are termed realistic. Cooper and Dunne found that social class and gender differences were greater when 'realistic' tasks were used. So they argue that pupils from lower social classes are more likely to get better results on a task that is not 'realistic' but is abstract. The reason for this is in part because they do not have the cultural experience or 'linguistic habitus' (Zevenbergen, Chapter 7) to understand the game of answering realistic questions. These questions are not part of the home experience and discourse of the lower social class pupils and therefore the middle class pupils are advantaged.

This is of concern at a time when some colleagues are arguing that there is a need for more realistic tasks in the National Curriculum tests.

Goos, Galbraith and Renshaw's research programme (Chapter 6) is based on sociocultural theory in which they are looking at the interactive and communicative conditions for learning. For them the idea of community is central where gaining knowledge is seen as the process of coming to know mathematics. In this community everyone is seen as having a voice and learners are author of their own mathematics. Their research shows that the roles of both teacher and learners need to change if the notion of a 'community of practice' is to take hold effectively.

Goos and colleagues found Vygotsky's notion of a Zone of Proximal Development *maths recov.* (ZPD) was a part-useful idea to work on as it highlighted the way in which pupils support each other so they are not fully reliant on the teacher. However, they also found that a teacher who does not have a good grasp of mathematics cannot see the links in order to help scaffold the pupils' learning. A combination of mathematics and pedagogic knowledge is needed by teachers in the form of long-term continuing professional development so that mathematics classrooms may become communities of learners.

Further reading

Buxton, L. (1981). *Do You Panic About Maths?* Heinemann, London.

Cooper, B. (1998). Using Bernstein and Bourdieu to understand children's difficulties with 'realistic' mathematics testing: An exploratory study. *International Journal of Qualitative Studies in Education,* 11(4), 511–532.

Murphy, P. and Gipps, C. (eds) (1996). *Equity in the Classroom: Towards an effective pedagogy for girls and boys,* RoutledgeFalmer.

Nickson, M. (1992). The culture of the mathematics classroom: an unknown quantity. In D. A. Grouws (ed.) *Handbook of Research on Mathematics Teaching and Learning,* Macmillan, New York, 100–114.

1   Images of mathematics, values and gender

A philosophical perspective

Paul Ernest

Abstract

This paper describes the widespread public image of mathematics as cold, abstract and inhuman, and relates it to absolutist philosophies of mathematics. It is argued that this image is consistent with 'separated' values (Gilligan, 1982) which help to make mathematics a 'critical filter' denying access to many areas of study and to fulfilling professional occupations, especially for women in anglophone western countries. In contrast, an opposing humanised image of mathematics, consistent with 'connected' values, finds academic support in recent fallibilist philosophies of mathematics. It is argued that although these two philosophical positions have a major impact on the ethos of mathematics classrooms, there is no direct logical connection. It is concluded instead that the values realised in the classroom are probably the dominant factor in determining the learner's image and appreciation of mathematics (and hence, indirectly, that of society).

A widespread public image of mathematics is that it is difficult, cold, abstract, theoretical, ultra-rational, but important and largely masculine. It also has the image of being remote and inaccessible to all but a few super-intelligent beings with 'mathematical minds'. Many persons operating at high levels of competency in numeracy, graphicacy and computeracy in their professional life in the UK still say 'I'm no good at mathematics, I never could do it'. In contrast to the shame associated with illiteracy, innumeracy is almost a matter of pride amongst educated persons in western anglophone countries.

In fact, many such persons are not innumerate at all, and it is school or academic mathematics, not everyday mathematics, that they feel they cannot do. Numeracy, contextual mathematics, even ethnomathematics are perceived to be quite distinct from school/academic mathematics, and the latter is understood to be 'real' mathematics. The popular image of mathematics sets it apart from daily concerns of the public, despite the many social applications of mathematics referred to daily in the mass media, from sports and weather to economic and social indicators. Thus the widespread public image of mathematics is largely a negative and remote one, alien to many persons' professional and personal concerns and their self-perceived abilities.

For many people the image of mathematics is associated with anxiety and failure. When Brigid Sewell was gathering data on adult numeracy for the Cockcroft Inquiry (1982), she asked a sample of adults on the street if they would answer some questions. Half of them refused to answer further questions when they understood it was about mathematics, suggesting negative attitudes. Extremely negative attitudes such as 'mathephobia' (Maxwell, 1989) probably only occur in a small minority in western societies, and may not be significant at all in other countries. Nevertheless it is an important phenomenon, and I have never heard of an equivalent 'literaphobia', although literacy is at least as important as numeracy.

The public image of mathematics is an important issue of concern for mathematics education. It is particularly important because of its social significance. Mathematics serves as a 'critical filter' controlling access to many areas of advanced study and better paid and more fulfilling professional occupations (Sells, 1973). This particularly concerns those occupations involving scientific and technological skills, but also extends far beyond this domain to many other occupations, including education, the caring professions and financial services. In addition, many adults leaving full-time education have not been empowered by their mathematics education as mathematically-literate citizens who are able to exercise independent critical judgements with regard to the mathematical underpinnings of crucial social and political decision-making.

If the image of mathematics is an unnecessary obstacle which blocks popular access to it, as well as failing to enable full participation in modern democratic society, then it is a great social evil. Of course, changing the image alone does little to address the problem. Instead the nature of the populace's encounters with mathematics needs to be changed, to be humanised. A semiotic analysis of mathematical language views much of it as coercive (Rotman, 1993). Traditional classroom tasks instruct the learner to carry out certain symbolic procedures; to do, not to think; to become an automaton, not an independent exerciser of critical judgement. This plays a key role in dehumanising mathematics and the learner. Resistance may involve the adoption of a negative stance towards mathematics. This analysis is the subject of my current research and I shall not develop it here. Instead, in this paper I explore how the conceptions or philosophies of mathematics which underpin and shape classroom experiences, coupled with the associated values of the teacher and the classroom, play a key role in determining the image of mathematics that the learner constructs for her/himself.

Absolutist philosophies of mathematics

The negative popular image of mathematics fits with a range of perspectives in the philosophy of mathematics which are termed 'absolutist'. These view mathematics as an objective, absolute, certain and incorrigible body of knowledge, which rests on the firm foundations of deductive logic. Among twentieth-century perspectives in the philosophy of mathematics, Logicism, Formalism, and to some extent Intuitionism and Platonism, may be said to be absolutist in this way (Ernest, 1991).

What must be emphasised is that absolutist philosophies of mathematics are not concerned to describe mathematics or mathematical knowledge. They are concerned with the epistemological project of providing rigorous systems to warrant mathematical knowledge absolutely (following the earlier crisis in the foundations of mathematics arising from the introduction of Cantor's infinite set theory). Many of the claims of absolutism in its various forms follow from its identification with rigid logical structure introduced for these epistemological purposes. Thus according to absolutism mathematical knowledge is timeless, although we may discover new theories and truths to add; it is superhuman and ahistorical, for the history of mathematics is irrelevant to the nature and justification of mathematical knowledge; it is pure isolated knowledge, which happens to be useful because of its universal validity; it is value-free and culture-free, for the same reason.

The outcome therefore is a philosophically sanctioned image of mathematics as rigid, fixed, logical, absolute, inhuman, cold, objective, pure, abstract, remote and ultra-rational, in short, the negative public image described above. If this is how many philosophers, mathematicians and teachers view their subject, small wonder that it is also the image communicated to the public. In my view, the philosophy of mathematics is at least partly to blame, because of its twentieth-century obsession with epistemological foundationalism.

An absolutist view may be communicated in school by giving students mainly unrelated routine mathematical tasks which involve the application of learnt procedures, and by stressing that every task has a unique, fixed and objectively right answer, coupled with disapproval and criticism of any failure to achieve this answer. This may not be what the mathematician recognises as mathematics, but a result is nevertheless an absolutist conception of the subject (Buerk, 1982). In some cases the outcome is also mathephobia (Buxton, 1981).

School mathematics versus mathematicians' mathematics

It would appear that the public image of mathematics is in many respects correct. However, some qualifications to this conclusion should be considered. Mathematics as a discipline (what professional mathematicians understand as mathematics) and school mathematics should be distinguished. School mathematics is not just a subset of the discipline of mathematics. It should instead be regarded as a different subject, comprising such elementary topics as number, measurement, algebra, geometry, statistics, probability, computing and problem-solving. All of these topics are studied not for their own sake but for their practical and cross-curricular applications, and as a basis for further study. Much of school mathematics is closer in content to numeracy, to contextual mathematics, to the mathematics of commerce and industry, than to the discipline of mathematics itself. The main concern of pure mathematics with axiomatic systems and the rigorous proof of theorems, for example, is largely irrelevant to school mathematics. Given this discrepancy, there is no need for school mathematics to communicate the negative image of mathematics described above. In fact the worldwide consensus of mathematics educators is that school mathematics must counter that image, and offer instead something that is personally engaging, and evidently useful or motivating in some other way, if it is to fulfil its social functions (NCTM, 1989; Howson and Wilson, 1986; Skovsmose, 1994). Mathematicians' views of mathematics should be considered as irrelevant to school mathematics, which should be humanised for purely utilitarian and social reasons (i.e. to better mathematically educate the public) irrespective of any views of the so-called 'true nature' of mathematics. However the power of mathematicians in moulding the mathematics curriculum must not be overlooked, and through the exercise of this power their images of the subject come into play. In part this is direct, through the selection of both form and content for national curricula in mathematics. In part this is mediated through the teaching of future mathematics educators, curriculum developers and teachers, i.e. communicating the culture of (academic) mathematics to those involved in the practice of mathematics education.

Second, there is a growing body of opinion that the absolutist philosophies of mathematics constitute a cul-de-sac, being based on the false hope of providing absolute and eternally incorrigible foundations for mathematical knowledge. Due to a range of profound philosophical and technical problems, including Gödel's incompleteness theorems, such foundations have not, and most would say cannot be provided (Davis and Hersh, 1980; Ernest, 1991; Kitcher, 1983; Lakatos, 1976; Tiles, 1991; Tymoczko, 1986). This 'loss of certainty' (Kline, 1980) does not represent a loss of knowledge. Just as in modern physics where general relativity and quantum uncertainty indicate the boundaries of current epistemology, so too the fallibilistic bounds of mathematical knowing represent an increase in meta-knowledge. Mathematical proofs remain the most certain warrants for knowledge in the possession of humanity. But we need to acknowledge that proofs vary in strength as knowledge warrants and not reify them into something timeless and absolute. For illustration, consider only the controversy over Andrew Wiles's proof of the Fermat Conjecture.

Third, in the past few decades a new wave of 'fallibilist' philosophies of mathematics have been gaining ground, and these propose a different and opposing image of mathematics as human, corrigible, historical and changing.

Fallibilist philosophies of mathematics

Kitcher and Aspray (1988) have described a 'maverick' tradition in the philosophy of mathematics which emphasises the practice of, and human side of mathematics. This position has been termed quasi-empiricist and fallibilist, and is associated with constructivist and post-modernist thought in education (Glasersfeld, 1995), philosophy (Rorty, 1979), and the social sciences (Restivo, 1992). A growing number of modern philosophers of mathematics and mathematicians espouse fallibilist views of mathematics (see Ernest, 1994b, and above).

Fallibilism views mathematics as the outcome of social processes. Mathematical knowledge is understood to be fallible and eternally open to revision, both in terms of its proofs and its concepts. Consequently this view embraces as legitimate philosophical concerns the practices of mathematicians, its history and applications, the place of mathematics in human culture, including issues of values and education – in short, it fully admits the human face and basis of mathematics. The fallibilist view does not reject the role of structure in mathematics. Rather it rejects the notion that there is a unique, fixed and permanently enduring hierarchical structure. Instead it accepts the view that mathematics is made up of many overlapping structures. These, over the course of history, grow, collapse, and then grow anew like icebergs in the Arctic seas or like trees in a forest (Steen, 1988).

Fallibilism rejects the absolutist image of mathematics described above as a misrepresentation. It claims instead that mathematics has both a front and a back (Hersh, 1988). In the front, the public are served perfect mathematical dishes, like in a gourmet restaurant. Here the impression of absolute mathematics is preserved, but in the back, mathematicians cook up new knowledge amid mess, chaos and all the inescapably associated features of human striving. Fallibilism admits both of these realms: the processes *and* the products of mathematics need to be considered an essential part of the discipline. For accuracy the false image of perfection must be dropped (Davis, 1972).

One of the innovations associated with a fallibilist view of mathematics is a reconceptualised view of the nature of mathematics. It is no longer seen as defined by a body of pure and abstract knowledge which exists in a superhuman, objective realm (the World 3 of Popper, 1979). Instead mathematics is associated with sets of social practices, each with its history, persons, institutions and social locations, symbolic forms, purposes and power relations. Thus academic research mathematics is one such practice (or rather a multiplicity of shifting, interconnected practices). Likewise each of ethnomathematics and school mathematics is a distinct set of such practices. They are intimately bound up together, because the symbolic productions of one practice are recontextualised and reproduced in another (Dowling, 1988).

It is important to distinguish between a fallibilist (or absolutist) epistemology of mathematics, and a fallibilist (or absolutist) account of the nature of mathematics. The former is a strictly defined philosophical position concerning the epistemological foundation and justification of mathematical knowledge. The latter is a looser descriptive account of mathematics in a broader sense. Usually these are linked, but strictly speaking, it is possible for an epistemological absolutist to promote aspects of a fallibilist view of the nature of mathematics: including, for example such views as: mathematicians are liable to error and publish flawed proofs, humans can discover mathematical knowledge through a variety of means, the concepts of mathematics are historical constructs (but its truths are objective), a humanised approach to the teaching and learning of mathematics is advisable, etc. Likewise, an epistemological fallibilist might argue that although mathematical knowledge is a contingent social construction, so long as it remains accepted by the mathematical community it is fixed and should be transmitted to learners in this way, and that questions of school mathematics are uniquely decidable as right or wrong with reference to its conventional corpus of knowledge. My argument is however that there is a strong analogy between epistemological absolutism (EA), absolutist views of the nature of mathematics (AV), and the cold, objectivist popular image of mathematics (OIM), but not a logically necessary connection. The forms of argument deployed, which are based on these links by analogy, include the double implication: EA ⟹ AV ⟹ OIM, used to support a fallibilist image (by reducing absolutism to absurdity). Another argument (which is logically equivalent) is that if mathematics is portrayed as fallible, humanly constructed, value-laden and context bound, then Not-OIM ⟹ Not-AV ⟹ Not-EA, i.e. mathematical knowledge is not objective and founded absolutely on logic. This is an absurdity from the epistemological absolutist perspective, and is used to attack fallibilism. My claim is that neither argument is logically valid, because the constituent implications are not correct. I shall return to the issue of what can be inferred from a philosophy of mathematics below.

Images of mathematics in school

Two philosophical views of mathematics have been described. Which of them reflects the image of mathematics in school? It must be said that the experience many learners have from their years of schooling confirms the absolutist image of mathematics as cold, absolute and inhuman. It is widespread for teachers and others and the experience of learning itself to confirm this view. Such an image is often (but not always) associated with negative attitudes to mathematics. A counter-example arose in my research on student teachers' attitudes and beliefs about mathematics. I found a subgroup of mathematics specialists who combined absolutist conceptions of the subject with very positive attitudes to mathematics and its teaching. However amongst non-mathematics-specialist future primary school teachers I found a loose correlation between fallibilist conceptions and positive attitudes to mathematics and its teaching (Ernest, 1988, 1989b). Thus the connections even just between beliefs and attitudes to mathematics are complex and multifaceted.

Research on children's attitudes towards mathematics in the past two decades shows fairly widespread liking of the school subject, certainly in the years of elementary schooling (Assessment of Performance Unit, 1985). In the later years of schooling attitudes in general become more neutral, although extreme negative attitudes are relatively rare. Presumably this downturn in attitudes is due to such things as adolescence, peer-attitudes, the impact of competitive examinations, not to mention the image of mathematics conveyed in and out of school.

However, the image of mathematics communicated in many enlightened schools and colleges is not the absolutist one and certainly does not have to be that way anywhere. Influential inquiries into the teaching of mathematics have propounded humanised and anti-absolutist (if not wholeheartedly fallibilist) views of school mathematics (Cockcroft, 1982; NCTM, 1980, 1989; NCC, 1989). The weight of informed educational opinion has likewise supported the progressive reform of mathematics in line with such views, for over a decade. Recently (1995) there has been a backlash from a group of mathematicians who claim that standards of mathematics students on entry to university has declined, and that this has been caused by progressives in mathematics education rejecting absolutism and promoting constructivism and investigative mathematics (Barnard and Saunders, 1994). Their observation that the competences of new entrants to mathematics degrees in the UK are declining may well be correct. However, there is no evidence to support the imputed cause for this, which might result from shifts in the school mathematics curriculum and assessment system, imposed by government. However a major factor is likely to be the fact that although an increasing number of students take A level exams in the UK at age 18, the number taking A level mathematics declines annually in absolute terms, and those who do succeed at it may be opting for medicine, economics, computer science, etc. The number opting for a mathematics degree course declines annually. So mathematicians may be having to recruit from the lower strata of a shrinking pool of applicants. Is this another effect of the society-wide negative image of mathematics?

Mathematics, values and gender

An important issue is that of the controversial relationship between mathematics and values. What can be asserted is that the popular image of mathematics is undoubtedly value-laden. This raises the question of whether there is any hidden agenda behind the widespread popular absolutist image of mathematics. There is a radical view that the kind of popular image of mathematics described above serves conservative interests in the mathematics community and in society in general. For if mathematics is viewed as difficult, cold, abstract, ultra-rational, important and largely masculine, then it offers access most easily to those who feel a sense of ownership of mathematics, of the associated values of western culture and of the educational system in general. These favour males, the middle classes, and white ethnic majorities (Walkerdine, 1988), at least in anglophone countries such as Australia, the USA, Canada and the UK. My remarks about mathematics, values and gender are restricted to these countries, and may well not apply to Latin or other Mediterranean countries like Cyprus. The problem seems to be more severe in Anglo-Saxon countries than in some others. For example, according to G. Greer 'there are [proportionately] five times as many female scientists in Latin American countries as there are in Anglo-Saxon' (Pile, 1993, p. 19).

For countries such as these the argument runs that the popular image of mathematics sustains the privileges of advantaged groups by favouring their entry, and putting an obstacle in the way of non-members' entry into higher education and professional occupations, especially where the sciences and technology are involved. How can this work? I shall offer a partial account of the relation between mathematics, values and gender.

First of all, much of the research on girls or females and mathematics concerns the problems caused by the stereotypical perceptions of mathematics as a male domain (Burton, 1986; Walkerdine, 1988; Walkerdine *et al.*, 1989). Gilligan (1982) has offered a theory of the gendered nature of values. According to this theory it is possible to distinguish stereotypically feminine values, which Gilligan terms 'connected', from stereotypically masculine values which she terms 'separated'. For each of these sets of values there is a cluster of associated descriptors. The 'connected' position is based on and valorises relationships, connections, empathy, caring, feelings and intuition, and tends to be holistic and human-centred in its concerns. The 'separated' position valorises rules, abstraction, objectification, impersonality, lack of feelings, dispassionate reason and analysis, and tends to be atomistic and thing-centred in focus. Gilligan's theory involves a series of stages of moral development based on the ethic of care (connection) which she contrasts with Kohlberg's (1969) theory of moral development based on justice, characterised as separation.

This theory must be treated with caution on a number of counts. First of all, it is not the case that separated values are men's values and connected values are those of women. They can be described as stereotypically masculine and feminine values, respectively. But every human being has both a masculine and feminine component to their nature. We are one species and male/female differences are not as profound as our commonalities.

Second, reviews of empirical evidence do not support any easy dichotomisation of male and female values. Bradbeck (1983) argues that differences in ethical views are much greater within than across sexes, based on a review of the published studies. Critical reviews of the evidence in Larrabee (1993) suggests that there are significant differences by late adolescence and adulthood, provided that the basis for moral reasoning, and not just Kohlberg's stages are considered. Indicative is Hoffman's (1977) finding that girls are more likely to be empathetic than boys in exhibiting emotional reactions to another's feelings.

Although both men and women have both a masculine and feminine side, the separated stereotypically masculine values have come to dominate many of the institutions and structures in western society, including mathematics and science, and men have been encouraged to develop and express these values as overriding parts of their identity. In the West separated values originate culturally with male, white, ruling or dominant classes, and they exclude many – perhaps most – human beings who often feel that mathematics is cold, remote, hard, uncaring, rejecting, neutral, unfeeling, impersonal, empty, inhuman, absolute, objective, rule-driven, perfectly rational, male, mechanical, soulless, dead, fixed and hierarchical.

Now the argument runs that because these separated values and mathematics are identified together in western culture, mathematics is identified as a stereotypically masculine domain, and as antithetical to the cultural stereotypes of femininity.

A number of researchers have offered models of how these values impact differentially on women, including Burton (1986), Fennema (1985), Walkerdine (1988), Walkerdine *et al.* (1989) and Ernest (1991). One of the most powerful models is due to Isaacson (1989) who coordinates a number of different factors including both in-school and out-of-school experiences which are mediated by their influence on girls' or women's belief systems. Central to her account are the terms 'double conformity' and 'coercive inducement'. Double conformity is a concept due to Delamont (1978). It describes the dilemma of a situation where there are two mutually conflicting sets of standards or expectations to which to conform. Since mathematics is stereotypically male, conforming to mathematical standards conflicts with standards of femininity. This, at its simplest, means that women must choose to be feminine or choose to be successful at mathematics. If they opt for both, they have to live with the contradiction Mathematics ≠ Feminine.

Coercive inducement is a way of describing the social pressures for women to conform with the stereotype of femininity. Women are rewarded for choosing the path of conventional femininity by social approval on all sides (from fathers, mothers, peers, boys, teachers, society, etc.). To reject this path is to give up very considerable rewards and inducements. Since approval is something widely craved, the inducements are coercive. Girls are 'forced' by needs to succumb to the overwhelming pressures and inducements to accept the conventional feminine role.

Isaacson argues that both double conformity and coercive inducement impact strongly on the girl or woman's internalised belief system, which includes the nature of femininity and a 'woman's role', and their relation with her identity as a gendered person (a woman). This belief system plays a key role in how the woman/girl views herself with regard to mathematics and performs as a learner of mathematics.

Figure 1.1 illustrates how such values, stereotypes and beliefs end up as a vicious cycle denying women equal opportunities. Figure 1.1 illustrates that girls' and women's lower participation rate in mathematics contributes to unequal opportunities

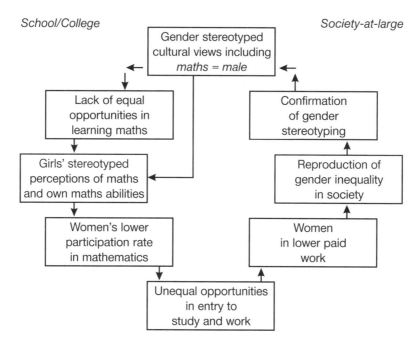

Figure 1.1 The reproductive cycle of gender inequality in mathematics education

in study and work (the 'critical filter' of Sells, 1973), leading to women in lower paid jobs. This reproduces gender inequality in society, reinforces stereotyping, and establishes a 'regime of truth' (Foucault, 1980) in which views such as *math = male, math feminine* and *female = inferior* are confirmed and sustained as 'lived truths'. The outcome is a lack of equal opportunities in school mathematics and lowered expectations for girls, with some girls' successes at mathematics being discounted (Walkerdine *et al.*, 1989). Girls internalise these stereotypes and myths, and the outcome is lower attainment and participation in mathematics, completing the vicious cycle. Only if every link in the circle is attacked can the reproductive cycle of gender inequality be broken. A hopeful sign is that during compulsory schooling girls have been catching up. In 1994 for the first time in the UK they outperformed boys in mathematics examinations at age 16. However, disproportionately few continue with mathematics afterwards, so the problem remains.

Philosophies of mathematics, values and their relation to teaching

Drawing together the disparate threads in the above account it is clear that there is, first of all, a strong parallel between the absolutist conception of mathematics, the negative popular view of mathematics, and the set of values described by Gilligan (1982) as separated. Likewise, a second parallel exists between the fallibilist conception of mathematics, the connected values described by Gilligan (1982) and the humanistic image of mathematics promoted by modern progressive mathematics education as accessible, personally relevant and creative (Cockcroft, 1982; NCTM, 1989).

The second parallel can be used to improve accessibility and the public image of mathematics. But the analysis cannot stop here. For the absolutist image of mathematics is precisely what attracts some persons to it. I described above how this was the case with some student teachers. Likewise, many mathematicians love mathematics just for its absolutist features. It is both consistent and common for teachers and mathematicians to hold an absolutist view of mathematics as neutral and value free, but to regard mathematics teaching as necessitating the adoption of humanistic, connected values. This raises the issue of the relationship between philosophies of mathematics, values and teaching.

A widely accepted position is that 'All mathematical pedagogy, even if scarcely coherent, rests on a philosophy of mathematics' (Thom, 1973, p. 204). Other articulations stress both that teaching approaches in mathematics incorporate assumptions about the nature of mathematics, and that any philosophy of mathematics has classroom consequences (Hersh, 1979; Steiner, 1987). Empirical research (e.g. Cooney, 1988) has confirmed claims that 'teachers' views, beliefs and preferences about mathematics do influence their instructional practice' (Thompson, 1984, p. 125). Thus it may be argued that any philosophy of mathematics (including personal philosophies) has many educational and pedagogical consequences when embodied in teachers' beliefs, curriculum developments, or examination systems. Elsewhere I have argued that teachers' personal philosophies of mathematics, understood as part of their overall epistemological and ethical framework, impact on their espoused conceptions of teaching and learning mathematics. These in turn, subject to the constraints and opportunities of the social context of practice, give rise to the realised theories of learning mathematics, teaching mathematics, and the related use of mathematical texts and curriculum materials in the classroom (Ernest, 1989c). Such a model is partially validated by empirical work.

However classroom consequences are not in general strictly logical implications of a philosophy, and additional values, aims and other assumptions are required to reach such conclusions (Ernest 1991, 1994a). Because the link is not one of logical implication, it is theoretically possible to consistently associate a philosophy of mathematics with almost any educational practice or approach. Both a neo-behaviourist or cognitivist (such as Ausubel, 1968) and a radical constructivist (such as Glasersfeld, 1995) may be concerned to ascertain what a child knows before commencing teaching, despite having diametrically opposite epistemologies (absolutist and fallibilist, respectively). Likewise a traditional purist mathematician and a social constructivist may both favour a multicultural approach to mathematics, but for different reasons (the former perhaps to humanise mathematics, the latter to show it as the social construction of all of humanity for social justice reasons).

Although there is no logical necessity for, say, a transmission-style pedagogy to be associated with an absolutist, objectivist epistemology and philosophy of mathematics, such associations often are the case (Ernest, 1988, 1991). This is presumably due to the resonances and sympathies between different aspects of a person's philosophy, ideology, values and belief-systems. These form links and associations and

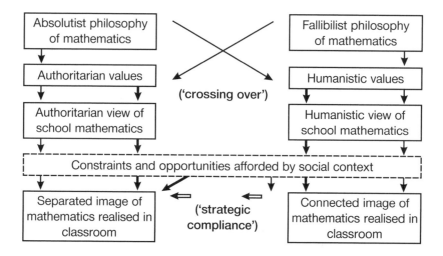

Figure 1.2 The simplified relations between personal philosophies of mathematics, values and classroom images of mathematics

become restructured in moves towards maximum coherence and consistency, and ultimately towards integration of the personality. (Of course compartmentalisation and 'splitting' are also possible.)

A further simplified model may be conjectured which suggests that the value-position of a teacher, curriculum development or school plays a vital role in mediating between personal philosophies of mathematics, and the image of mathematics communicated in the classroom. Figure 1.2 shows how an absolutist philosophy of mathematics combined with separated, thing-centred or authoritarian values can give rise to an authoritarian view of school mathematics.

This, subject to the constraints and opportunities afforded by social context of schooling, often results in a separated classroom image of mathematics. Likewise, a fallibilist philosophy of mathematics combined with connected, person-centred and humanistic values can give rise to a humanistic view of school mathematics. Subject to the same constraints, this can result in a connected classroom image of mathematics. These two possible sets of relations are shown by bold vertical arrows. They represent the most straightforward relationships between philosophies, values and classroom images of mathematics.

The figure also illustrates 'crossing over': how an absolutist philosophy of mathematics if combined with connected, humanistic values can give rise to a humanistic view of school mathematics. This, subject to social constraints, may be realised as a connected classroom image of mathematics. A deep commitment to the ideals of progressive mathematics education can and frequently does coexist with a belief in the objectivity and neutrality of mathematics, especially amongst mathematics teachers and educators. Fallibilism has no monopoly on this. In cases like these, connected values are often associated with education and the conception of *school* mathematics, rather than with *academic* (mathematicians') mathematics. This is illustrated in the figure by the thin black arrows.

It is theoretically possible that a fallibilist philosophy of mathematics can combine with separated values, resulting in an authoritarian view of school mathematics. This, subject to contextual constraints and opportunities, can give rise to a separated image of mathematics realised in the classroom. This is shown by the outline arrows, and is probably infrequent, because of the common association of fallibilism with progressive pedagogical views in the mathematics education community.

Finally, it is possible for the various constraints of the social context of schooling to be so powerful that a teacher with humanistic values and a humanistic view of school mathematics is nevertheless forced into 'strategic compliance' (Lacey, 1977), so that the image of mathematics realised in the classroom is a separated one. This may be a temporary consequence of contextual constraints, but if permanent, leads to tensions and stress. This state of affairs is indicated in the diagram by the bold and thin arrows deviating left towards a separated classroom image under the impact of the social context. These arrows may originate with either an absolutist philosophy (thin arrows), or a fallibilist philosophy (bold arrows), but in both cases they cross over. Empirical research has confirmed that teachers with very distinct personal philosophies of mathematics (absolutist and fallibilist) have been constrained by the social context of schooling to teach in a traditional, separated way (Lerman, 1986).

Much work in the philosophy of mathematics education pertains to exploring the link between the philosophies of mathematics implicit in teachers' beliefs, in texts and the mathematics curriculum, in systems and practices of mathematical assessment and in mathematics classroom practices and ethos, and the results with learners. There is a growing literature base, especially on teachers' beliefs, images of mathematics and related attitudes (Ernest, 1988, 1989a, 1989b, 1989c, 1991; Hoyles, 1992; Lerman, 1986). A few researchers have looked at students' images too (Hoyles, 1982; Kouba and McDonald, 1987, 1991). Whilst much progress has been made, much work remains to be done in the area, and it is clear that the relationships are complex and non-deterministic.

Conclusion

I have sketched a series of dichotomies: traditional versus humanistic public images of mathematics, absolutist versus fallibilist philosophies of mathematics, separated versus connected sets of values, mathematics classrooms promoting separated versus connected images of mathematics. There have been two main threads of argument. First, that these dichotomies are all to some extent parallel, so that traditional cold images of mathematics, absolutist philosophies of mathematics, separated values, and mathematics classrooms with a separated image of mathematics all work together and reinforce each other. Presumably the widespread negative public images of mathematics are the outcome of what I termed a separated classroom image of mathematics. Similarly positive, inviting public images of mathematics, fallibilist philosophies of mathematics, connected values, and classrooms promoting a connected image of mathematics are linked and mutually reinforcing. Ignoring the mediating factors, this analysis suggests that if we want to change a widespread negative public image of mathematics then we must change the image communicated by the mathematics classroom. This is an unsurprising but important conclusion, which might help to redress some of the gender-related problems described above for mathematics and perhaps also for science and technology.

The second thread of argument cuts across any simplistic understanding and acceptance of the first. It appears that the values (plus the conception of school mathematics) rather than the philosophy of mathematics embodied in the teacher or classroom are the dominant factors in determining the image of mathematics communicated in the classroom and hence ultimately the public image of mathematics. Perhaps this is not surprising, since the realisation of such values will embody the type of teacher–pupil relations, the degree of competitiveness, the extent of negative weight placed on errors, the degree of public humiliation experienced in consequence of failure, and other such factors which powerfully impact on the young learner's self-esteem and self-concept as a learner of mathematics.

Of course, like any analysis made in terms of dichotomies, the above account is oversimplified, perhaps even simplistic. Human beings do not fall neatly into two boxes. In my analysis of mathematics curriculum ideologies (Ernest, 1991) I suggested five basic ideological types and distinguished over a dozen components for each ideology, and that model was a simplification. Nevertheless, such simplified models can suggest the way that important theoretical factors impact on the teaching and learning of mathematics and suggest ways forward in terms of both practice and research (Ernest and Greenland, 1990).

Finally, I wish to point to another social division which in some respect parallels that of gender, but may be of more significance on the international scale. This is the division according to class or socio-economic status. Some of the work on separated values found them positively associated with educational level (Larrabee, 1993). Research by Mellin-Olsen (1981) and others indicates that the preferred learning styles of apprentices is for the concrete (connected), whereas that of academic students is for the abstract, theoretical (separated). Recent data from Australia suggests that students in the last two years of compulsory schooling are twice as likely to opt to study mathematics and science if they are from the higher socio-economic status bands, than from the lower (Maslen, 1995). Given the above discussion, the image of mathematics may play a significant role in the reproduction of such differences.

References

Assessment of Performance Unit. (1985). *A Review of Monitoring in Mathematics 1978 to 1982* (2 volumes), Department of Education and Science, London.

Ausubel, D. P. (1968). *Educational Psychology, a cognitive view*, Holt, Rinehart and Winston, New York.

Barnard, T. and Saunders, P. (1994). Is school mathematics in crisis? *The Guardian*, 28 December, 18.

Bradbeck, M. (1983). Moral judgement. *Developmental Review*, 3, 274–291.

Buerk, D. (1982). An experience with some able women who avoid mathematics. *For the Learning of Mathematics,* **3**, 2, 19–24.

Burton, L. (1986). *Girls into Maths Can Go,* Holt, Rinehart and Winston, London.

Buxton, L. (1981). *Do You Panic About Maths?* Heinemann, London.

Cockcroft, W. H. (1982). *Mathematics Counts,* Her Majesty's Stationery Office, London.

Cooney, T. J. (1988). The issue of reform. *Mathematics Teacher,* **80**, 352–363.

Davis, P. J. (1972). Fidelity in mathematical discourse: Is one and one really two? *American Mathematical Monthly,* **79**, 3, 252–263.

Davis, P. J. and Hersh, R. (1980). *The Mathematical Experience,* Penguin, London.

Delamont, S. (1978). The contradictions in ladies' education. In S. Delamont and E. Duffin (eds) *The Nineteenth Century Woman: Her cultural and physical world,* Croom Helm, Beckenham.

Dowling, P. (1988). The contextualising of mathematics: Towards a theoretical map. In M. Harris (ed.) (1991) *Schools, Mathematics and Work,* Falmer Press, London, 93–120.

Ernest, P. (1988). The attitudes and practices of student teachers of primary school mathematics. In A. Borbas (ed.) *Proceedings of PME-12,* Veszprem, Hungary, **1**, 288–295.

Ernest, P. (1989a). The knowledge, beliefs and attitudes of the mathematics teacher: A model. *Journal of Education for Teaching,* **15**(1), 13–33.

Ernest, P. (1989b). Mathematics-related Belief Systems. Poster presented at *PME-13,* Paris.

Ernest, P. (1989c). The impact of beliefs on the teaching of mathematics. In P. Ernest (1989d), 249–254.

Ernest, P. (1989d). *Mathematics Teaching: The state of the art,* Falmer Press, London.

Ernest, P. (1991). *The Philosophy of Mathematics Education,* Falmer Press, London.

Ernest, P. (1994a). The philosophy of mathematics and mathematics education. In R. Biehler, R. W. Scholz, R. Straesser and B. Winkelmann (eds) *The Didactics of Mathematics as a Scientific Discipline,* Kluwer, Dordrecht, 335–349.

Ernest, P. (1994b). *Mathematics, Education and Philosophy: An international perspective,* Falmer Press, London.

Ernest, P. and Greenland, P. (1990). Teacher belief systems: Theory and observations. In S. Pirie and B. Shire (eds) *BSRLM 1990 Annual Conference Proceedings,* BSRLM, Oxford, 23–26.

Fennema, E. (1985). Explaining sex-related differences in mathematics: Theoretical models. *Educational Studies in Mathematics,* **16**, 303–320.

Foucault, M. (1980). *Power/Knowledge,* C. Gordon (ed.). Pantheon Books, New York.

Gilligan, C. (1982). *In a Different Voice,* Harvard University Press, Cambridge, MA.

Glasersfeld, E. von. (1995). *Radical Constructivism: A way of knowing and learning,* Falmer Press, London.

Hersh, R. (1979). Some proposals for reviving the philosophy of mathematics. *Advances in Mathematics,* **31**, 31–50.

Hersh, R. (1988). Mathematics has a front and a back. Paper presented at *The 6th International Congress of Mathematics Education,* Budapest, 27 July–4 August.

Hoffman, M. (1977). Sex-differences in empathy and related behaviours. *Psychological Bulletin,* **84**, 712–722.

Howson, A. G. and Wilson, B. (1986). *School Mathematics in the 1990s,* Cambridge University Press.

Hoyles, C. (1982). The pupil's view of mathematics learning. *Educational Studies in Mathematics,* **13**, 4, 357–372.

Hoyles, C. (1992). Illumination and reflections: Teachers, methodologies and mathematics. In W. Geeslin and K. Graham (eds) *Proceedings of PME-16,* Durham, New Hampshire, **3**, 263–286.

Isaacson, Z. (1989). Of course you *could* be an engineer, dear, but wouldn't you *rather* be a nurse or teacher or secretary? In P. Ernest (1989d), 188–194.

Kitcher, P. (1983). *The Nature of Mathematical Knowledge,* Oxford University Press.

Kitcher, P. and Aspray, W. (1988). An opinionated introduction. In W. Aspray and P. Kitcher (eds) *History and Philosophy of Modern Mathematics*, University of Minnesota Press, Minneapolis, 3–57.

Kline, M. (1980). *Mathematics: The loss of certainty*, Oxford University Press.

Kohlberg, L. (1969). *Stages in the Development of Moral Thought and Action*. Holt, Rinehart and Winston, New York.

Kouba, V. and McDonald, J. L. (1987). Students' perceptions of mathematics as a domain. In J. C. Bergeron, N. Herscovics and C. Kieran (eds) *Proceedings of PME-11*, University of Montreal, **1**, 106–112.

Kouba, V. and McDonald, J. L. (1991). What is mathematics to children? *Journal of Mathematical Behaviour,* **10**, 105–113.

Lacey, C. (1977). *The Socialization of Teachers*, Methuen, London.

Lakatos, I. (1976). *Proofs and Refutations*, Cambridge University Press.

Larrabee, M. J. (1993). *An Ethic of Care*, Routledge, London.

Lerman, S. (1986). *Alternative Views of the Nature of Mathematics and their Possible Influence on the Teaching of Mathematics*. Unpublished Ph.D. thesis, King's College, University of London.

Maslen, G. (1995). Posh boys and girls choose physics. *The Times Educational Supplement,* 27 January, 15.

Maxwell, J. (1989). Mathephobia. In P. Ernest (1989d), 221–226.

Mellin-Olsen, S. (1981). Instrumentalism as an educational concept. *Educational Studies in Mathematics,* **12**, 351–367.

NCTM. (1980). *An Agenda for Action*, National Council of Teachers of Mathematics, Reston, VA.

NCTM. (1989). *Curriculum and Evaluation Standards for School Mathematics*, National Council of Teachers of Mathematics, Reston, VA.

NCC. (1989). *Mathematics, Non-Statutory Guidance*, National Curriculum Council, York.

Pile, S. (1993). King's College: what went wrong with the bluestocking revolution? *The Daily Telegraph,* 15 March, 19.

Popper, K. R. (1979). *Objective Knowledge* (Revised Edition), Oxford University Press.

Restivo, S. (1992). *Mathematics in Society and History*, Kluwer, Dordrecht.

Rorty, R. (1979). *Philosophy and the Mirror of Nature*, Princeton University Press, Princeton, NJ.

Rotman, B. (1993). *Ad Infinitum The Ghost in Turing's Machine: Taking God out of mathematics and putting the body back in*, Stanford University Press, Stanford, CA.

Sells, L. (1973). High school mathematics as the critical filter in the job market. *Proceedings of the Conference on Minority Graduate Education*, University of California, Berkeley, CA, 37–49.

Skovsmose, O. (1994). *Towards a Philosophy of Critical Mathematics Education*, Kluwer, Dordrecht.

Steen, L. A. (1988). The science of patterns. *Science*, **240** (4852), 611–616.

Steiner, H. G. (1987). Philosophical and epistemological aspects of mathematics and their interaction with theory and practice in mathematics education. *For the Learning of Mathematics*, 7, 1, 7–13.

Thom, R. (1973). Modern mathematics: Does it exist? In A. G. Howson (ed.) *Developments in Mathematical Education*, Cambridge University Press, 194–209.

Thompson, A. G. (1984). The relationship between teachers conceptions of mathematics and mathematics teaching to instructional practice. *Educational Studies in Mathematics*, **15**, 105–127.

Tiles, M. (1991). *Mathematics and the Image of Reason*, Routledge, London.

Tymoczko, T. (1986). *New Directions in the Philosophy of Mathematics*, Birkhauser, Boston.

Walkerdine, V. (1988). *The Mastery of Reason*, Routledge, London.

Walkerdine, V. and the Girls and Mathematics Unit. (1989). *Counting Girls Out*, Virago, London.

2 Towards a sociology of learning in primary schools

Andrew Pollard

Abstract

In this paper the aim is to highlight the absence of a sociology of learning in relation to primary education. Further, it is argued that there is considerable scope for cooperation between psychologists and sociologists in tackling this issue and one way will be explored in which this could be achieved by drawing on social constructivist psychology and symbolic interactionist sociology. In support of this suggestion, some brief illustrative material is presented, drawn from a longitudinal ethnography of a pupil cohort progressing through a primary school in the UK.

The limitations of disciplinary boundaries

One could argue that the division of labour between the academic disciplines which make up the social sciences has justified itself over the years by the quality of descriptions and depth of analyses which have been produced. There are processes of research, publication and debate which foster such refinement. Thus, within each discipline, dominant perspectives tend to come and go as development takes place and each decade witnesses new 'taken for granteds' and discrete progress within the disciplines.

However, the demarcations between disciplines must be seen as socio-historical products, maintained by people and institutions who had, and have, enormous personal, cultural and material investments in them and who must respond to the specific circumstances which they face. This throws up the danger that the reliance on detailed intra-disciplinary development could result in the establishment of theoretical perspectives and empirical procedures which in fact fail to engage with the more complex and enduring realities of social processes and phenomena. Indeed, I would argue that, as our understanding of the social world becomes more sophisticated, it is becoming increasingly apparent that the validity of the study of many issues cannot be maximised unless each of the relevant disciplines is drawn on in sustained study.

Interestingly, such more complex and enduring issues are often those which are regarded as being particularly important by practitioners – by the people who live out the processes which academic analysts study – and, indeed, by policy makers – people who have to make decisions of great significance with whatever information and understanding is available to them at the time. From the perspective of such groups, social scientists are often seen as myopic pedants, locked into their theoretical thought-worlds with little grasp of 'practical realities'. The underlying message here, on offer to those who are actively listening, is that the lack of an integrated analysis, comparable to the integrated nature of experience, denies the validity and thus the credibility of the academic account.

At the same time though, it would be a churlish observer of the social sciences who did not recognise that each discipline has particular strengths for addressing particular social phenomena and issues. It might thus be concluded that ways of drawing on such strengths should be found and, in the first place, it might reasonably be argued that academics should cooperate across disciplinary boundaries. Only this can begin to ensure that the issues which we address are tackled in more valid and transferable ways.

The issue of learning in primary schools provides a case in point.

Learning in primary schools

A review of the sociology of primary schooling and of the psychology of young chil-dren's learning over the past twenty years or so reveals a curious picture. On the one hand, sociologists have continued, in one way or another, to focus their attention on issues of social differentiation. Certainly the emphasis has developed from that of social class to include increasing attention to issues of race and gender, and theoretical refine-ments have accumulated too. However, the overriding impression left by work such as Hartley (1985), Pollard (1985), Sharp and Green (1975), Lubeck (1985), King (1978) and King (1989), is that learning processes are, at best, tangential to issues such as typification, group formation and the consequences of differentiation. Returning over a decade earlier, and to a different theoretical perspective, reveals a similar story – as is illustrated by the way in which Dreeben's *On What is Learned in School* (1968) concerns itself with socialisation of children into norms but makes no attempt to consider the sociological factors which influence the learning of knowledge, concepts and skills.

Sociologists' focus on differentiation in the past has, until recently, been matched by the naive individualism of much child psychology which derived from the work of Piaget. Piaget's work was directed, in an overarching sense, towards the study of 'genetic epistemology', but the route towards this analysis was through many detailed studies of children's thinking and behaviour. Careful development and use of the clinical method over many years enabled Piaget to generate a model of learning processes based on the interaction between individuals and their environment and involving development through successive stages of equilibration, each of which was taken to be associated with particular capacities and ways of thinking. This model was powerfully adopted by primary school teachers in the UK in the years following the Plowden Report (CACE, 1967) and was used as a professional legitimation for 'progressive' classroom practices which, ostensibly, gave children a large degree of control over their learning.

However, whilst it is impossible to overestimate Piaget's influence within develop-mental psychology over the past decades, it is also true to say that Piaget's ideas have increasingly been modified by the gradual emergence of a new paradigm – 'social constructivism'.

Thus, the previously dominant model, which implicitly conceptualised children as *individual* 'active scientists', has begun to be superseded by an image of children as *social* beings who construct their understandings (learn) from social interaction within specific socio-cultural settings. They are thus seen as intelligent social actors who, although their knowledge base may be limited in absolute terms, are capable in many ways. For instance, processes of 'intellectual search' have been identified in young children (Tizard and Hughes, 1987) as have children's capacities to develop sophisticated forms of representation for meaning and understanding. Such findings are being found with younger and younger children as research goes on.

The theoretical basis of such psychological research is strongly influenced by Vygotsky (1962, 1978). Of particular importance is his comparative work on the interrelations of thought, language and culture and, at another level, on the role of adults in scaffolding children's understanding across the 'zone of proximal development' – the extension of understanding which can be attained with appropriate support from others. According to Bruner and Haste (1987), this social constructivist approach has brought about a 'quiet revolution' in developmental psychology in the last decade and this is certainly borne out by the impact in education of work such as that by Donaldson (1978), Hughes (1986), Bruner (1986) and Edwards and Mercer (1987).

A key thrust of such new approaches is to recognise the way in which the social context influences perspectives and behaviour. One particularly interesting way of conceptualising this has been provided by Helen Haste (1987) in her model of 'intra-individual', 'interpersonal' and 'socio-historical' factors affecting learning (Figure 2.1).

The intra-individual domain is the province of the cognitive psychologists who have accumulated so many insights into the ways in which individuals assimilate experiences and construct understanding. The interpersonal is the domain of social interaction – the area in which meanings are negotiated and through which cultural norms and social conventions are learned. The socio-historical is the domain of culturally defined and historically accumulated justification and explanation. It is a socio-historical resource for both interpersonal interaction and intra-individual reflection.

Such conceptualisation of factors and domains affecting learning begins to make it possible to break out of the individualist assumptions which have been common in child psychology, so that wider social issues can be addressed. Sociologists could have much to offer here for, as Apple (1986) has argued:

> We do not confront abstract 'learners' in schools. Instead, we see specific classed, raced and gendered subjects, people whose biographies are intimately linked to the economic, political and ideological trajectories of their families and communities, to the political economies of their neighbourhoods.
>
> (Apple, 1986, p. 7:5)

In other words, intra-individual learning cannot really be understood without reference to both interpersonal experiences and socio-historical circumstances.

I suspect that there is some way to go in the development of working relationships and analytical tools before psychologists and sociologists concerned with children's learning are able to take on the full import of Haste's framework and Apple's suggestion

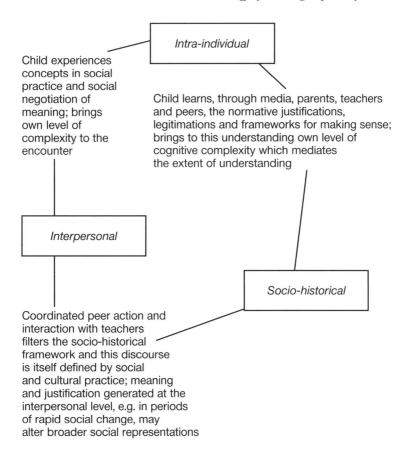

Figure 2.1 The relationship between intra-individual, interpersonal and socio-historical factors
in learning

Source: Haste (1987, p. 175).

in detailed empirical investigations. However, a growing consensus about the inter-relatedness of such factors does seem to be emerging and this is underpinned, not just by theory and empirical research, but also by the common sense and lived experiences of millions of children, teachers, parents and others. If we are to investigate the issue of learning in valid ways, then our first problem, as social scientists, is really to find ways of bridging the artificial disciplinary boundaries which dissipate our energies.

I want to suggest that one way of developing such collaborative work could be through the linking of social constructivist psychology and symbolic interactionist sociology.

These approaches share a basic assumption that people are active and make decisions on the basis of meanings. However, whilst social constructivist work has begun to identify the processes by which people 'make sense' in social situations, and thus come to 'know', symbolic interactionist studies promise to provide more detailed and incisive accounts of the dynamics and constraints of the contexts in which learning takes place. The two approaches are, arguably, complementary.

Some years ago I began to toy with this potential sociological contribution through the publication of a collection of papers which highlighted the influence of social contexts in schools on children's thinking and learning (Pollard, 1987). This collection of case studies includes material from 3–12 year olds and provides a degree of 'thick description' which invites further theorisation regarding the nature of such complementarity – a task which I have begun through the work on an ethnography and which is reflected in this paper.

However, before addressing the study and the theoretical issue directly, it is appropriate to place the topic of 'learning in primary schools' in the context of recent policies in England and Wales and in relation to other approaches to classroom teaching/learning processes. In particular, I will have regard below to the work of Neville Bennett because of the sustained quality and impact of his research into classroom teaching and learning over many years.

Policy and substantive contexts

In recent years, major thrusts of Government policy in England and Wales have been directed towards the streamlining of the management of schools, increasing the effectiveness and accountability of teachers and restructuring the curriculum (e.g. Education Act, 1986; Education Reform Act, 1988). We do not yet know whether such initiatives will achieve their aims in terms of the delivery of the curriculum. However, irrespective of this, it can be argued that far too little attention has been paid to the actual reception of the curriculum by learners. Indeed, by focusing on the issue of learning, one could claim to be anticipating a policy debate of the future – a claim based on the proposition that when the dust of reforms of teacher and curriculum management has settled and we are still chasing that ever-receding Holy Grail of 'educational standards', more detailed attention to learning and the learners in schools will be perceived as necessary.

The issue also has implications for teachers in primary schools in a more general way concerning the theoretical underpinning of practice. Over the past decade or so, there has been a gradual erosion of the primacy of the Plowden Report's (CACE, 1967) philosophy of 'child centredness', which underpinned much primary school practice. As Piaget's work has been questioned and research evidence has accumulated about actual classroom behaviour, so primary school practice has begun to be seen to lack a 'theoretical base' (Sylva, 1987). I would suggest that a fusion of social-constructivism and symbolic-interactionism, suitably applied, has the potential to offer a new legitimation – indeed, I think there are many forms of innovative curriculum practice which, perhaps unwittingly, appear to be based on such precepts.

In the past twenty years a considerable amount of research has been conducted with the aim of identifying factors which enable teachers to be 'effective'. However, as Bennett (1987) has argued, whilst the initial work, emphasising teaching styles, identified some interesting patterns and descriptions, it lacked explanatory power and made few connections with actual practice. It was superseded in the mid-1970s by an

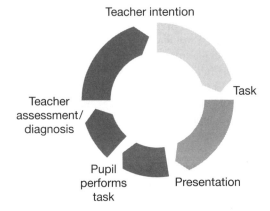

Figure 2.2 A model of classroom task processes

Source: Bennett and Kell, 1989, p. 27.

'opportunities to learn' model in which the teacher was seen as the manager of the attention and time of the pupils. A key indicator became the amount of time which the pupil was 'on task'. More recently the focus has also turned to the analysis of what is termed 'quality' of classroom tasks – defined in terms of the degree of appropriate match with children's capacities (e.g. Bennett *et al.*, 1984).

Neville Bennett's work represents a sustained and consistent attempt to develop and test a model of teaching and learning. His successive studies have focused on different parts of an emerging model and his work continues through his present Leverhulme Project on the quality of teacher's subject knowledge and ability to diagnose learning difficulties.

Bennett, and his co-author, Joy Kell, express the model particularly clearly below:

> Teaching is, we argue, a purposeful activity: teachers provide tasks and activities for their children for good reasons. These reasons or, as we call them in the model, teacher intentions, will inform the teacher's selection of tasks/activities. Once chosen these are presented to children in some way, e.g. to individuals, groups or the whole class, together with the necessary materials. The children then get on with their work, demonstrating, through their performances, their understanding (or misconceptions) of it. When they have completed their activity it might be expected that the teacher will assess it in some way in order to judge children's developing competencies, and it might also be expected that the information gained from those assessments will inform the teacher's next intentions.

The very important point which Bennett has empirically documented is that breakdowns can and do occur regularly between each stage in the 'task process cycle' and it is unfortunate that this can sometimes come across as an unappreciative critique of teachers. Rather, I would suggest that it should be seen, more constructively, as providing a detailed testimony of just how difficult the job is.

Having said that though, I would also argue that such work seriously underplays the importance of the socio-cultural situation in which teaching and learning take place and fails to trace the full impact of the subjectivity of the participants. There is no specific emphasis on learners with reference to their responses to the social influences and teaching/learning situations which they experience. The model thus appears as a technical model of teaching – one which is dominated by the teacher, with pupils 'performing' to externally determined tasks.

In terms of the issues raised by Helen Haste, Bennett's analysis is very partial. It is worthwhile and necessary, but it is not sufficient and should be complemented by other work – work which is more informed by sociological perspectives.

Among other related issues which have emerged regularly in recent research and in HMI surveys has been that of the routine nature of many of the activity structures and classroom tasks in which children engage – particularly in the 'basic' curriculum areas (Alexander, 1984). In an attempt to address this issue and to be appreciative to the concerns of teachers, Woods (1990) has drawn on coping strategies theory (e.g. Pollard, 1982) to identify problems of the limited 'opportunities to teach' in classrooms. These are constrained by the inadequate resourcing of schools and by the enormous current expectations of teachers.

However, it is also clear that the routinisation of tasks and activity structures is not simply the result of a transmission process for which teachers are solely responsible. Indeed, Doyle (1979) has suggested that many pupils seek tasks which are 'low risk' and 'low ambiguity' and both the ORACLE researchers' identification of 'intermittent working' and 'easy riding' (Galton *et al.*, 1980) and my own identification of pupil 'drifting' (Pollard and Tann, 1987) suggest that pupils' learning stances and strategies could be of considerable significance. Arguably, this is particularly important in the context of the national concern for improvement in the level of learning achievements, given the psychological evidence on the contribution of risk-taking to learning (Claxton, 1984) and Dweck's socio-cognitive research on motivation (1986). As Galton's (1987) review of the field in the last twenty years concludes:

> ... if advances (in our understanding) are to be made, there will (need to) be greater concentration on the social factors affecting pupil learning and (on) the ways in which teachers can create classroom climates which allow situations of 'high risk' and 'high ambiguity' to be coped with successfully.
>
> (Galton, 1987, p. 44)

This statement underlines a key point in social constructivist models of learning about control of the learning process. Since understanding can only be constructed in the mind of the learner, it is essential that learners exercise a significant degree of control of the process – a point to which I will return below.

I turn now though, to introduce the empirical study around which my thinking on this topic has developed.

A longitudinal ethnography

In 1987 I began a research programme, a longitudinal ethnography, which was designed to explore the potential for linking social interactionism and social constructivism.

I aimed to monitor the primary school careers of a small cohort of ten children at one primary school by using a variety of qualitative methods and I started from the children's entry to the school at the age of four. I particularly focused on the social factors which were likely to influence the children's stance, perspectives and strategies regarding learning. Data was thus collected from parents about family life, sibling relationships and the children's emergent identities; from peers and playground contexts concerning peer-group relations; and from teachers with regard to classroom behaviour and academic achievements.

At the heart of the study was regular classroom observation so that the progression of organisation, activity structures and routine tasks in each class which the children passed through could be documented – together with the responses of the children to such provision. The main sources of data were: field notes from participant-observation, interviews, teacher records, parent diaries, school documents, photographs, video recordings, sociometry and examples of children's work.

This work built on the sociological studies of teacher/pupil coping strategies in schools which have developed over a number of years (e.g. Woods, 1977, Hargreaves, 1978; Pollard, 1982; Beynon, 1985; Scarth, 1987), with their strong influence of symbolic interactionism. Since that work has been generally accepted as a means of conceptualising and analysing macro–micro linkages as they affect school processes, I judged that it might also prove to be capable of bearing the weight of analysis of socio-historical factors in learning, as raised by Helen Haste (see Figure 2.1), in addition to the interpersonal factors which are the more obvious provenance of symbolic interactionism.

I also hoped that the study would develop existing work on coping strategies substantively because of the focus on children as pupils developing through schools. This focus was designed to complement the considerable amount of work which is now available on teacher strategies and careers (Ball and Goodson, 1985; Sikes *et al.*, 1985; Nias, 1989). Additionally, of course, the study was intended to provide a more explicit focus on learning than is evident in previous sociological work, which, as I argued earlier, has tended to be primarily concerned with differentiation.

The main aims of the study were thus:

1   to trace the development of a cohort of young children's stances, perspectives and strategies regarding learning, through consideration of home, playground and classroom settings;
2   to investigate pupil career, in terms of emergent identities and the influences on them, as children move through different teachers and classrooms within their school;
3   to develop the analytic potential of combining social constructivist models of children's learning and symbolic interactionist models of school processes.

In the course of gathering data, I attempted to code and analyse it with the intention of generating grounded theoretical models and concepts (Glaser and Strauss, 1967;

Hammersley and Atkinson, 1983) which could contribute to both professional and academic debate. In keeping with other, earlier work, I do not aspire to 'prove' relationships, believing this too inappropriate with regard to such subtle issues (or indeed to many aspects of social science more generally). However, through the detailed analysis of the data, I aimed to highlight the most significant issues and patterns in the social relationships which seem to affect pupil learning and career. Others can then relate this analysis to their own circumstances.

This paper represents my first public attempt to begin to make sense of my work. It remains tentative in many respects, but certainly indicates the direction in which my thinking is leading.

By the spring of 1990, I had studied nine children (one child had moved schools) over their first three school years with regard to three major social settings (classroom, playground, home). I had collected a large amount of data and faced analytical problems which I aimed to address through the comparison of the nine cases which the children represented.

Before I focus directly on the emerging analysis, an indication of the data is provided below by a brief illustrative account of the educational experiences, over their first two school years, of just two of the children whom I studied.

This is a highly condensed 'account', in almost narrative form, and was written initially for an audience of governors and parents (Pollard, 1990). The judgements expressed in it rest on a detailed analysis of data, but the main point which I wish to make requires a holistic understanding, for which narrative documentary is a proven vehicle. I thus hope that the account below serves its purpose in highlighting the importance of contextual factors in learning and in providing a bridge to the theoretical analysis in the final section of this paper. More complete substantive documentation and analysis will appear in due course.

Learning and developing an identity

The two children on whom this illustration is based began their school careers together, with 24 others, in the same 'reception' class.

The first child, a girl called Sally, was the youngest of the two children of the school caretaker. Her mother also worked in the school as a School Meals Services Assistant and as a cleaner. Her parents had always taken enormous pleasure and pride in Sally's achievements. They celebrated each step as it came but did not seem to overtly press her. Life, for them, seemed very much in perspective. Sally was physically agile and had a good deal of self-confidence. She had known the school and the teaching staff for most of her life. She felt at home. She was very sensitive to 'school rules' and adult concerns and she engaged in each new challenge with zest. Over the years, with her parents' encouragement, she had developed a considerable talent for dancing and had won several competitions. In school she had also taken a leading role in several class assemblies and had made good progress with her reading and other work. The teachers felt she was a delightful and rewarding child to teach – convivial and able, but compliant too. Her friends were mainly girls though she mixed easily. She was at the centre of a group which was particularly popular in the class and which, over the years since playgroup, had developed strong internal links and friendships through shared interests, for instance, in 'My Little Pony', playing at 'mummies and daddies' and reciprocal home visits.

The second child, Daniel, was the fifth and youngest in his family. His father was an extremely busy business executive and his mother had devoted the previous 16 years to caring for their children, which she saw as a worthwhile but all-absorbing commitment. She was concerned for Daniel who had had some difficulties in establishing his identity in the bustle of the family with four older children. She also felt that he had 'always tended to worry about things' and was not very confident in himself. For many years he had tended to play on being the youngest, the baby of the family, a role which seemed naturally available. At playgroup he was particularly friendly with a girl, Harriet, who was later to be in his class at school. However, over their first year at school, distinct friendships of boys and girls began to form. It became 'sissy' to play with girls. Daniel, who had found the transition from the security of home hard to take and who had to begin to develop a greater self-sufficiency, thus found the ground rules of appropriate friendships changing, as the power of child culture asserted itself. He could not play with Harriet because she was a girl, but nor was he fully accepted by the dominant groups of boys.

This insecurity was increased when he moved from the structured and 'motherly' atmosphere of his reception class into the more volatile environment of his 'middle infant' class. There were now 31 children in his class, most of whom were from a parallel reception class – within which a group of boys had developed a reputation for being 'difficult'. The new teacher thus judged that the class '... needed a firm hand to settle them down after last year' and, as a caring but experienced infant teacher, decided to stand no nonsense. It also so happened that this teacher was somewhat stressed, as a lot of teachers in England and Wales have been in the late 1980s. She sometimes acted a little harshly and in other ways which were against her own better judgement.

The environment which Daniel experienced was therefore one which was sometimes a little unpredictable. Whilst he was never one of the ones who 'got into trouble', he was very worried by the possibility that he might 'upset Miss'. Daniel would thus be very careful. He would watch and listen to the teacher, attempting to 'be good' and do exactly what was required. He would check with other children and, on making a first attempt at a task, try to have his efforts approved before proceeding further. Occasionally, at work with a group and with other children also pressing, the teacher might wave Daniel away. He would then drift, unsure, watching to take another opportunity to obtain the reinforcement which he felt he needed. As the year progressed, Daniel became more unhappy and increasingly unwilling to go to school.

Daniel's mother was torn as this situation developed – was the 'problem' caused by Daniel's 'immaturity' or was it because he was frightened of the teacher? She felt it was probably a bit of both but school-gate advice suggested that discussion in school might not go easily. She delayed and the situation worsened, with Daniel making up excuses to avoid school, insisting on returning home for lunch and becoming unwilling to visit the homes of other children. Daniel's mother eventually and tentatively visited the school where the issues were aired.

Over the following weeks the teacher worked hard to support Daniel and to help him settle. Daniel's confidence improved a little, particularly when he found a new friend, a boy, from whom he then became inseparable. Even so, as his mother told me towards the end of the year, 'we are holding on and praying for the end of term'.

These two children attended the same school and were part of the same classes – yet as learners they had quite different characteristics. Whilst Sally was confident, keen to 'have a go' and would take risks, Daniel was insecure, fearful lest he 'got things wrong' in a world in which he felt evaluated and vulnerable. The accident of birth into a small or large family may have been an influence too, with Sally having had the psychological space to flourish and the day-to-day support of both her parents all around her, whilst Daniel had to establish his place in a large family in which both parents faced considerable pressure in their work – be it in an office or domestically. Perhaps too, Daniel's initial solutions to his position, which had carried him in good stead in his infancy, whilst at home, would simply not transfer into the less bounded environment of school.

Towards an analytical framework

The data which underpins an account such as that reviewed above is highly complex and, in attempting to make sense of it, one can easily lose direction or become distracted. For the purposes of this study, it was crucial to retain the focus on identity and learning whilst also structuring the comparison of cases across settings – with 27 interrelated data sets formed by the nine children and three major settings. Building on what I take to be key interactionist and constructivist principles, I evolved a simple analytical formula Figure 2.3 which I found to be powerful and which could be applied to data and cases derived from any setting.

Figure 2.3 Individual, context and learning: an analytic formula

The relationship between self and others expresses the key symbolic interactionist focus, with its recognition of the importance of social context in the formation of meaning and self. A sense of control in social situations is seen as a product of this. It is an indication of the success, or otherwise, of a child's coping strategies in the politico-cultural context of any particular social setting – home, classroom, playground – and thus reflects the interplay of interests, power, strategies and negotiation. However, it is also a necessary element of the learning process as conceived by social constructivist psychologists. Only children themselves can 'make sense', understand and learn. They may be supported and instructed by others, but, once their understanding has been scaffolded in such ways, it must stand on its own foundations – foundations which can only be secure when the child has been able to control the construction itself.

Teaching and other forms of support by adults are necessary, but they are not sufficient. Learning also requires conditions which enable each child to control the assembly and construction of their understanding[1].

I have elaborated below (Figure 2.4) a model by Rowland (1987) in order to express this point.

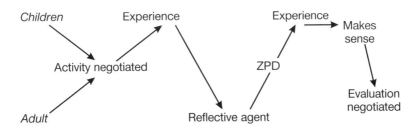

Figure 2.4 A social-constructivist model of the teaching/learning process

It is worth dwelling a little on the importance of the role of an adult as a 'reflective agent' in this model, providing meaningful and appropriate guidance and extension to the cognitive structuring and skill development arising from the child's initial experiences. This, it is suggested, supports the child's attempts to 'make sense' and enables them to cross the zone of proximal development (ZPD).

Their thinking is thus *restructured* in the course of further experiences. Of course, the concept of 'reflective agent' is not unrelated to that of 'reflective teaching' (Pollard and Tann, 1987), which is becoming a new orthodoxy in terms of course rationales for teacher education in the UK. However, as with sociology of education, present work on reflective teaching is relatively weak on the issue of learning itself[2]. Of great interest too, is the fact that carrying out the role of a reflective agent effectively is dependent on sensitivity *and* accurate knowledge of each child's needs. It thus places a premium on formative, teacher assessment (TGAT, 1988) and could be greatly facilitated in England and Wales by the requirements of new legislation – if it is appropriately implemented, a condition which, unfortunately, we cannot take for granted.

To recap – in Figure 2.4, we see the need for appropriate adult support and instruction and its relationship to children's control over their learning. The two are not contradictory. Indeed, I would argue that both are necessary but neither is sufficient for high quality learning. In the cases of Sally and Daniel, Sally was able to negotiate, control and cope with the variety of domestic, classroom and playground settings which she encountered with relative ease. She was confident in tackling new learning situations and achieved a great deal. Daniel found things much more difficult in each setting, but particularly in the classroom. He developed two key strategies regarding this learning. First, to watch, check and recheck to make sure that he 'was doing it right' so that he could avoid 'trouble with Miss'. Second, to stay away from school. His learning achievements over the two years were relatively modest.

Of course, the simple formula (Figure 2.3) and the social constructivist model of interaction in learning (Figure 2.4) express only a small part of the story, and I have developed them further to begin to reflect on the outcomes and consequences of the learning process.

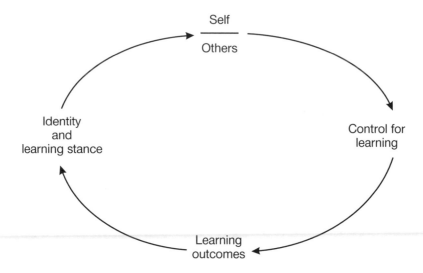

Figure 2.5 A model of learning and identity

This model Figure 2.5 expresses the recursive nature of experience. Self-confidence, together with other attributes and other contextual factors (e.g. Bennett's work on the quality of tasks set), produces particular learning outcomes – successful or otherwise – and with them associated perspectives. These, it is suggested, contribute cumulatively to each child's sense of identity and to their learning stance, and it is with these which, for better or worse, they enter the next setting. Over time, as this cycle moves forward, it tends to develop in patterned ways into what can be identified more clearly as 'pupil career'.

Thus, in the case of Sally and Daniel, we might speculate that Sally's pupil career will go from strength to strength, founded on the confidence of her learning stance, whilst Daniel's progress may be more halting. In fact, of course, such speculation is premature. Time will bring new social contexts and experiences and the factor of social class may influence the children's development. This is where the longitudinal design of the study should be significant.

Whatever the empirical outcomes, the nature of the patterns in pupil learning and career is of consequence for both psychologists and sociologists. For psychologists, it highlights processes of learning in context. For sociologists, it begins to relate factors such as social class, gender and race, through the processes of learning and identity formation, and on to long-term social differentiation, career and life chances.

I am attempting to apply the basic formula, Figure 2.3, in relation to the settings of classrooms, playground and the home, through the application of some key elements of the model of coping strategies which I developed some years ago (Pollard, 1985). Four important aspects of this are:

1   An individual's structural position: their power, influence and capacity to take active decisions.
2   An individual's interests-at-hand: the immediate concerns of a person in processes of interaction, given their goals and structural position within a particular social setting.
3   The working consensus: the social rules and understandings which tend to become established in any particular setting as a result of interaction. Such understandings often involve a negotiated 'trade-off' between the participants.
4   Strategic action: strategies used by individuals as a means of coping with different settings. These include conformity, negotiating and rejecting and may or may not be transferred across different settings.

In the cases of both the children illustrated, we see the influence of each of the three major social settings and significant others in their lives – family, peers and teachers.

For Sally, the particular, overlapping configuration of the self/other relationship between home and school gave her self-confidence on which she was able to build in her relationships with her peers and which enabled her to exercise considerable control over her classroom learning. Other data clearly show how this control was obtained, in large part, through her social awareness and negotiating skills. She contributed directly to the working consensus in both classes. Her structural position was strong, her interests-at-hand could be accommodated within teacher goals and she acted with skill and strategic awareness to achieve expected learning outcomes and a positive identity – despite the risks associated with life in her second class.

For Daniel, the situation was more difficult. His structural position was weak both in his family and then, almost as a knock-on effect of his strategies in the home setting, amongst his peers. He felt insecure, in one way or another, in each of the three main settings in his life and he thus developed relatively defensive strategies in order to protect his interests. At its most obvious, this involved trying to avoid coming to school but, once there, it was manifested by extreme caution in his dealings with teachers and a reluctance to take any sort of risk or exercise control over his learning. Preferring to keep a low profile, he participated little in the establishment of classroom understandings and the working consensus.

Learning outcomes were affected and with them Daniel's identity began to develop and to be registered with both his teachers, parents and peers.

Of course, these patterns are related to the particular classroom settings in which Daniel worked and to the teachers concerned and, unfortunately, the teacher of Daniel's middle infant class seemed to compound some of his difficulties. It remains perfectly possible that Daniel will develop more poise and belief in himself as he gets older and he has many abilities and social advantages. The question is an empirical one about which, for the moment, we must be open-minded.

The story of these two children is not just about learning in a narrow academic sense. Additionally, it is about the ways in which Sally and Daniel began to develop their identities as people. As was suggested by Figure 2.5, identity and self-confidence in stances towards future learning develop alongside skills, knowledge and other learning outcomes. They thus feed back, recursively, into future actions and experiences and as the biography and career of each child is gradually constructed.

This brief illustration of the cases of Sally and Daniel demonstrates the importance of the social context in which learning takes place and suggests that it will impact on children irrespective of their individual capabilities. Interestingly, it also reinforces the suggestion that there is no necessary connection between social class factors or income levels and the quality of the learning environment which parents can provide.

There are many further aspects of this attempt to generate theoretical models of the social factors affecting learning which could be discussed. However, in a paper such as this there is little space to do them justice and they must therefore await elaboration elsewhere.

Summary and conclusion

In this paper I firstly suggested that many social phenomena require interdisciplinary analysis if they are to be studied in ways which are valid – and thus practically useful. Learning in primary schools provided a case in point and I reflected on the strange absence of a sociological account and on the partial nature of other analyses because of this omission. I then began to explore the potential for drawing on symbolic interactionism and social constructivism to construct an integrated analysis and showed how I have attempted to begin this through the analysis of data gathered from a longitudinal ethnography of a small group of children in one school.

This analysis has significant policy implications for parents, teachers and school governors since they bear very heavy responsibilities for children's learning and careers. This is so because children develop their perspectives, strategies and, thus, identities in response to their need to cope with circumstances which such adults control. If adults fail to cooperate, to liaise, to negotiate or to think their actions through, then it is the children who will suffer. Their lives are, literally, an ongoing test of the continuity and support which adults provide. Certainly such vulnerability deserves our attention and can, I would argue, best be addressed by focusing on the nature of the learning provision in different settings and by recognising the integrated nature of experience.

It is interesting that, at the present time in England and Wales, such issues are far down the educational agenda – an agenda which is dominated by curriculum, assessment, accountability and management issues. One day, when policies are sought with a more secure foundation on learning processes, it is to be hoped that sociologists will be able to contribute to the available understanding about this extremely important issue.

Acknowledgements

I would like to thank all the children, parents, teachers and governors of the school from whom case study data are drawn in this paper. Without their consistent trust, openness and support the study on which this paper is based would not have been possible.

I am grateful to Bristol Polytechnic for supporting this project over several years and to Cassell for permission to publish some material from my book, *Learning in Primary Schools* (1990).

I would also like to thank Charles Desforges, Peter Kutnick and Peter Woods for their helpful comments on the design of this project and Neville Bennett and two anonymous BJSE referees for useful comments on a draft of this paper.

Notes

1   Neville Bennett, in helpfully commenting on a draft of this paper (personal communication, May 1990), has advised that he 'knows of no data which would argue that pupil choice of work is more positively related to elaborated schema than, say, teacher given work'. I am still thinking about this statement because at first sight it appears to beg the issue of motivation and its relationship to learning. Clearly more discussion is necessary to clarify this important issue.

2   In the case of my own book with Sarah Tann, *Reflective Teaching in the Primary School* (Cassell, 1987), a new edition, due 1991, will correct this.

References

Alexander, R. J. (1984). *Primary Teaching*, Holt Saunders, London. Revised second edition, Cassell, London, 1988.

Apple, M. (1986). *Teachers and Texts*, Routledge, London.

Ball, S. and Goodson, I. (1985). *Teachers' Lives and Careers*, Falmer Press, Lewes.

Bennett, N. (1987). The search for the effective primary school teacher. In S. Delamont (ed.) *The Primary School Teacher*, Falmer Press, Lewes.

Bennett, N. *et al.* (1984). *The Quality of Pupil Learning Experiences*, Lawrence Eribaum, London.

Bennett, N. and Kell, J. (1989). *A Good Start? Four Year Olds in Infant Schools*, Basil Blackwell, Oxford.

Beynon, J. (1985). *Initial Encounters in the Secondary School*, Falmer Press, Lewes.

Bruner, J. (1986). *Actual Minds, Possible Worlds*, Harvard University Press, London.

Bruner, J. and Haste, H. (1987). *Making Sense*, Methuen, London.

CACE. (1967). *Children and their Primary Schools* (The Plowden Report), HMSO, London.

Claxton, G. (1984). *Live and Learn*, Harper and Row, London.

Donaldson, M. (1978). *Children's Minds*, Fontana, London.

Doyle, W. (1979). Classroom tasks and student abilities. In P. Peterson and H. Walberg (eds) *Research on Teaching: Concepts, findings and implications*, McCutchan, Berkeley, CA.

Dreeben, R. (1968). *On What is Learned in School*, Harvard, London.

Dweck, C. (1986). Motivational processes affecting learning. *American Psychologist,* October, pp. 1040–1048.

Edwards, D. and Mercer, N. (1987). *Common Knowledge*, Methuen, London.

Galton, M. (1987). An OrACLE Chronicle: A Decade of Classroom Research. In S. Delamont (ed.) *The Primary School Teacher*, Falmer Press Lewes.

Galton, M., Simon B. and Croll, P. (1980). *Inside Primary Schools*, Routledge, London.

Glaser, B. and Strauss, A. (1967). *The Discovery of Grounded Theory*, Aldine, Chicago.

Hammersley, M. and Atkinson, P. (1983). *Ethnography: Principles into Practice*, Tavistock, London.

Hargreaves, A. (1978). The significance of classroom coping strategies. In L. Barton and R. Meighan (eds) *Sociological Interpretations of Schooling and Classrooms*, Nafferton, Driffield.

Hartley, D. (1985). *Understanding Primary Schools*, Croom Helm, London.

Haste, H. (1987). Growing into rules. In J. Bruner and H. Haste (eds) *Making Sense*, Methuen, London.

Hughes, M. (1986). *Children and Number*, Basil Blackwell, Oxford.

King, R. A. (1978). *All Things Bright and Beautiful*, Wiley, London.

King, R. A. (1989). *The Best of Primary Education*, Falmer Press, Lewes.

Lubeck, S. (1985). *Sandbox Society*, Falmer Press, Lewes.

Nias, J. (1989). *Primary Teacher's Talking*, Routledge, London.

Pollard, A. (1982). A model of coping strategies. *British Journal of Sociology of Education*, **3**, No. 1, pp. 19–37.

Pollard, A. (1985). *The Social World of the Primary School*, Cassell, London.

Pollard, A. (1987). *Children and their Primary Schools: A New Perspective*, Falmer Press, Lewes.

Pollard, A. (1990). *Learning in Primary Schools*, Cassell, London.

Pollard, A. and Tann, S. (1987). *Reflective Teaching in the Primary School*, Cassell, London.

Rowland, S. (1987). Child in control. In A. Pollard (ed.) *Children and their Primary Schools*, Falmer Press, Lewes.

Scarth, J. (1987). Teacher strategies: A review and critique. *British Journal of Sociology of Education*, **8**, No. 3, pp. 245–262.

Sharp, R. and Green, A. (1975). *Education and Social Control*, Routledge, London.

Sikes, P., Measor, L. and Woods, P. (1985). *Teacher Careers: Crises and continuities*, Falmer Press, Lewes.

Sylva, K. (1987). Plowden: History and prospect – research. *Oxford Review of Education*, **13**, No. 1, pp. 3–11.

Task Group on Assessment and Testing. (1988). *National Curriculum Report*, Department of Education and Science, London.

Tizard, B. and Hughes, M. (1987). The intellectual search of young children. In A. Pollard (ed.) *Children and their Primary Schools: A new perspective*, Falmer Press, Lewes.

Vygotsky, L. (1962). *Thought and Language*, Wiley, New York.

Vygotsky, L. (1978). *Mind in Society*, Harvard, London.

Woods, P. (1977). Teaching for survival. In P. Woods and M. Hammersley (eds) *School Experience*, Croom Helm, London.

Woods, P. (1990). *Teacher Skills and Strategies*, Falmer Press, Lewes.

3　Learners as authors in the mathematics classroom

Hilary Povey and Leone Burton with
Corinne Angier and Mark Boylan

Introduction

In this chapter we explore authoring as the means through which a learner acquires facility in using community-validated mathematical knowledge and skills. As an author, the learner uses his or her mathematical voice to enquire, interrogate and reflect upon what is being learned and how. What does it mean to say that a learner of mathematics is an author? For the majority of classrooms, authorship appears to be vested in the mathematicians who determine what is to be learned, and the texts through which that mathematics is conveyed. We believe that such a view ignores what is known about the process of coming to know, which, far from being one of cultural transmission, is necessarily one of interpretation and meaning negotiation in the context of current personal 'knowing' as well as knowledge situated in the community. This we believe to be a lifelong struggle to accord meanings to the narratives that describe the personal, the socio-cultural and, inevitably, the political. Without such meanings, it is difficult to make sense of why so many people fail in, or discard, their attempts to learn mathematics and, in particular, why so many of these unsuccessful learners are predominantly found in particular communities.

This leads us to ask three questions, which will guide the development of this chapter.

- How does characterising mathematics learners as authors help us to uncover what might be liberatory discursive practices in the classroom?

To answer this question, we invoke models of different ways of coming to know in order to allow us better to theorise the learning of mathematics as located within peda-gogical practices that support critical mathematics education.

- In what ways does understanding mathematics as narrative help to change the classroom experiences of learners?

We explain our understanding of mathematics as a socio-cultural artefact similar to language. Any particular 'piece' of mathematics can then be located, spatially and in time, and be 'understood' within its cultural context. One outcome of this approach is to take away some of the mysticism and power of mathematics and to relocate respect to the learners, as well as those who have discovered or invented the culturally powerful tools and knowledge.

- What are the classroom discourses and practices that foster or deny the authorship of learners of mathematics?

We use empirical data to explore this question in order to embed our theorising in classrooms.

Coming to know mathematics

Three contrasting epistemological perspectives, three different 'ways of knowing' (Belenky *et al.*, 1986) are found in the mathematics classroom (as elsewhere): *silence, external authority* and *author/ity.* We are not claiming that these perspectives cover every epistemological stance or that a learner will, inevitably and irretrievably, be located in just one of them. But viewing classroom experiences through this lens helps us to understand how different pedagogical practices are experienced by learners.

The first perspective, that of *silence,* is where learners experience themselves as 'mindless and voiceless and subject to the whims of external authority' (ibid., p. 15). It cuts off the knower from all internal and external sources of intelligence. Such learners do not see themselves as developing, acting, learning, planning or choosing. They may have no vantage point outside the self from which to view their situation or may see themselves only as the object of such a gaze. They feel 'deaf' because they cannot learn the words of others and 'dumb' because they have no voice. The perspective is immobilising, making the mind blank so that the sense of knowing is lost. It is accompanied by fear, loss of a sense of agency and feelings of powerlessness (Buerk, 1985; Buxton, 1981; Isaacson, 1990). By its nature, although apparently so widespread, it is unlikely that, as teachers, we 'hear' this way of knowing in our classrooms. It is illustrated when learners find their voice again and can look back on the experience of silence: 'it is like a stainless steel wall – hard, cold, smooth, offering no handhold' (Buerk, 1985), 'the wall comes up ... down comes the blanket like a green baize cover over a parrot's cage' (Buxton, 1981, p. 4); 'if unable to answer some fate worse than death would be waiting' (Isaacson, 1990, p. 23). Laurie Buxton pointed to a key link between the generation of this state of silence and the presence of authority external to the learner. It is a way of knowing likely to be experienced in a classroom that is predicated on an epistemology of *external authority,* to a description of which we now turn.

The second epistemological perspective, possibly more commonly experienced than any other in mathematics classrooms, is that of *external authority.* Authority is experienced as external to the self and belonging to the 'experts'. Meaning is taken as given and knowledge is assumed to be fixed and absolute rather than contextual and changeable. The knower is deeply dependent on others, especially authoritative others. This is the voice that asks 'Is it an add, miss?' (Brown and Kuchemann, 1976) and it is the one to which many mathematicians from the hegemonic group would have us listen:

> A common cause for concern is that there is far too much emphasis on self-discovery rather than the presentation of material as a body of knowledge.
>
> (Professor Crighton, *Times Higher Education Supplement,*
> 24 February 1995, p. 6)

Much, even in those practices advocated as 'discovery', is predicated upon external authority as the appropriate way of knowing; indeed the learner is understood to be discovering the already known mathematics just as the mathematician is deemed to discover mathematics, which is implicit to the system:

> Nearly all research mathematicians believe that mathematics is discovered. This is subjectively how it feels when one is working.
>
> (David Epstein, 1994, private communication)

The authority for the learner rests in the content. The authority for the mathematician rests in the subject. In both cases, the authority is external. Paul Cobb, Terry Wood, Erna Yackel and Betsy McNeal (1992) gave an account of a teacher striving to work with her students in a 'discovery' mode, offering practical activities intended to evoke for the learners the mathematics to be learnt. However, a fundamental assumption behind the pedagogy was that the children's purpose when they engaged in mathematical activity was to match the teacher's intellectual expectations, in a sense to retell the teacher's story. In particular, 'Every challenge identified was made by the teacher, and, in this sense, she acted as the sole validator of what could count as legitimate mathematical activity' (p. 587). (See Edwards and Mercer, 1987, for a sensitive account of similar practices within the science classroom and Barbara Jaworski, 1999, for a sympathetic discussion of this difficulty for teachers.) More commonly, of course, 'delivery' of the teacher's knowledge is not simply implied by the pedagogy: it is explicitly given as the goal.

The third epistemological perspective is that of *author/ity* (Povey, 1995). Teachers and learners sharing this way of knowing work implicitly (and, perhaps, explicitly) with an understanding that they are members of a knowledge-making community. (The authors of each of the other chapters in this section have useful things to say about how such community meaning-making might be conceptualised and/or practised.) As such, meaning is understood as negotiated. External sources are consulted and respected, but they are also evaluated critically by the knowledge makers, those making meaning of mathematics in the classroom, with whom *author/ity* rests. Such a way of knowing opens up the possibility of understanding knowledge as constructed and meaning as contingent and contextual, and personal in the sense that it reflects the positionings of the knower. The teacher and the learner meet as epistemological equals. They work together to comprehend the world and to forge more adequate representations of it, which may include de-naturing the present and revisioning and re-envisaging the future (Kenway *et al.*, 1994, p. 202). It is therefore potentially emancipatory.

Within author/ity, we want to use the epistemological perspective suggested by Patricia Hill Collins (1991). She offers four dimensions that help to assess knowledge claims: *concrete experience as a criterion of meaning, the use of dialogue, the ethic of caring* and *the ethic of personal accountability*. We believe that these four dimensions comfortably describe author/ity, as we understand it, as well as give us a useful tool for making judgements about the efficacy of the mathematics classroom.

Concrete experience as a criterion of meaning allows for 'subjectivity between the knower and the known' (ibid., p. 211), relying upon her direct experience as a valid form of creating, testing and affirming meaning. Affirming the links between the concrete and the mathematical abstractions that are drawn from that concrete seems a necessary part, to us, of building mathematical competence and confidence.

The use of dialogue in assessing knowledge claims demands that such claims be subject to both connectedness and critique within a community of knowers. We understand the progess of making meaning, with Deborah Hicks, as that:

> ... of the child as actor within emergent and non-deterministic discourse contexts. As the child moves within the social world of the classroom, she appropriates (internalises) but also reconstructs the discourses that constitute the social world of her classroom. This creative process is what I would term learning.
>
> (Hicks, 1996, pp. 108–9)

The ethic of caring suggests to Patricia Hill Collins 'that personal expressiveness, emotions, and empathy are central to the knowledge validation process' (Collins, 1991, p. 215). In the context of the mathematics classroom, this relocates author/ity within the learner(s), respecting them for what they bring to the struggle for meaning, rather than reserving respect for the authorities who validate the communal knowledge. Between the personal expressions and the empathy of other learners lies the space for establishing similarity and difference, for drawing out analogy or establishing the boundaries within which a statement is valid. The ethic of caring requires that critique within the classroom to be both a requirement *and* a responsibility, which students and teachers accept in offering positive intellectual and emotional support while, at the same time, pointing out discrepancies and/or difficulties in argumentation.

The ethic of personal accountability calls upon learners to justify, to engage in debate, to provide an evidential basis for their knowledge claims and to be willing to participate in such activities as fully responsible members of the community of learners. (There are resonances here with Terry Wood and Tammy Tumer-Vorbeck, 1999.) Ways can then be found for mathematical knowledge claims in classrooms to 'stand the test of alternative ways of validating truth' (ibid., p. 219).

Author/ity and critical mathematics education

Author/ity as a way of knowing can be further explored through a concept of narrative. We all use narrative 'to make sense of our life experiences ... to give meaning and some semblance of coherence to our lives' (Clark, 1993, p. 32). Mathematics can be appropriately construed as narrative because it is 'an essentially interpretive activity' (Brown, 1994, p. 141), mathematical expressions being thus understood not as objects with internal inherent meaning but as hermeneutic acts uttered within a social space that is contingent upon context, culture and coherence. If mathematics is understood as the 'telling of a story', then each of us gains greater autonomy as an author of that mathematics, but not at the expense of a deep commitment to the social context of life and meaning-making. The very notion of telling a story presupposes at least an audience and at best an active community of meaning-makers.

[N]arrative always communicates within a community involving story teller(s), sometimes listeners, or readers, and sometimes participants. It engages others in the attempt not only to tell but also to explain and, ultimately, to understand the experience which has provoked it.

(Burton, 1996, p. 30)

The notion of mathematics as narrative helps us to 'see' the authors of mathematics within a community. This human meaning-making has been expunged from the accounts of mathematics that appear in standard texts; the contents are then portrayed in classrooms as authorless, as independent of time and place and as that which learners can only come to know by reference to external authority. The teacher becomes

a Pythagorean educator wishing to reveal to children the eternal Divine Forms of which children's experience must inevitably be but a confused anticipation or a pale reflection.

(Winter, 1992, p. 91)

Because the author(s) of the narrative remain hidden, mathematics becomes a cultural form suffused with mystery and power, a discourse that mystifies the basis for cultural domination. (See Winter, 1992; Skovsmose, 1994; and Burton, 1996 for a discussion.)

Understanding mathematics as narrative opens up the possibility of a more equal relationship between the teacher and the taught in mathematics classrooms. Nicholas Burbles and Suzanne Rice (1991) have noted that 'teacher authority, even if it is adopted with beneficial intent, takes significance against a pervasive background of relations of domination' (p. 396) and therefore needs constantly to be re-examined and called into question in an emancipatory classroom. If the task of learners in the mathematics classroom is to be, jointly or severally, the authors of their own mathematics, the culture of the classroom must be one in which an epistemology of author/ity is fostered. Constructing a narrative, acquiring authorship, cannot be done on the basis of the external authority of others, but needs the participant(s) to understand themselves as the makers of knowledge, tested out within their community of validators (Cobb *et al.*, 1992, p. 594). It also, of course, requires that such participants are not silenced in the sense outlined above, but have a personal voice.

Such a classroom is one in which teachers and learners strive to approximate to the ideal speech situation posited by Jurgen Habermas and summarised by his translator:

[T]he structure (of communication) is free from constraint only when for all participants there is a symmetrical distribution of chances to select and employ speech acts, when there is an effective equality of chances to assume dialogue roles. In particular, all participants must have the same chance to initiate and perpetuate discourse, to put forward, call into question, and give reasons for and against statements, explanations, interpretations, and justifications. Furthermore, they must have the same chance to express attitudes, feelings, intentions and the like, and to command, to oppose, to permit and to forbid, etc.

(McCarthy, 1975, quoted in Carr and Kemmis, 1986, p. 143)

In such a space, learners can tell their own stories about mathematics, the differing accounts and interpretations being subjected to productive dialogue in the search for more adequate descriptions of reality. The classroom changes. It is no longer a drill ground 'reflecting the commands put forward in the curriculum and made audible by the teacher' (Skovsmose, 1994, p. 185), which practises 'a system of oppression [which] draws much of its strength from the acquiescence of its victims who have accepted the dominant image of themselves and are paralysed by a sense of helplessness' (Murray, quoted in Collins, 1991, p. 93). It becomes a space for the inculcation and acquisition of the communicative virtues (Burbles and Rice, 1991, p. 411) which, in turn, are predicated on relationships of equality and respect for each of us as authors.

In mathematics classrooms in which learners are the author/ity of knowledge, they have the opportunity to use their personal authority both to produce and to critique meanings, to practise caring in a dialogic setting where the effectiveness of their own narrative(s) and also those of others is refined. The teacher and the learners will (implicitly) understand that they have 'constituted mathematical truths in the course of their social interactions and that acts of explaining and justifying were central to this process' (Cobb *et al.*, 1992, p. 592). When the learner's understandings do not fit with those of others, they are encouraged to engage in 'talk, discussion, suggestions and conjectures and refutations, or shifts of thought through resonance' (Lerman, 1994, p. 196), that is, to engage in the practice of critique, a practice fundamental to creating potentially emancipatory discourse.

Author/ity in practice

We wish to embed this theorising into the practices of the classroom, to try to make it 'fact-laden' (John Mason, 1999). But, as will be obvious, exemplifying the classroom discourses that foster the authorship of learners of mathematics is unlikely to be successfully done by presenting 'authorless' snippets of teachers and learners at work. *The meanings for the teachers* of their actions in the classroom are going to be central to understanding, in practice, how they foster author/ity: how they nurture respect for concrete experience as a criterion of meaning, how they promote dialogue, how they help to generate an ethic of caring and of personal accountability. We offer here extracts from the reflective writing of two secondary teachers who are committed to such a perspective. We invited them to read the chapter thus far and to use the ideas as a stimulus for thinking about their own classroom practices. We then wove their writing and ours together to construct the rest of this section.

Striving for clarity about what one wants to achieve is a starting point. Corinne is concerned to move her students from fearful mathematical silence to an epistemological location where they have the opportunity to express their author/ity. She writes:

> As a teacher I find that the children in my classroom are desperate for dialogue on all sorts of levels. The challenge for me is to provide them with the space in which to develop their mathematical voices and not to drown out their efforts in a cacophony of discordant demands. As a friend, a parent, a sibling, I find it much easier to allow dialogue on somebody else's terms. I happily participate in

hundreds of conversations with my own children that lead into blind ends; a luxury I rarely afford the children I teach. In the classroom there is always the curriculum, the lesson plan, the implications for classroom management, most of all there is the fear of anarchy ...

This starting point allows her to focus on the narrative usually constructed in mathematics classrooms and to critique her own actions as they reflect current practice.

I remember a mixed ability lesson on percentages with my class of 11-year-olds.

ME: What does per cent mean?

Five hands shoot up. (I seem to have forgotten the strategy of tell the person next to you, now tell your table and so on.) Twenty-five people are already feeling voiceless. I select one hand.

CHILD A: It means in the shops you get 50 per cent off.

How can, how should, I reply to this? The child has stated what percentage means to him at the moment. He is therefore right but on the other hand the lesson exists to move his understanding on and so he is not right enough! What might have happened if I had responded as a person not a teacher?

ME: Yes, that's right I expect everybody has seen those kinds of signs up in the shops. What were you going to say?
CHILD B: It means if its 10 per cent off then that's 10p in every £1.
ME: Very good, it does. That's something to do with how many pence there are in a pound. Does anybody know what cent means in French? (I write cent on the board.)
ANONYMOUS VOICE: One hundred.
ME: That's right. What were you going to say?
CHILD C: Does it mean out of 100?

Child C clearly felt that the initial question had not been answered, that the class had not yet produced the desired result. I greeted her answer with enthusiasm, which the class picked up on as meaning that's it, we've cracked it. All of us then breathed a collective sigh of relief. Had any of us really achieved anything at all?

This incident draws attention to a very real difficulty with teacher questioning: teacher questions seem to imply answers and those then seem to be both predetermined and already known.

As well as enabling her to see differently some practices currently accepted, Corinne's starting point also allows the possibility of understanding 'deviant' practice differently and of recognising the need to renegotiate the complex space within which students can pursue meaning-making.

Later in the lesson, after a number of activities, child C shouted out, '10 per cent is not really very much, is it?' Child B joined in, 'No, they just do that to make you think you are getting a bargain.' I joined in with their cross-class chat by suggesting that 10 per cent of a large lottery win might be quite a lot of money. More people joined in and a far more meaningful discussion took place – or perhaps a disruptive girl pulled half the class off task? It was, of course, bad classroom practice; children should not shout out, they should not have conversations across the room and certainly the teacher should not join in and hence condone such behaviour. How can teachers provide space for children to express the things they've just thought of?

Taking seriously the notion of children as authors of mathematics involves a more fluid and responsive structure to mathematics lessons. Building such a classroom culture takes a considerable amount of time.

Mark had been working with the same class for more than a year and had a number of experiences that were significant in moving himself and the class forward. In these reflections on a particular lesson with them, we see glimpses of what it can mean for students to be the authors of mathematics and the significance of this for them as learners.

I have come to identify with a radical tradition in education that seeks to develop educational practice in such a way that it can help to nourish personal development ... A significant concern is how can I create the conditions whereby my students think more critically about mathematics, themselves as learners, the learning process, schooling and society ... One incident that helped me think about how the gap between my theory and practice might be closed arose out of a lesson on infinity and the students' response to it ... I was stuck for a lesson for the last lesson with my class of 15-year-olds on the last Friday of a long half-term. The tradition was to play some sort of mathematical game. (It is an indictment of our National Curriculum [in the UK] that its effect is so unexciting that a game is seen by teachers and students as a relaxing release from its pressure and, by implication, that maths lessons being enjoyable is a rarity.) However I had the idea that I wanted to do something different and decided that a lesson on infinity was a much better idea. The students took some convincing that 'going lobster fishing' wasn't a better choice!

The lesson was investigative and largely orally based. It was clear during the lesson that many students had thought deeply about the concept, even if it was on the part of some students to deny its reality. This was a 'good' lesson in the sense that our current regime of inspectors teaches us how to think about lessons in that nearly all students remained on task throughout the lesson, they used and learned mathematics at the higher levels of the National Curriculum (calculating with fractions, deriving sequences by iteration, summing to a limit). This was important to me because in the short-term it feels necessary to show that teaching in a different way ought to be successful in those terms as well as giving more besides. Feeling a little carried away by its success, I set them a homework to do over half-term (much moaned about at the time) on the lesson. I asked them to do two sides of A4 on infinity. The choice of the content was up to them, they might choose to investigate some infinite series of their own, to write about the history of the idea, their own ideas about infinity or to write a poem (no takers for this one but that's hardly surprising as the number of poems by 'proper poets' on the subject is not very large).

The students' response was qualitatively different from previous pieces of work ... I was teaching in a working-class school set in a large council estate with high levels of poverty and unemployment. The students' image of themselves as learners is generally low ... In addition there exists a counter culture in the school which derides achievement and interest in learning; this is particularly prevalent amongst boys in the school. The students' responses were the most individual pieces of work I had received. I felt that I had set them a difficult task and they had responded very well. I felt pleased with what had happened but did not spend too long thinking about it.

Later in the year students had to write formative records of achievement and select one piece of work that they felt most proud of. To my surprise the majority of students chose the work they had done on infinity ... When I discussed their choices of work with them I realised that for a number of them their view of learning and themselves as learners had changed in a small but important way.

Mark also offers an account of a more 'commonplace' lesson, a surface description of which might have much in common with classrooms predicated on a very different epistemology. We have to read through the lines in order to hear the validation of specific experience, the centrality of dialogue for building shared meaning, the respect for what the learners bring and the call to justify their knowledge claims within a community of learners.

I think my students get a lot from the collective strength of tackling a problem together ... One lesson I wanted my 14-year-old students to get practice in using Pythagoras' theorem, a new topic for them. I saw an opportunity to explore trial and improvement methods at the same time. I didn't have a clear idea of exactly where the lesson was going to go, preferring to let the students' response guide me.

I started by setting out a problem from recreational maths. Sue, a forest ranger, is 300 m east from a river when she sees smoke from a fire 1000 m north and 400 m east from her. She has to run to the river, collect a bucket of water and then run to the fire to put it out. Obviously she needs to do this in the shortest time possible and so must run the shortest distance from her position to the river and then to the fire.

The students' first task was to agree in pairs on a diagram that would model the problem. We then shared these on the board. A class discussion then followed on what might be the best solution, some students asserting that she should run directly east and then diagonally to the fire, others stating that she run diagonally to the river and then go east, whilst the rest argued for two diagonal runs. The students came and drew diagrams on the board of their proposed solutions, identified right-angled triangles and quickly realised that all of their proposals would need to be tested by using Pythagoras. We worked through one triangle together to make sure everyone was happy about applying the rule in this context.

They set to work in pairs to calculate distances for their preferred solutions... Comparing answers we agreed that we couldn't be certain that any of the solutions was the shortest distance. A little nudging led to the idea of searching for a solution and we agreed on steps of 50 m. The work was divided up and more distances calculated.

We collected the solutions in a table. The design of the table provoked some controversy but the majority wanted as much information as possible in it. All possibilities were attempted by at least two pairs and this meant that the class checked each other's results. When differences of opinion occurred we all worked through the triangles and had the chance to discuss some common errors. In the situation of a shared goal the error makers didn't seem particularly embarrassed but rather valued for adding a useful contribution to the experience. Examining the table led to the decisions to narrow the range of the search and we tackled the problem again at 5 m intervals and then finally we narrowed the solution down to the nearest metre.

We discussed some extensions and most students worked through the problem again setting their own initial distances at home. One pair tried to see if they could find the point Sue would get to the river given the total distance and another decided that Sue wouldn't be able to run as fast once she was carrying a bucket full of water and with some guidance found a new solution to the original problem taking this into account – although their assumed running speeds would have made Sue a world record middle distance runner by a long way! All homeworks were completed on time – a very unusual occurrence with this class.

Tasks that can be approached in a variety of ways and that depend upon a range of different responses can provide a particular opportunity for nurturing an alterative epistemology. Mark and Corinne were together involved in two lessons when a class of 15-year-old students, during a visit to the university, worked on the idea of geometric construction. In groups, the students spent part of the time using a variety of materials – geostrips, tissue paper circles, pairs of compasses – to construct a square in as many different ways as they could, sharing their results later with one another and explaining what they had produced. They were also asked to reconstruct a particular figure (of an equilateral triangle produced by two circles) using dynamic geometry software, to set themselves the task of constructing some other constrained triangle (for example, isosceles or right-angled) and finally some polygon(s) of their choice. Groups compared and contrasted their approaches and needed only a little encouragement to believe that alternative paths might lead equally to success. The fact that all the pairs set themselves to work with a will, and had no difficulty in setting themselves a task and tackling it, is a result of patterns of working that Mark had established over time. Nevertheless, the students noted and valued particular features of these sessions. Lucy said:

> I liked doing them circles best, the ones with the triangle, we thought about trying to do a scalene triangle but we didn't have time. We thought that were good when we were trying to work out about why [the equilateral triangle] did that ... it took us

more than once to try and work out the first time and then once we'd got that we could like go on to other things ... I liked it because we had to experiment.

The students were asked to write up their reflections on the experience.

> JOANNE: The work we did was quite challenging and I enjoyed it a lot. I enjoyed puzzling things out and trying my ideas. I also enjoyed being part of the 'group' and knowing that I was there to not just work on my own but to work with someone I could talk to, work with and relate to. It also felt good to be able to talk to other people about my work.
>
> PATRICK: I also learnt that maths isn't just writing, there are lots of practical things you can do.
>
> MATTHEW: I also learnt a lot about myself. I learnt that I can work with a partner and in groups to solve problems, and I can work on a puzzle until it is solved, correcting mistakes I make and learning from them.
>
> ZOE: ... the work we did involved more thinking and remembering what we had done, at school we usually write everything that we learn or have learnt in the past.

Mark, in turn, reflected on the students' responses.

> Studies have shown that students from working-class schools spend a significantly greater amount of time than other students writing. The approaches to learning that the students described and valued have been an important part of the way I have tried to work. Nevertheless the unspoken realities and culture of school life have nudged me in the direction of 'write it down'. There is a strong fear that if there is not a written record of work done then the work will be less valid. I recognise how this displays a lack of confidence that students really will learn more through discussion: they had better have a written record to help them 'revise' in case the content is not learnt ... Is the current emphasis in the [UK] National Curriculum on record keeping, evidence, inspection and testing a pressure away from the oral and group work these students so enjoyed? ... It is ironic that the students who were critical of their usual diet of 'writing things down' were much more enthusiastic when writing their own record of the visits: here the process of writing was a creative individual act.

These visits helped Mark in his attempts to look behind the taken-for-granted practices of schooling and the epistemology on which they are based, which restricts the use of a caring and accountable dialogue in the construction of mathematical meaning. Corinne describes how a pupil-shadowing exercise illuminated for her how those practices inhibit the voice of the student and neglect the potential of the knowledge-making community, which is the class.

> I was involved recently in a shadowing exercise, following a 14-year-old pupil, which amongst other issues brought home to me just how 'silencing' the

classroom environment is. In an art lesson, I watched as a teacher tried to interest her students in a display of lettering whilst they were otherwise occupied. Eventually one of the girls listened and started to 'argue/discuss' but she was reprimanded for talking out of turn even though she was the only person willing to engage. The message goes out that sitting and silently ignoring a teacher is more commendable than taking issue. This observation was repeated in technology where again a girl made a pertinent observation and started asking insightful questions but was ignored then fobbed off. Later in science it was the same story when a boy started to question the structure of the atom. Just the same thing happens in maths lessons. We appear to be determined to make our classes walk along predetermined paths that are called lesson plans, schemes of work and so on.

During my pupil-shadowing day I talked to three 14-year-old students for an hour. I asked them to tell me about any experience in school where they felt they had really learned something. One of the boys described a lesson the previous week when a supply teacher had taken them for science and he had answered all of the boy's questions, engaging in conversation and discussion for nearly an hour. I asked one of the other students whether this hadn't been a bit boring for the rest of the group. 'Oh no', he replied, 'it was great. We were all listening and joining in a bit, it's just that Tim asked most of the questions'. It is a classical way of learning. It is how most pre-school learning takes place and fortunate children have a parent or friend who is willing to go on engaging in discussion on the child's terms. It seems to be a rarity in school. We are so locked into an ideology of performance and testing that we dare not depart into the realms of true enquiry. We do not allow ourselves the time to meander in directions chosen by our pupils.

Skovsmose notes that 'when the orientation is decided by the child, an epistemic 'energy' is released' (Skovsmose, 1994, p. 69). This epistemic energy can be seen 'as something people possess which must be annexed in order for larger systems of oppression to function' (Collins, 1991, p. 166, drawing on the work of Audre Lorde). This epistemic energy needs to be released if mathematics classrooms are to be the site of critical education.

Conclusion

In this chapter we have explored how the characterisation of mathematics learners as authors can help us uncover aspects of liberatory classroom practice. We have argued that fostering an epistemological perspective of *author/ity* among teachers and learners will support a renegotiation of the relations of dominance embedded within current conceptions of the nature of mathematical knowledge. Such an epistemological perspective takes the concrete and the personal as the starting point for meaning-making; it recognises the vitality and significance of dialogue in the process of knowledge construction within a community; it relocates the privileging of the read *and* written in the mathematics classroom into a more coherent approach drawing upon speaking, listening, reading and writing and emphasising meaning construction and negotiation; and it nurtures within that community an ethic of care and of personal accountability. Sal Restivo (1992) has written,

> Some of the representations of dominant groups are likely to be labelled as self-evident, and put to use to enforce conformity, put a subject beyond dispute, and deal with ambiguities and anomalous events.

(p. 125)

Much mathematics has functioned as such a representation. It is our hope that the ideas in this chapter will support a challenge to mathematics thus viewed and will help open up the power of the subject to learners within communities to whom it has so far largely been denied.

References

Belenky M. F., Clinchy, B. M., Goldberger, N. R. and Tarule, J. M. (1986). *Women's Ways of Knowing: The Development of Self, Voice and Mind*, Basic Books, New York.

Brown, M. and Kuchemann, D. (1976). Is it an add, miss? *Mathematics in Schools*, 5, 5, pp. 15–17.

Brown, T. (1994). Towards a hermeneutical understanding of mathematics and mathematical learning. In P. Ernest (ed.) *Constructing Mathematical Knowledge: Epistemology and Mathematics Education*, Falmer Press, London.

Buerk, D. (1985).The voices of women making meaning in mathematics. *Journal of Education*, 167, 3, pp. 59–70.

Burbles, N. and Rice, S. (1991). Dialogue across differences: Continuing the conversation. *Harvard Educational Review*, 61, 4, pp. 393–416.

Burton, L. (1996). Mathematics, and its learning, as narrative – a literacy for the twenty-first century. In D. Baker, J. Clay and C. Fox (eds) *Challenging Ways of Knowing in English, Mathematics and Science*, Falmer Press, London.

Buxton L. (1981). *Do You Panic about Maths?* Heinemann, London.

Carr, W. and Kemmis, S. (1986). *Becoming Critical: Education, Knowledge and Action Research*, Falmer Press, Lewes.

Clark, C. (1993). Changing teachers through telling stories. *Support for Learning*, 8, 1, pp. 31–34.

Cobb, P., Wood, T., Yackel, E. and McNeal, B. (1992). Characteristics of classroom mathematics traditions: An interactional analysis. *American Educational Research Journal*, 29, 3, pp. 573–604.

Collins, P. Hill (1991). *Black Feminist Thought: Knowledge, Consciousness, and the Politics of Empowerment*, Routledge, London.

Edwards, D. and Mercer, N. (1987). *Common Knowledge: The Development of Understanding in the Classroom*, Routledge, London.

Hick, D. (1996). *Discourse, learning, and schooling*, Cambridge University Press.

Isaacson, Z. (1990). 'They look at you in absolute horror': Women writing and talking about mathematics. In L. Burton (ed.) *Gender and Mathematics: An International Perspective*, Cassell, London.

Jaworski, B. (1999). Tensions in Teachers' Conceptualizations of Mathematics and Teaching. In L. Burton (ed.) *Learning Mathematics: From Hierarchies to Networks*, Falmer Press, London.

Kenway, J., Willis, S., Blackmore, J. and Rennie, L. (1994). Making 'hope practical' rather than 'despair convincing': Feminist post-structuralism, gender reform and educational change. *British Journal of Sociology of Education,* **15**, 2, pp. 187–210.

Lerman, S. (ed.) (1994). *Cultural Perspectives on the Mathematics Classroom,* Kluwer, Dordrecht.

McCarthy, T. (1975). *Legitimation Crisis,* Beacon Books, Boston.

Mason, J. (1999). The Role of Labels for Experience in Promoting Learning from Experience Among Teachers and Students. In L. Burton (ed.) *Learning Mathematics: From Hierarchies to Networks,* Falmer Press, London.

Povey, H. (1995). Ways of knowing of student and beginning mathematics teachers and their relevance to becoming a teacher working for change. Ph.D. thesis, University of Birmingham, School of Education.

Restivo, S. (1992). *Mathematics in Society and History,* Episteme 20, Kluwer, Dordrecht.

Skovsmose, O. (1994). *Towards a Philosophy of Critical Mathematics Education,* Kluwer, Dordrecht.

Winter, R. (1992). 'Mathophobia', Pythagoras and roller-skating. In M. Nickson and S. Lerman (eds) *The Social Context of Mathematics Education: Theory and Practice,* South Bank Press, London.

Wood, T. and Turner-Vorbeck, T. (1999). Developing Teaching of Mathematics: Making connections in practice. In L. Burton (ed.) *Learning Mathematics: From Hierarchies to Networks,* Falmer Press, London.

4 Paradigmatic conflicts in informal mathematics assessment as sources of social inequity

Anne Watson

Abstract

Mathematics teaching in the UK has undergone several major externally imposed changes during the last decade. Current practices display a range of epistemological and pedagogical assumptions and behaviours, depending on teachers' interpretation of, adoption of and belief in current statutory requirements for teaching and assessment. This paper examines in detail differences within the informal assessment practices of 30 UK mathematics teachers. It is found that these illustrate several of the paradigmatic differences that permeate studies of human behaviour on a grander scale. Since informal assessment decisions can lead directly or indirectly to differentiated access to the curriculum and high-stakes grading, the use of teacher assessment as a focus for examining differences illuminates the possible inequities which might arise for pupils. Examination of differences within one system and one society gives information about effects of different educational practices which, were they to show up between societies, might be attributed to other social and cultural factors.

Introduction

The recent publication of the TIMSS report (1997) has generated much interest in international comparisons of the mathematical performance of school children. Many attempts have been made to make sense of different outcomes relative to features of national culture, such as predominant teaching styles, social structures, educational intentions and so on (Jaworski and Phillips, 1999). In this paper I will look closely at a subgroup of differences of practice within one highly structured national system, that of the UK National Curriculum (NC), in order to show a range which cannot be explained solely by national features. These differences reveal a collection of paradigmatic conflicts within one national culture, expressed as variations in classroom cultures.

In the context of educational research Gage (1989) suggests that 'paradigm differences do not require paradigm conflict'. He shows how it should be possible for three apparently unreconcilable perspectives, which I shall roughly classify *positivist, relativist* and *emancipatory,* to contribute three compatible forms of knowledge about teaching, learning and schools. The kinds of questions one can pose within each paradigm, and the ways one might answer, are different but the ultimate purpose of improving education is the same. However, Brown (1993) describes conflicts that arise when these different paradigms are used to design usable curricular and assessment systems. She collates the subjective and emancipatory paradigms and describes how an interpretivist/relative/subjective view of knowledge, such as one might need for the problem-solving aims of the mathematics NC, can be emancipatory for learners by allowing them to use pragmatic forms of knowledge they have developed outside school, or for the specific purpose of solving the current problem. These approaches inevitably clash with the absolutist/positivist/objective approach which led to the structures of the NC and require mathematics to be a formal, abstract, testable, hierarchical body of knowledge (Lawton, 1993). Cresswell and Houston (1989) examine contextual assessment tasks for mathematics, introduced in an attempt to reconcile these views, and conclude that the effect of context on performance led them to be 'less accurate, reliable and fair' in producing abstract statements of achievement than conventional assessment proce-dures, which are well known to be unfair (Gipps, 1994). Cooper and Dunne (1998) provide evidence of inequities created by contextual mathematics test questions demanding situational and linguistic flexibility which appears to discriminate along class and gender lines (see also Bernstein, 1990). In other words, some methods of summative assessment which have the appearance of supporting an interpretivist view of knowledge can be as unfair as positivist approaches, thus challenging Brown's implied collation of interpretivist and emancipatory approaches within the current system.

Individual classroom cultures are, however, created only in part by the external system within which teachers operate; teachers' interpretation of statutory requirements in prac-tice varies according to their own beliefs and philosophies. As Thom (1973) said: 'All mathematical pedagogy, even if scarcely coherent, rests on a philosophy of mathematics', a point elaborated in Thompson's (1992) substantial review of the relationship between teachers' beliefs and their practices. Beliefs are expressed in a range of ways, most power-fully in how (and in what circumstances) the teacher evaluates and responds to students' attempts to express their mathematical understanding, for it is partly through these mech-anisms that learners decide what mathematics is (Nickson, 1994). In recognition of the importance of classroom beliefs, Steiner (1987) has called for the development of:

> A meta-theory (of mathematics) which is based on a systems approach based on human activity and social interaction ... a system from the point of view of human object-related cooperative activities.

Similarly, Ernest (1998) has attempted to develop a philosophy of mathematics which includes an adequate account of how it is learnt, arguing that any philosophy which excludes such features cannot account for the development and use of the subject.

The aspect of classroom culture discussed in this paper is teachers' informal, ongoing assessment of students' mathematics. Assessment both contributes to, and is partly formed by, the classroom culture as a whole. The mechanisms of assessment reflect what is valued by teachers and others, explicate such values, bestow status and also shape classroom activities so that valued behaviour is generated. 'We interpret, theorise, teach, test, assume, expect, measure and thus confirm our initial expectations of children' (Lerman, 1994, p. 192).

In the UK educational system informal assessment practices contribute to discrimi-natory curriculum decisions from an early age through grouping, tracking and setting practices which, according to OFSTED (1994), are used increasingly. They also contribute to grading decisions at 7, 11 and 14, which may be used for high-stakes decisions, and to high-stakes decisions at 16+. Teachers' assessments, as well as structuring and reflecting what is valued in school mathematics, therefore partly control access to the curriculum and hence to future educational and social opportunity. Indeed it is usually in-school assessments which generate the information used to place pupils in differentiated groups for mathematics teaching, groups which tend to fracture the student cohort in terms of class and ethnicity (Boaler, 1997). For these reasons it is important to look at informal assessment to see if, and how, inequities might arise in its associated practices.

Research

Thirty primary and secondary teachers were interviewed about their informal assessment practices over a period of three years during which they were using an early version of the Mathematics National Curriculum which was very prescriptive both in terms of what has to be studied, and in the detail of the accompanying assessment criteria. The sample was selected to represent primary, middle and secondary school teachers of Years 6 and 7 in three local authorities. Early interviews were arranged through personal contacts and a balanced total sample was achieved by approaching other schools by letter, sampling from appropriate lists. To a certain extent all the teachers were self-selected as being interested in talking about their assessment practices. All the teachers had received some training in the objectives, content and assessment requirements.

The NC provides a framework for UK mathematics teaching which emphasises process as well as product, expects understanding as well as performance, and encourages the development of practical, problem-solving and investigative skills alongside knowledge of the conventional canons of the subject (DfE, 1995). Within this system of a prescribed curriculum, detailed assessment criteria and trained teacher-assessors it will be instructive to look at varieties of practice. However, it must be emphasised that the assessment criteria required by the NC were summative statements of capability, understanding and performance; while what teachers look for in their informal assessment includes, as well as these features, useful working habits and notions of 'ability' and 'potential' which help a teacher decide what to say, and how, to whom (Lorenz, 1982; Ruthven, 1987; Dunne, 1994; Watson, 1996).

Interviews typically lasted an hour, taking place after a day's observation and support in the teacher's classroom, and were semi-structured around a core question and a core prompt: 'How do you find out and recognise what children know and can do in mathematics? Tell me about <child's name>'s mathematics'.

Interview transcripts were analysed in several ways, including an analysis of the interviewer's role. Firstly, many features of the teacher's narratives about assessment were identified and coded. Then these were grouped into categories that describe assessment practices from various perspectives. The relevant process for this paper was the recognition of several levels of power in the practice of teachers-as-assessors. These were identified by looking for features of the reported assessment practices in which teachers exercised choice, explicitly or implicitly, and where they reported having to 'fit in' with real or perceived constraints, as they interpreted them, imposed by various authorities. In this analysis the teacher is seen as subordinate or superordinate to some of the components of teacher assessment, thus exercising power over or being subject to the power of others. For instance, the teacher is subordinate in the NC assessment structure, being the servant of the government and answerable to it through inspection. The teacher is subordinate to the school governing body, carrying out its policies, working within the staffing structure it provides, and answerable to it through league tables and appraisal. The teacher is superordinate to the pupils; they are expected to learn through her actions, obey her, fulfil her expectations, and will be assessed by her and have certain decisions about futures made by her, and yet they also bring aspects of other parts of their lives and other knowledge into the classroom.

Figure 4.1 describes these power relationships, producing a network of relations in the classroom. It is not a complete picture of power relations in the classroom, because it only sets out to describe those that affect the actions and intentions of the teacher-as-assessor. For the purposes of this illustration I have taken 'mathematics' to be an academic structure in which the teacher is servant to a higher notion of mathematics as an academic subject; this is represented to the teacher by the NC and the statutory assessment requirements. I have selected this view of mathematics so that Figure 4.1 presents the maximum possible power superordinate to the teacher, and hence describes the teacher as under most pressure to conform to outside influences. The final powerfulness of the teacher is expressed through interpretation of the pupils' work, leading to an assessment judgement. Of course, the teaching process does not end there; such judgements then affect teachers' actions, pupils' dispositions, and possibly, eventually, teachers' own attitudes.

This structure having been suggested by an initial analysis of the interviews, the transcripts were then re-analysed with this framework in mind. Statements about actions, methods, systems, beliefs from the 30 interviews were sorted within the structure of relationships, and the reported practices then examined for similarities and differences within each grouping. This proved to be an effective method of exposing differences within the collected practices of all 30 teachers, showing how far intentions and actions were shared between the teachers, and what sort of differences could occur. The differences I report here are those which emerged from this analysis and might lead to inequity. By inequity I mean the making of different decisions and the offering of different opportunities, in similar circumstances, by different teachers, in ways which might affect pupils' futures. Operational differences which were explicitly mentioned by the interviewees are dealt with elsewhere (Watson, 1998). Similar contradictions appeared in several places in the data, so I will report them under the following headings rather than as features of the power relationships:

- differences in perception of how pupils can change;
- differences in teaching practices which can affect assessment;
- differences in assessment practices which could lead to different outcomes;
- different learning styles of students;
- differences in desired learning outcomes;
- different views of mathematics; and
- different personal experience.

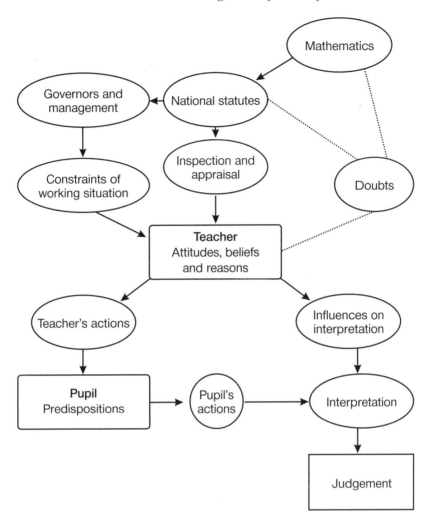

Figure 4.1 Power relationships

Differences in perception of how pupils can change

Teachers differ in their perceptions of stability of certain traits in their students. For instance, impoverished socio-economic background was sometimes given as a reason for underachievement, yet some teachers had high expectations as a norm and did not mention background as relevant. For some teachers motivation, interest, boredom, confidence and preferred learning styles were treated as given, but other teachers regarded it as part of their job to affect these through their expectations or teaching styles.

The influence of the teacher's existing knowledge of a pupil is important. Some teachers were aware that they would react differently to different pupils doing the same thing because they had formed judgements about the capability in advance. The expectation that pupils will follow patterns of learning behaviour, and that the teacher can get to know these patterns thoroughly enough to spot when an incident is a manifestation of normal behaviour, and when it is an aberration, is high. One teacher was sure he would know whether an error was evidence of misunderstanding, or merely a 'slip-up', because of who had made it. The question here is whether real changes in learning behaviour will be interpreted as such by a teacher who already has a strong opinion of a pupil.

Differences in teaching practices which can affect assessment

All teachers used investigative activities for assessment of mathematical processes, although some only used them for assessment purposes. Some teachers gave regular tests and practice sessions for national tests, while others did not. Some teachers give practical tasks as an assessment tool, believing application to be the ultimate demonstration of understanding. Others give practical work first to motivate the topic. Those students who are encouraged often to work investigatively or practically, or have practice tests will, presumably, be better at working that way when being assessed, or applying their knowledge with different strengths in different circumstances.

Teachers talked of different groupings and expectations of pupils, offering different levels of challenge and expecting different outcomes. It is well known that this approach creates or confirms difference as well as responding to it (e.g. Nash, 1976). For instance, a teacher's actions generate similar behaviours for most pupils who conform to a notional norm, but noticeably different behaviour in those who do not fit the norm (Walkerdine, 1984). The tension here could be between individual and group approaches to education, but could also be between the maintenance or improvement of past standards.

In teaching interventions some teachers prefer to show similar examples, similar explanations to the ones which have previously failed to help the pupil understand, while others look for different approaches and examples. The teacher who uses a transmission model of teaching offering pupils opportunities to fill in gaps of a message previously received, and the teacher who expects the pupils to construct their own meanings offering a variety of metaphors to aid construction, encourage different learning styles. The former may lead to a solely procedural view of mathematics, the latter to a broader, more adaptable view of mathematics.

Many teachers acknowledged that working from written texts is difficult and they have to mediate frequently, very often the difficulty being with the text and not with the mathematics. It was found that often the same teachers use texts not just as sources of questions and ideas but as a major teaching method thus further disadvantaging pupils already recognised as having difficulty.

Differences in assessment practices which could lead to different outcomes

Many teachers were doubtful about the use of tests: they are 'limited' and 'not the be all and end all'. Others regarded them as a way to verify what they already knew in a way that would be acceptable to outside eyes. Many teachers referred to well-known problems with regard to national tests, for instance, they believed that use of contexts could bias results for certain students; some students reacted badly to test pressure; tests could only test certain things and not tell you about the whole of a student's achievement; test questions can be ambiguous; and so on. But they did not raise the same issues about their own 'home-made' tests.

Time was a huge problem; teachers frequently said that assessment of individual pupils required time to be done accurately, and time was not realistically available. Therefore they had to prioritise. Teachers vary in how they prioritise what they want to find out about new pupils. For instance, some wanted to know first how pupils work, especially in investigative situations. Others wanted to find out what pupils already know by using specially designed assessment. Thus teachers gain different kinds of knowledge about individuals during the early lessons of a course and may therefore base their initial assessments on different kinds of evidence.

Different learning styles

Teachers talked of achievement and display of understanding as an exploratory, discursive and reflective practice which nevertheless could cause frustration in some students. They described students who are goal oriented and dislike explaining before moving on to something else; who prefer a conformist approach and linear progress through textbooks; who aim for mastery; who need to see how a concept could be useful. In contrast, teachers used words like 'imagination' and 'intuition' to describe good learners of mathematics. But in general there was more concern voiced about those who could not work in unstructured, relational or creative ways, than those who could not work in structured or instrumental ways. Learners with some preferred styles of learning may not be encouraged to develop a repertoire of other ways to learn (Scott-Hodgetts, 1986).

Differences in desired learning outcomes

One difference in desired outcomes is the perceived importance of pupils' own methods. Almost all teachers valued these, but traditional layouts are taught and given higher status by teachers because they believe these to be the desired artefacts of the prevailing assessment culture. Teachers have largely adopted the aims expressed throughout the NC, of understanding, explaining and valuing own methods. But these aims cause problems with some pupils, especially those who find writing about their mental processes hard, and conflict with a perceived aim of producing traditional algorithms.

There are different views about written work: some only accepting it if accompanied by discussion or other oral work, others seeing it as the summit of achievement. In the end, disembodied written communication is important in exams and tests, yet most teachers say that there is a gap between understanding, successful doing of mathematics and being able to write it appropriately. The order in which teachers expect work done (oral–written or written–oral) varies. Quality of written work may be confused with good presentation, and very messy work is not always a demonstration of failure to understand. These differences may lead to different classroom practices for similar pupils, and different judgements being made about the mathematics represented by written work.

Teachers make judgements about pupils' normal achievements in classrooms, and these are influenced by their own values in mathematics. Several different aspects of doing maths in classrooms have to be balanced. For instance, ad hoc problem-solving skills and replicable mathematical skills, memory for rules and ability to adapt rules, may be valued differently by different teachers. Even with similar views of mathematics, teachers may interpret evidence differently because their idea of how mathematics should be represented may differ. If the ultimate aim of an activity is an algebraic expression in correct form, other forms of that expression (diagrammatic, verbal, unconventional algebra, etc.) may or may not be valued, depending on the teacher.

Language weaknesses may mask the level of understanding. Some teachers might say that if a pupil understands they will be able to communicate it, others that these are separate processes and understanding may precede communication.

Different views of mathematics

Strong links exist between teachers' views of mathematics, how they teach it, how they interact with pupils about mathematics, and therefore how the pupil views mathematics, does mathematics and achieves in mathematics (Thompson, 1992; Nickson, 1994). Hence there is an inevitable link between views of mathematics and ideas about its assessment. There are differences in views about order in mathematical learning so that a display of understanding will lead to different assumptions, made by different observers, about what else the pupil knows. Also views of understanding may vary. For instance, a teacher with a *utilitarian* view of mathematics may see successful use as indicative of understanding, where one with a *logicist* view might require a full explanation of meaning or deduction (Ernest, 1990). Hence achievement may be 'measured' differently.

Different personal experience

Some of the interviewed teachers seemed implicitly to be assuming that those who could follow their expectations, or communicate in a way they understood, or responded well to them in class, were the 'able' ones. One teacher, a highly qualified and articulate mathematician, described the 'good' ones as 'the ones who always answer, and have the right answers', but another teacher believed that struggle and discomfort were an essential part of her learning, and that work should be difficult. A third teacher pointed out that some of her students do not answer, but follow painstaking, insecure, logical pathways that demonstrate their mathematical ability. Yet another teacher knew from her own experience that one can make leaps into the abstract that are so different from the way others work that one can be ridiculed for doing so. So different teachers' own experience of learning leads them to value, and devalue, different kinds of effort.

Summary

To summarise, therefore, there are several differences in the practices of teachers-as-assessors. One might query whether there exists a professional understanding of common practice. In terms of political positioning there is; it is at the interface between politicians, assessment authorities, industry, parents and pupils. Teachers form a clear group who administer the wishes of the first two groups, have to fulfil the desires of the next two groups and do their best for the last group. There is no reason why such a community should not have its internal tensions and contradictions, but those described above affect the futures of the pupils because they all contribute towards assessment decisions which would lead to different pedagogic, organisational and social choices. It would be possible for the same pupil producing the same work in different circumstances with different teachers to have the work, and her future, assessed differently.

Underlying each of the differences described above there appear to be six major contrasting beliefs and perceptions which are manifested in various ways. These may look like dichotomies below, but should really be seen as spectra represented by two ends of a range of views:

1   *Personal change is a result of natural maturation, or education.* The sections above on perception of change, teaching practices and learning styles show differences between teachers who think they can affect change, that it is part of their job to influence change, and those who accept personal traits and learning habits as 'given'. This is a manifestation of a 'nature versus nurture' debate, a version of the difference between psychology and anthropology, or of the difference between positivist and emancipatory views of education.

2   *Mathematical knowledge is universal and transferable, or situationally specific.* The discussions above about teaching practices, assessment styles and desired learning outcomes show contrasts between those who see mathematics as generated in and for a specific situation and those who expect it to be transferred without problem to other situations; this is most marked in cases where the assessment styles differ markedly from usual teaching and learning styles, and in the suggestion that number is easiest to assess. This is a manifestation of the difference between positivist and relativist views of mathematics, and of Brown's demonstration of the emancipatory power of valuing ad hoc approaches to mathematics.

3   *Students learn through transmission, or through construction.* The discussion about teaching practices, assessment methods, desired outcomes and views of mathematics shows contrasts between actions which 'fit' a transmission metaphor of teaching and those which 'fit' a constructivist approach (e.g. Jaworski, 1994). However, the above discussion of learning styles shows a strong understanding of constructivism as a learning approach, but this is not necessarily carried through into the assessment practices which may function as if knowledge is transmitted in unchanged forms. This is a manifestation of a conflict between positivist and relativist/transformative views of learning.

4   *Education is for development of individuals, or for the development of the group.* Contrasts in teaching and assessment practices reflect this confusion of purpose.

Most marked is the expectation that students will have different assessment outcomes, rather than a description of successful teaching as 'everyone achieved the objectives of the lesson'. As well as illustrating differences between a psychological and social approach to education, this also questions whether individual emancipation will be more likely in private or social domains.

5   *Thought and language develop consecutively or together.* This contrast is manifested through the role oral work plays in assessment, and how much it is encouraged and deliberately developed in lessons. Again, here we have a difference between the private and the social domains of learning.

6   *Mathematics is a set of rules and correct procedures, or is a way of thinking.* This contrast shows itself in teaching and assessment methods, and in teachers' own experience; most often it is manifested in the different weighting given to processes or products by teachers explicitly or implicitly. Here is another manifestation of the positivist/interpretative difference.

It is not the case that each teacher is positioned similarly on each of the spectra. For instance, a teacher may believe that her role is to educate individuals, but may see mathematics as a set of tools to be used in the socio-economic activities of the community. However, this is not to say that Gage's (1989) vision of coexisting paradigms is possible. Differences in assessment lead to social inequity and can thus more usefully be seen as conflicting than as coexisting. Conflicts and inequities partly result from positivist, summative, assessment outcomes (used mainly for accountability and selection purposes) being applied within a NC framework which purports to value discussion, reasoning and mathematical thinking. Furthermore, national targets for minimal cohort achievement (social) are applied to an education system which is constructed to provide differentiated expectations and differentiated outcomes (individual). Further conflicts result from teachers' different interpretations and adaptations of the system, as shown above.

Conclusion

This research revealed differences in assessment practice which could result in social inequity, that is that students acting in similar ways might be assessed and treated differently by different teachers so that future opportunities which are available to some are not to others. Inequities due to measurement, labelling and irreversible decision-making which arise from one end of each of the six spectra above are often in accordance with the operation of NC assessments and league tables. These might therefore be avoided to some extent by a change of assessment policy. Inequities arise because of the social effects of assessment, so those which appear to be due to unavoidable factors (there is no single right way to view mathematics or bring about its learning) could be separated from inequitable decision-making by a review of the purposes and uses of assessment. In particular, one could hope for a separation of assessment for pedagogic purposes from assessment for the purposes of selection, management and accountability. However, policies do not solely determine systems.

It should be remembered that all the differences in belief and practice described above take place within one system which has a detailed national curriculum, universal assessment criteria, frequent national testing, frequent inspection, with competition between students, teachers, schools and regions structurally encouraged. Yet fundamental conflicts between different paradigms of human endeavour still run through this small but important subset of teachers' actions. Psychological, linguistic, sociological, and epistemological arguments about the nature of knowledge, its universality and situatedness, and the determination of human behaviour individually or in social groups all emerge in the above analysis of teachers' assessment, even in such a highly regulated system. This analysis confirms the centrality of the classroom culture created by the teacher's interpretation of roles and policies, seen through her own beliefs and perspectives, in influencing children's futures (Thompson, 1992; Lerman, 1994). The teacher acts out the summative assessment requirements of the state while valuing, selecting, and advantaging according to local and personal beliefs. In the absence of shared philosophies about the teaching of mathematics, such as those advocated by Steiner and Ernest, inequities can therefore occur which may be exacerbated by the apparent formalism of the system, rather than removed by it.

The overarching finding of this research is that a highly regulated national system, with closely defined curricula and a universal testing regime, does not result in a monoculture of mathematics teaching and assessment. An obvious final question is whether such a monoculture is desirable at all, given that it is not achievable.

References

Bernstein, B. (1990). *The Structuring of Pedagogic Discourse*, Routledge, London.

Boaler, J. (1997). *Experiencing School Mathematics: Teaching Styles, Sex and Setting*, Open University Press, Buckingham.

Brown, M. (1993). Clashing epistemologies: The battle for control of the National Curriculum and its assessment. *Teaching Mathematics and its Applications*. **12**, pp. 97–112.

Cooper, B. and Dunne, M. (1998). Social class, gender, equity and National Curriculum tests in mathematics. In P. Gates (ed.) *Proceedings of the 1st International Mathematics Education and Society Conference*, University of Nottingham.

Cresswell, M. J. and Houston, J. G. (1989). Assessment of the National Curriculum: Some fundamental considerations. *Educational Review*, **43**, pp. 63–78.

Department for Education (DfE). (1995). *Mathematics in the National Curriculum*, HMSO, London.

Dunne, M. (1994). The construction of ability: A critical exploration of mathematics teachers' accounts. Unpublished PhD thesis, University of Birmingham.

Ernest, P. (1990). *The Philosophy of Mathematics Education*, Falmer, London.

Ernest, P. (1998). *Social Constructivism as a Philosophy of Mathematics*, SUNY, Albany.

Gage, N. L. (1989). The paradigm wars and their aftermath: A 'historical' sketch of research on teaching since 1989. *Teachers College Record*, **91**, pp. 135–150.

Gipps, C. (1994). *Beyond Testing: Towards A Theory of Educational Assessment*, Falmer, London.

Jaworski, B. (1994). *Investigating Mathematics Teaching: A Constructivist Enquiry*, Falmer, London.

Jaworski, B. and Phillips, D. (eds) (1999). *Comparing Students Internationally: Research on Practice in Mathematics and Beyond*, Symposium Books, Wallingford.

Lawton, D. (1993). Political parties, ideology and the National Curriculum. *Educational Review*, **45**, pp. 111–118.

Lerman, S. (1994). Changing focus in the mathematics classroom. In S. Lerman (ed.) *Cultural Perspectives on the Mathematics Classroom*, Kluwer, Dordrecht.

Lorenz, J. H. (1982). On some psychological aspects of mathematics achievement assessment and classroom interaction. *Educational Studies in Mathematics*, **13**, pp. 1–19.

Nash, R. (1976). *Teacher Expectations and Pupil Learning*, RKP, London.

Nickson, M. (1994). The culture of the mathematics classroom. In S. Lerman (ed.) *Cultural Perspectives on the Mathematics Classroom*, Kluwer, Dordrecht.

OFSTED. (1994). *Science and Mathematics in Schools: A Review*, HMSO, London.

Ruthven, K. (1987). Ability stereotyping in mathematics. *Educational Studies in Mathematics*, **18**, pp. 243–253.

Scott-Hodgetts, R. (1986). Girls and mathematics: the negative implications of success. In L. Burton (ed.) *Girls into Mathematics*, Cambridge University Press.

Steiner, H. G. (1987). Philosophical and epistemological aspects of mathematics and their interaction with theory and practice in mathematics education. *For the Learning of Mathematics*, 7, pp. 7–13.

Thom, R. (1973). Modem mathematics: does it exist? In A. G. Howson (ed.) *Developments in Mathematical Education*, Cambridge University Press.

Thompson, A. G. (1992). Teachers' beliefs and conceptions: A synthesis of research. In D. A. Grouws (ed.) *Handbook of Research on Mathematics Teaching and Learning*, Macmillan, New York.

TIMSS. (1997). Mathematics achievement in the middle school years. *The 3rd International Mathematics and Science Study*, Chestnut Mill, MA.

Walkerdine, V. (1984). Developmental psychology and the child-centred pedagogy: The insertion of Piaget into early education. In J. Henriques (ed.) *Changing the Subject: Psychology, Social Regulation and Subjectivity*, Methuen, London.

Watson, A. (1996). Teachers' notions of mathematical ability in their pupils. *Mathematics Education Review*, **8**, pp. 27–35.

Watson, A. (1998). Potential sources of inequity in teachers' informal judgements about mathematics. In P. Gates (ed.) *Proceedings of the 1st International Mathematics Education and Society Conference*, Nottingham, September.

5   Constructing the 'legitimate' goal of a 'realistic' maths item

A comparison of 10–11- and 13–14-year-olds

Barry Cooper and Máiréad Dunne

Introduction

Sociological approaches to assessment have taken a variety of forms. Broadly macro-structural perspectives have focused on the relations between the criteria for assessment, social selection and the wider, socio-economic context (for example, Bowles and Gintis, 1976). Broadly micro-structural perspectives have focused instead on the ways in which assessment outcomes are constructed within classrooms or testing contexts (for example, Mehan, 1973; Newman *et al.*, 1989). Both of these approaches have produced important contributions to our understanding of the origins, the practice and the consequences of assessment. Notwithstanding their different emphases these authors have had many useful things to say about the *relations* between social structure, culture and the processes of meaning construction in the contexts in which assessment actually occurs. Bourdieu's work (for example, Bourdieu, 1974) on the nature of assessment practices in French higher education serves as an early example of work of this type. Turning to maths education, there has been a considerable body of research in recent years focusing on the ways in which the contexts within which mathematical problem-solving occurs can affect radically both the processes and the products of such cognitive activity (Nunes *et al.*, 1993; Lave, 1988). In parallel, there has also been much research on children's 'failure' to take a 'realistic' perspective during mathematical problem-solving when it would seem appropriate to do so (for example, Säljö, 1991). Our recent research on maths assessment, on which we will draw here, is intended as a contribution to these relational and contextual approaches to the study of assessment in maths (for example, Cooper, 1998b; Cooper and Dunne, 2000; Dunne, 1994).

We will draw on our research programme on the assessment of the mathematical knowledge and understanding of 10–11- and 13–14-year-old children in England. This research was partly motivated by a concern that the national testing of children's mathematics mainly via 'realistically' contextualised items might have a variety of unintended consequences, especially for the validity of the assessment of working-class children's knowledge and understanding. Children are often required by 'realistic' test items to make quite subtle judgements about the relevance to the process of solution of their everyday knowledge and experience (Cooper, 1992, 1994). There are sociological grounds for expecting working-class children to find it more difficult to make these judgements in ways in which the designers of school maths tests define as legitimate (Holland, 1981; Bernstein, 1996; Bourdieu, 1986). There have also been suggestions that girls might find particular types of 'realistic' items more difficult to negotiate than boys (for example, Boaler, 1994). Exploratory empirical work had confirmed that children's confusion about the boundary between the everyday and the 'mathematical' could lead sometimes to an underestimation of their mathematical knowledge when it is tested by 'realistic' items (Cooper, 1998a, 1998b). This problem seemed worthy of further research, which we have subsequently been able to undertake in three primary and three secondary schools.[1]

In these six schools, this programme of research has collected performance data on UK National Curriculum tests from more than 600 children, as well as data from some 250 individual interviews, in which a subsample of the same children have responded to a subset of test items (Cooper and Dunne, 2000). We have also collected data on children's social class backgrounds, sex and measured 'ability'. This dataset has enabled statistical analyses of children's comparative performance on 'realistic' and 'non-realistic' items. We have defined 'realistic' items as those which place mathematical operations within contexts including everyday objects, events and people. 'Non-realistic' items, which we have termed 'esoteric', do not. An example of each can be seen in Figures 5.1 and 5.2. Our analyses have shown, for example, that for 10–11-year-olds, both social class and sex differences in performance are greater when 'realistic' rather than 'esoteric' items are used to assess children in the group testing context. These social class differences in performance are large enough to produce substantial differences between the social classes when entered into two simulations of an educational selection process using, respectively, either the 'esoteric' or the 'realistic' scores achieved by these children (Cooper and Dunne, 2000). Twice as many of the working-class 10–11-year-old children in our sample win through in a process selecting the top-performing quarter of the sample when scores from the 'esoteric' rather than the 'realistic' subsets of test items are employed as the basis for judging performance (Cooper and Dunne, 2000). We have also been able to use a comparison of our qualitative interview data with our test data to show that children's actually existing mathematical knowledge and understanding is not always validly accessed by 'realistic' items in test contexts – and that this results at least partly from the problems some children experience in reading the 'everyday'/'esoteric' boundary in ways defined as 'legitimate' by the test designers (Cooper and Dunne, 1998).

We intend here to examine the responses of children to one 'realistic' test item originally intended as a 'difficult' item for 10–11-year-olds, but which we also have used in our research with 13–14-year-olds. The item (Figure 5.2) concerns an imaginary tennis competition. The 'Statement of Attainment' which this item was intended to assess is: *Identify all the outcomes of combining two independent events.* The marking scheme gave this solution:

n stands for a number

$n + 7 = 13$

What is the value of $n + 10$?

Figure 5.1 Finding '*n*': an 'esoteric' item

Source: SCAA (1996).

Organising a competition

David and Gita's group organise a mixed doubles tennis competition. They need to pair a boy with a girl.
They put the three boys' names into one bag and the three girls' names into another bag.

Find all the possible ways that boys and girls can be paired. **Write the pairs below.** One pair is already shown.

Rob and Katy

Figure 5.2 Tennis pairs: a 'realistic' item

Source: SEAC (1993).

Rob and Katy
Rob and Ann
Rob and Gita
Rashid and Katy
Rashid and Ann
Rashid and Gita
David and Katy
David and Ann
David and Gita

There should be exactly nine pairings, all different. One way to check is as follows:

Are there three with Bob? Are they all different?
Are there three with Rashid? Are they all different?
Are there three with David? Are they all different?

We might note that an 'esoteric' version of the item might have been: *Find the Cartesian product of the sets* {*a, b, c*} *and* {*d, e, f*}. It is an indication of the shift in the climate of opinion in maths education circles since the heyday of 'abstract' algebraic approaches in the 1960s that it is the tennis competition rather than these sets that children meet in their tests (Cooper, 1985). It is partly with the consequences for the validity and fairness of assessment of this shift from the 'esoteric' to the 'realistic' as the context for assessment in mathematics that our research has been concerned. In the case of the tennis item, a child has first of all to *see through* the 'noise' of the setting in order to realise the intended meaning of the item which, as can be seen from the marking scheme, concerns a Cartesian product with 'names' acting as the tokens which are to be arranged in pairs.

Several other features of the tennis item and its marking scheme can be noted straightaway. First of all, it is possible that not all children will make sense of the reference to 'mixed doubles'. Second, where they do, they may be misled by the 'realistic' context with the result that they produce just three pairs using the six names rather than the expected nine pairs. After all, these three pairs would form a basis for proceeding with games of tennis and are also the type of outcome children might be familiar with from televised draws for sports competitions (Cooper, 1994). The fact that the pair 'Rob and Katy' is given – and in bold type – might help to overdetermine such a response if children believe they should not disturb this pair. Third, children might, and do, respond to the item in terms of 'ways' of producing pairs (process) rather than in terms of the pairs themselves (product). Lastly, it is interesting to note the particular 'esoteric' manner in which the pairs are set out in the model answer. This given arrangement of the names seems to bear no relation to the tennis context. However, a child might also set out nine pairs in a more 'realistic' manner thus:

David and Ann	David and Gita	David and Katy
Rashid and Katy	Rashid and Ann	Rashid and Gita
Rob and Gita	Rob and Katy	Rob and Ann

Here, each grouping of three pairs using all six names could engage in a series of mixed doubles, as long as one pair was willing to act as spectators! We have coded children's responses in our interviews as 'esoteric' or 'realistic' on the basis of whether they have set out nine pairs in one or other of these ways. It should be noted that a child who has produced three pairs, but used each of the six names just once, has his or her response coded as 'realistic'. We will now describe children's responses to and performances on this item, beginning with 10–11-year-olds. Since we have already reported the responses of these younger children elsewhere (Cooper and Dunne, 1998), we will summarise their case here before moving on to consider the responses of 13–14-year-olds in more detail.

10–11-year-olds

The first point we might note is that many 10–11-year-old children do not respond to the tennis item as if the names are merely 'realistic' tokens representing abstract elements of sets of items. Indeed, when asked in interviews to explain why they had chosen particular sets of three pairs, children referred, amongst other things, to the assumed ethnicity or nationality of the children (Cooper and Dunne, 1998). One working-class boy, for example, argued against putting Rashid with Gita on the grounds that 'Rashid and Gita sound like different country names, so that it wouldn't exactly be fair if Rashid and Gita got together, because you've got to give them a chance to meet other people'. Other children, on the other hand, thought they should go together for similar reasons. The crucial point here is that, in the sense of Bernstein's (1996) recognition rules for reading the specialised nature of contexts, these children are not 'recognising' the intentions of the designers of this item 'correctly'. The marking scheme, with its 'esoteric' setting out of nine pairs, makes no reference whatsoever to such issues as the children's origins or methods of choosing pairs; but children, when accounting for their choices, often do. We have argued earlier that responses of three pairs, as well as nine pairs set out in a tennis-friendly manner, can be seen as 'realistic' responses to this item. Bernstein (1996) has argued that children from working-class backgrounds are more likely than children from middle-class backgrounds to misrecognise the intended nature of specialised problem-solving contexts. With his co-workers he has shown, for example, that when children are asked to sort food items into groups, there are modal differences in the ways in which working- and middle-class children sort items (Holland, 1981). Working-class children were found to more often sort these by reference to the ways the items of food appeared together in their everyday life settings or, in our terms, 'realistically'.

We have been able to explore whether comparable social class differences (and analogous sex differences) appear in the case of 'realistically' contextualised maths test items. For this purpose, we have categorised children's social class by reference to the occupations of their fathers and mothers using the 'dominance' approach set out by Erikson and Goldthorpe (1993) (see the appendix at the end of this chapter). We have collapsed the underlying categories of the social class schema used by these authors into three broad categories: a service class, an intermediate class and a working class. For the tennis item, we have categorised children's initial responses in the interview context as either 'esoteric', 'realistic' or 'other' (a category which typically involves a setting out of the pairs which mixes elements of an 'esoteric' and a 'realistic' approach). The 28 responses of these 120 10–11-year-olds coded as 'realistic' include four cases where children have not produced pairs but, instead, make various points concerning how they would go about choosing pairs if they were actually undertaking the 'real' task. The remaining 24 'realistic' responses comprise 18 sets of three pairs, one set of six pairs and five sets of nine pairs.

Table 5.1 sets out the relation between a child's initial response and social class, while Table 5.2 shows the relation between initial response and sex. While there is no evidence in Table 5.2 of any overall difference between the sexes in the nature of the initial response on our chosen dimension, Table 5.1 shows considerable differences between children from the three social class groupings. Working-class children are nearly three times as likely as service-class children to produce 'realistic' pairings (including, we should recall, a set of three pairs using each of the six names). A further breakdown of the data, which we will not reproduce here, shows that this pattern of social class differences holds when boys and girls are considered separately. However, the sex differences are not constant across the three social class groups. Within the service class, girls are more likely to be 'realistic' responders than boys (girls: 16.0 per cent, boys: 11.8 per cent). Within the intermediate class this is reversed, with boys being more likely than girls to respond 'realistically' (girls: 23.1 per cent, boys: 29.4 per cent). Similarly, in the working class, boys are more likely to respond to this item 'realistically' (girls: 33.3 per cent, boys: 42.1 per cent).

The distribution of marks awarded for children's initial response to this item in the interview is shown in Table 5.3. There is a clear relation between mark and social class for both boys and girls. Part of this relationship can be 'explained' via the greater tendency of working-class children than others to produce three pairs, coded by us as 'realistic', and which gains no mark. What we want to briefly consider, now, however, is whether the children who produced three pairs were capable of producing the required nine, had they not apparently misrecognised the demands of the item as more 'realistic' than 'esoteric'. In our interviews, when a child had produced three

Table 5.1 Response strategy on the tennis item (interview) by class (10–11 years)

	'Esoteric' pairings	Other (typically mixed)	'Realistic' pairings	Totals
Service class	47	4	8	59
Percentage	79.7	6.8	13.6	
Intermediate class	20	2	8	30
Percentage	66.7	6.7	26.7	
Working class	14	5	12	31
Percentage	45.2	16.1	38.7	
Totals	81	11	28	120
Percentage	67.5	9.2	23.3	

Table 5.2 Response strategy on the tennis item (interview) by sex (10–11 years)

	'Esoteric' pairings	Other (typically mixed)	'Realistic' pairings	Totals
Girls	34	5	11	50
Percentage	68.0	10.0	22.0	
Boys	47	6	17	70
Percentage	67.1	8.6	24.3	
Totals	81	11	28	120
Percentage	67.5	9.2	23.3	

Table 5.3 Marks achieved (one mark available) on the tennis item in the interview context: initial response (10–11 years)

	Female		Male		Total	
	Mean	*Count*	*Mean*	*Count*	*Mean*	*Count*
Service class	0.84	25	0.85	34	0.85	59
Intermediate class	0.77	13	0.82	17	0.80	30
Working class	0.75	12	0.63	19	0.68	31
Total	0.80	50	0.79	70	0.79	120

pairs and seemed to have finished her or his response, we asked whether s/he was sure that all the possible pairs had been found. Given this cue, 12 of the 18 children who had produced three pairs produced another six, to give nine. Here is an example, an intermediate-class girl, who writes the three pairs thus:

Rob and Katy
Rashid and Gita
David and Ann

MD: Done that one?
SARAH: Yeah.
MD: OK, so tell me how you worked that one out.
SARAH: I put those two names and – so I did those two there can and I did those.
MD: David and Ann, Rashid and Gita, OK.
SARAH: Mm.
MD: OK, see where it says there find all the possible ways that girls and boys can be paired, do you think you've found all the possible ways?
SARAH: No.
MD: You could find some more?
SARAH: Yeah.
MD: OK, let me just do that, so I'll know where you stopped for the beginning. [The interviewer adds a mark at this point to indicate the first response (for later coding)] OK, go on then. [Sarah works at the problem, silently. She then adds six pairs to give:]

Rob and Katy	Gita and David	Katy and David
Rashid and Gita	Gita and Rob	Ann and Rob
David and Ann	Katy and Rashid	Ann and Rashid

MD: OK, so have you finished that one now?
SARAH: Mm.
MD: And you think you've got all of them?
SARAH: Yeah.

MD: OK, do you know? – when you first did it you stopped, after three, why did you stop after three?

SARAH: I don't know.

MD: You don't know, but why didn't you continue?

SARAH: I didn't think that you were supposed to.

MD: OK, that's a good reason, but why didn't you think you were supposed to?

[The interview continues with Sarah being apparently unable or unwilling to give a reason.]

We cannot be sure why Sarah chose three pairs initially. However, we have shown elsewhere that the relation between the choice of a 'realistic' or 'esoteric' approach and class holds for other items and we have also shown that there is a positive correlation between children's choice of either a 'realistic' or 'esoteric' strategy on tennis and on an item concerning a traffic survey (Cooper and Dunne, 2000). We believe it is plausible that children like the one quoted above are, at the level of practical consciousness, captured by Bourdieu's concept of a social class linked *habitus,* misrecognising the actually 'esoteric' demands of test items because of a cultural predisposition to engage 'realistically' with problems (Bourdieu, 1986). We have shown elsewhere that it is working-class and intermediate-class children in our sample who are more likely to fall into the group who initially produce three pairs but then produce nine after the cue (Cooper and Dunne, 1998). The result of this can be seen in Table 5.4, which shows marks achieved *after* children had been cued to reconsider their initial response. This table shows a quite different relation between class and success than Table 5.3. Here, social class differences are reduced and sex differences become greater. Overall success is higher. This tennis item seems therefore to have the potential to underestimate children's actually existing understanding of and skills in 'mathematics'. The children concerned are more likely to be from working and intermediate class backgrounds. For 10–11-year-olds, the item seems to be differentially valid by class. Interestingly, however, while both boys and girls from the working- and intermediate- classes improved their mark after being offered a second chance, it is girls in these two groups whose scores have improved the most between the two tables.

13–14-year-olds: overall results

We have shown that, for some children, the intended goal of the problem setters as set out in the marking scheme is not immediately perceived and/or chosen as their own. We will return to this issue of the 'obviousness' or otherwise of the goal of the item below, but first we wish to compare the overall nature of the responses of the older children with those of the younger children. Having had three more years of experience of schooling – and of the culture of school maths – are these older children less likely to read the item 'realistically' as indexed by the 'inappropriate' production of three pairs?

Tables 5.5 to 5.8 are the parallel tables for the older children to Tables 5.1 to 5.4 for the 10–11-year-olds. Table 5.5 shows a markedly higher frequency of 'realistic' responses from the working-class children than others, as did Table 5.1 for the 10–11-year-olds. In absolute terms, however, the percentage of the working-class children[2] responding in this

Table 5.4 Marks achieved (one mark available) on the tennis item in the interview context after cued response (10–11 years)

	Female		Male		Total	
	Mean	*Count*	*Mean*	*Count*	*Mean*	*Count*
Service class	0.92	25	0.88	34	0.90	59
Intermediate class	1.00	13	0.94	17	0.97	30
Working class	1.00	12	0.74	19	0.84	31
Total	0.96	50	0.86	70	0.90	120

Table 5.5 Response strategy on the tennis item (interview) by class (13–14 years)

	'Esoteric' pairings	*Other (typically mixed)*	*'Realistic' pairings*	*Totals*
Service class	31	3	2	36
Percentage	86.1	8.3	5.6	
Intermediate class	25	3	3	31
Percentage	80.6	9.7	9.7	
Working class	40	3	9	52
Percentage	76.9	5.8	17.3	
Totals	96	9	14	119
Percentage	80.7	7.6	11.8	

Table 5.6 Response strategy on the tennis item (interview) by sex (13–14 years)

	'Esoteric' pairings	*Other (typically mixed)*	*'Realistic' pairings*	*Totals*
Girls	51	4	5	60
Percentage	85.0	6.7	8.3	
Boys	45	5	9	59
Percentage	76.3	8.5	15.3	
Totals	96	9	14	119
Percentage	80.7	7.6	11.8	

Table 5.7 Marks achieved (one mark available) on the tennis item in the interview context: initial response (13–14 years)

	Female		Male		Total	
	Mean	*Count*	*Mean*	*Count*	*Mean*	*Count*
Service class	1.00	17	0.95	19	0.97	36
Intermediate class	0.87	15	0.88	16	0.87	31
Working class	0.86	28	0.88	24	0.87	52
Total	0.90	60	0.90	59	0.90	119

Table 5.8 Marks achieved (one mark available) on tennis item in the interview context: after cued response (13–14 years)

	Female		Male		Total	
	Mean	Count	Mean	Count	Mean	Count
Service class	1.00	17	1.00	19	1.00	36
Intermediate class	0.87	15	0.94	16	0.90	31
Working class	0.89	28	0.96	24	0.92	52
Total	0.92	60	0.97	59	0.94	119

manner has dropped dramatically between Table 5.1 and Table 5.5 (from 38.7 per cent to 17.3 per cent). Turning to sex, Table 5.6 shows twice as many boys as girls responding realistically. The sex difference is much greater here than it had been amongst the younger children (Table 5.2). Considering the social class distribution of responses for boys and girls separately, as we did for the 10–11-year-olds, we have found that the class differences in 'realistic' responding hold for both boys and girls. Within each class taken separately, boys more often respond 'realistically'. No service-class girls respond 'realistically', though two of the 19 service-class boys do. Here it is boys who, on our coding of responses, are more likely to fall into the trap of responding 'inappropriately'.

Of the 14 older children who responded 'realistically', ten produced three pairs and four nine pairs. Of the ten children producing three pairs, four then produced nine after being encouraged to consider their response further. Of the remaining six, one produced the 'super-esoteric' response of 18, two produced six pairs, two produced eight pairs, and one stuck at three. Two of the five girls, and three of the five boys, moved from an initial three to a final nine or 18 pairs. These five children comprised one each from the service and intermediate class, and three from the working class.

Summing up, we can see by comparing Tables 5.1 and 5.5 that, amongst the older children, fewer within each social class group initially read this item 'realistically'. Similarly, a comparison of Tables 5.2 and 5.6 shows that both boys and girls, taken separately, were less likely initially to respond 'realistically' at the older age. Children at 13–14 years of age seem to have a better 'feel for the game' (Bourdieu, 1990). Nevertheless, some children apparently remain unaware of these rules, and a comparison of Tables 5.7 and 5.8 shows that, as in the case of the younger children, some older children did succeed in improving their mark when encouraged to reconsider their initial response. For some older children, as for some younger children, this item seems to have underestimated their combinatorial capacities.

13–14-year-olds: three individual cases

In the remainder of this chapter, we will examine in depth several older children's accounts of their problem-solving in order to bring out more clearly which features of the item, in interaction with what the children bring to the situation, produce these problems of invalidity. We will look in detail at some interview transcripts, concentrating on those where children did recover from their initial 'choice' of three pairs. We will start with Charlie, an intermediate-class boy, who almost recovered from his initial three pairs, moving on to obtain nine pairs, but with one repeat, with the result that he produced eight valid pairs. Now, it is the 'obviousness' of this question's demands that seems clear to some children and not to others. For those for whom it isn't 'obvious' that this is a request for 3 × 3 pairs, an activity of extended sense-making has to be undertaken in collaboration with the interviewer. In the case of Charlie we can follow his thought processes fairly readily. He began, as did a number of children, by being confused by the wording of the question, thinking that he should address the issue of what process might be used to choose pairs (line 5 of transcript following). The interviewer helps him remedy this reading of the question (lines 10–16). Charlie then writes down two pairs, to give as his initial response:

Rob and Katy
Rashid and Gita
David and Ann

In answer to the question why he had chosen Rashid and Gita, he produces an explanation which refers to the way the names are placed on the page (lines 23–24). This works for Rashid and Gita who, like Rob and Katy, can be seen as diagonally related. It does not work for the residual pair David and Ann (line 26). So far, what we see is Charlie apparently undertaking something akin to Popper's (1963) conjecturing and refuting, or in other words, a form of scientific reasoning.

When the interviewer invites him to consider whether he has found all the possible pairs (lines 29–33), his response brings out another aspect of the item which those who consider its demands to be 'obvious' might miss. **Rob and Katy** appear in the item in bold print. They are given, and the bold type seems to lend this pairing some special authority, some fixedness. Charlie asks (line 34) 'What, still having Rob and Katy as that one ... and these four?' (pointing, one assumes, to the pair in bold type and then to the other four names). The interviewer, who seems not to have considered this 'problem', comes to understand Charlie's perspective and explains that Rob and Katy can be changed around as well. It might not be stretching the data too far to say that Charlie seems not to believe he has the right to disturb Rob and Katy, defined by the authority of the text as a pair in advance of his thinking. Charlie then adds three pairs to his original three to give:

Rob and Katy	David and Ann
Rashid and Gita	Rashid and Katy
David and Ann	Rob and Gita

As he verbalises these, he also asks, 'and some more?', apparently seeking either instruction or permission from the interviewer to proceed further. His second three pairs form a set which could engage in tennis, but he has reused a pair already chosen (David and Ann). When the interviewer suggests that, if Charlie can think of any more, he should add them, he adds four pairs to give:

Here is a dice with faces numbered 1 to 6.

Here is a drawing pin.

The dice can land with any face up.
The drawing pin can land on its **side**, or on its **top**.

The dice and the drawing pin are dropped at the same time.

 List all the possible ways that the dice and the pin can land. One pair has been done for you.

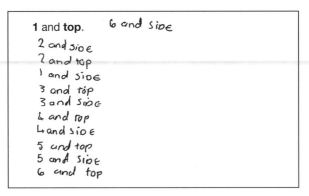

Figure 5.3 Die/pin item and Charlie's written response

Source: SCAA (1994).

Rob and Katy	David and Ann
Rashid and Gita	Rashid and Katy
David and Ann	Rob and Gita
David and Gita	David and Katy
Rob and Ann	
Rashid and Katy	

It appears that the interviewer did not notice that, alongside the repeated *David and Ann*, there was also a repeated *Rashid and Katy*. It also seems likely that the interviewer, but perhaps not Charlie, was concerned about the production of *different* pairs (line 52). The final eight pairs have been co-constructed by the child and the interviewer. Later in the interview, Charlie was asked to tackle an item whose structure was very similar to that of the tennis item, shown in Figure 5.3, with his response. While we have not coded this item as 'esoteric', it does seem to be one step further away from everyday life than a tennis competition. This may be one reason why Charlie produces the wanted response of 12 pairs straightaway in this case, and in a systematic fashion. It is also the case that the die/pin item does not seem to invite quite as strongly as the tennis item a response in terms of 'method' as opposed to 'pairs'. However, Charlie has also been encouraged, earlier in the interview, to take the required approach in the tennis item, and he may have drawn on this very recent experience in responding to the die/pin item. It is worth discussing this further, in the light of the analysis of similar combinatorial tasks presented to children by Newman *et al.* (1989).

1 CHARLIE: Does this mean like, er, *you* put, you can *choose them by putting*
2   them in a bag, and you can choose them another way, not in a
3   bag, choose them all different ways?
4 BC: So what would you need to write down then do you think?
5 CHARLIE: Oh right, you can like, muddle them up and like put them in a
6   box and you could pick 'em out together or you could like put
7   them on a table and like close your eyes and like pick two.
8 BC: Ah-ha!
9 CHARLIE: Muddle them up and pick two.
10 BC: Right, OK, well you're saying that because it says find all the
11   possible ways aren't you?
12 CHARLIE: Yeah.
13 BC: You're thinking of ways, but then it says, so it says find all the
14   possible ways that boys and girls can be paired, then it says, write
15   the pairs below. One pair is already shown, Rob and Katy, so I
16   think what it's actually thinking is
17 CHARLIE: just in the bag
18 BC: write the result down, what the pairs would be.
19 CHARLIE: Rob and Katy, Rashid and Gita, and Ann and David, I'm not sure.
20 BC: Well, write down what you think they'd be, go on.
21 CHARLIE: [writes]
22 BC: OK, any special reason why you put Rashid and Gita together?
23 CHARLIE: Because like, er, Rob and Katy are like diagonals going like
24   that, and that's why I done Rashid and Gita,
25 BC: Right, is it ...
26 CHARLIE: but I didn't know about David and Ann.
27 BC: OK, now, you've got three pairs yeah?
28 CHARLIE: Yeah.
29 BC: It says find all the possible ways that boys and girls can be paired,
30   write the pairs below. Do you think there are any other pairs you
31   could get, do you think there are any other pairs you could get if
32   I said, write all the possible pairs you could get, do you think
33   there are any others?

34 CHARLIE: What, still having Rob and Katy as that one ...

35 BC: Well I'm thinking of all the possible ...

36 CHARLIE: ... and these four.

37 BC: I'm thinking of all the possible pairs you could get, changing
38   them around.

39 CHARLIE: What, changing them around using Rob and Katy as well?

40 BC: Yeah.

41 CHARLIE: Oh! right having 'em going across like that to each other.

42 BC: Well could you write any more, if I call that your first three pairs,
43   can you think of any others, as many as you can.

44 CHARLIE: You could get David and Ann, Rashid and Katy, and Rob and
45   Gita – and some more?

46 BC: If you can think of some more, yeah, you've got six so far.

47 CHARLIE: [Charlie writes some further pairs.]

48 BC: Right, any more you can get? Do you think?

49 CHARLIE: Mm-hm ...

50 BC: Umm, what's that one?

51 CHARLIE: David and Katy.

52 BC: Are you sure you haven't got that one already?

53 CHARLIE: Yeah, David and Ann, David and oh, I've done it, I've got David
54   and Ann twice.

55 BC: Oh I see right, OK, so take, right do you want to take one of the
56   David and Anns out then, take

57 CHARLIE: Just take that one out

58 BC: I'll just put a little dotted line through one of your David and
59   Anns, so, right.

60 CHARLIE: David and Katy, so I can't get any more.

61 BC: OK.

Newman *et al.* compared children's responses to several tasks. These tasks included one task in which children had to produce, working with the experimenter, all the possible pairs of cards picturing movie stars, and in which the children were 'trained' by the experimenter to answer the question. Here the 'problem' of finding pairs was made explicit to the children. They did not have to discover it for themselves. Then, in a subsequent 'isomorphic' task, children were given four household chemicals and had to explore, in small groups, what happened when pairs of these chemicals were mixed. Here they needed to discover the 'problem', that is, of finding all the possible pairs, for themselves 'as they began to run out of pairs of chemicals to mix' (1989, p. 33). Newman *et al.* describe the contrasting situations in these terms:

> In the laboratory setting, we expect the task to be presented clearly to the subject. It is part of the experimenter's job. We conduct pilot studies to find out how to do this effectively; we arrange training on the task and choose criterion measures that let us know whether the subject 'understands' the task that we have constructed. These procedures are certainly socially constructed. In everyday situations people

are not always presented with clearly stated goals. They often have to figure out what the problem is, what the constraints are, as well as how to solve the problem once they have formulated it. In other words, in everyday situations people are confronted with the 'whole' task. There is no experimenter responsible for doing the presentation part ... This broader conception of the whole task is important to our analyses of the transformation of a task when it is embedded in different social settings. When we look for the 'same task' happening outside of the laboratory, we have to look for how the work of specifying and constraining the task is getting done and who is doing it. This kind of analysis provides us with the basis for arguing that the practical methods of maintaining control in the laboratory veil a crucial process: formulating the task and forming the goal.

(Newman *et al.*, 1989, pp. 33–34)

The key point here is that there is no one problem embedded in the text, but rather a whole range of possible problems which might be constructed by children. Earlier we have referred to Bernstein's concept of recognition rules as one way of making sense of children's use or otherwise of 'everyday' knowledge in responding to test items. What these remarks of Newman *et al.* remind us is that, within the choice of an 'everyday' or 'esoteric' response mode, there are still other issues for the child to confront. In Charlie's case he had to work through, with the interviewer, several possibilities. Was the item about 'methods' of producing pairs? Was he allowed to disrupt the given pair? It seems likely that without the intervention of the interviewer he would not have resolved these issues so as to produce something like the 'right' goal for the problem, and therefore that he would not have produced more than three pairs. He wrote nothing in the pre-interview group test for this item, and probably had not reached it. We can not therefore compare his two responses, aided and unaided. It does, however, seem quite likely that the work done by the interviewer, with Charlie, in trying to construct the 'right' goal for the tennis problem provided the basis for Charlie to construct the 'right' goal for the die/pin item. Taking responses to both items together, it seems that he can undertake the required combinatorial task with some degree of success, but that this would not have become known as a consequence of his attempting the tennis item in an unaided group testing context.

We will look now at a child who recovered from producing three pairs, in this case fully, to produce nine pairs. In the group test, Emma, a working-class girl, had written nothing for this item, but had attempted subsequent questions. In the interview, she initially wrote:

Rob and Katy
Rashid and Gita
David and Ann

She is worried that her three pairs do not constitute a complete answer, but her worry perhaps concerns 'methods' (lines 8–9 of the transcript). As she says, the item asks for 'all the possible ways' as well as referring to 'pairs' (lines 15–16). Her subsequent remark, 'I thought it meant write these pairs below, in the bag', is open to a number of plausible interpretations. One is that she has set up pairs to play tennis, and that this is a 'goal' which has been successfully addressed. Another is that she has read the item as asking her to copy the pairs in the bags, though the diagonal placing of Rob and Katy in the bags makes this less likely. However, whatever her interpretation is, when the interviewer tries to explain what the 'goal' of the item is not, and stresses 'all the pairs' (lines 28–34), Emma quickly responds 'there are loads of other names that you could do' (line 35). The following exchanges make it clear that Emma has now formulated a 'goal' which is broader than that intended by the test designers, one in which she can draw on the whole universe of boys' and girls' names (line 47). The interviewer limits the population (lines 48–49). There is laughter, of recognition. Emma checks her understanding (line 50). She then decides a pair starting with a girl's name is not different from the corresponding pair starting with a boy's (lines 58–62). Only then does she proceed to produce her nine pairs, systematically, thus:

Rob and Katy   Rob and Ann
Rashid and Gita   Rob and Gita
David and Ann

David and Gita
David and Katy
Rashid and Katy
Rashid and Ann

1 EMMA: What have we got to do, explain, 'cos I've never done this one,
2   I've done that one and the others, but I think I've skipped this one.
3 BC: What you don't think you did that one at all?
4 EMMA: No.
5 BC: So, you've done three pairs, yeah?
6 EMMA: Yeah.
7 BC: What are you worried about now, what you have to
8 EMMA: Well, what do you have to do, like find out a way how they can
9   be paired up together?
10 BC: Er, well, it says write the pairs below, have you written the pairs
11   below do you think?
12 EMMA: Yeah.
13 BC: Right, so what, I'm not quite sure what you're thinking of, what are
14   you thinking of exactly?
15 EMMA: Well, it says find all the possible ways, that boys and girls can be
16   paired.
17 BC: Yeah, write the pairs below.
18 EMMA: I thought it meant write these pairs below, in the bag.
19 BC: Ah, well, what I'm going to say to you is that, if I call this your
20   first answer yeah,
21 EMMA: Mm.
22 BC: Because you think, you've more or less finished there haven't you?

23 EMMA: Mm.

24 BC: Do you agree, you think?

25 EMMA: Mm.

26 BC: Er, what it is, you've found three pairs haven't you?

27 EMMA: Mm.

28 BC: When it says find all the possible ways that girls and boys can be
29   paired, sometimes people think that means what method you
30   could use, you know, put your hand in, blindfold people, swing
31   them about, that sort of thing, what it actually means is find all
32   the possible pairs, and the answer, the question is do you think
33   you've found all the pairs you could make out of boys and girls
34   or do you think there are others that you could do?

35 EMMA: There are loads of other names that you could do.

36 BC: What, other pairs, OK, if you can think of some more, write
37   them down outside my

38 EMMA: What, just names?

39 BC: Pairs of names, boys and girls pairs, like those.

40 EMMA: Yeah, but they're just two names ain't they?

41 BC: Give me an example of what you're thinking.

42 EMMA: They're just names, like David and Katy.

43 BC: Yeah.

44 EMMA: They're just names and Rashid and Gita, they're just names and
45 Robert and Ann.

46 BC: Yeah, well, they're pairs aren't they of names, yeah? Two together.

47 EMMA: You could go on for ages though, thinking of names.

48 BC: Well see how, well, you're only allowed to use the names that are
49   here.

50 EMMA: Oh, only the names that are there.

51 BC: Oh, I see, you were thinking that you could use others.

52 EMMA: Yeah.

53 BC: OK [laughter]

54 EMMA: Shall I do, can you use the same ones that I've put here, or
55   different ones from there?

56 BC: Well, don't use the same pairs, but you can use names again, but
57   you've got to mix them up into new pairs, yeah?

58 EMMA: Mm-hm [thinking] Don't need to do it the other way round for
59   the girls do you, 'cos the girls are like already there look?

60 BC: What you mean you don't have to do Ann and Rob, because
61   you've got Rob and Ann already.

62 EMMA: Yeah.

63 BC: I agree you don't. OK, and one more question about this one, if I
64   cover those up

65 EMMA: Mm.

66 BC: including the pair they had already, how many pairs do you think
67   you've got altogether.

68 EMMA: Nine.

69 BC: How do you know?

70 EMMA: Because there's six and you've got three to each one, because

71   there's only three girls, so it's nine.

72 BC: OK, now, when you started you did three, that's the right answer,

73   nine, why do you think you only did three and didn't do nine

74   straight away?

75 EMMA: Because I didn't understand what they were saying.

76 BC: Right, a lot of people do this, they do three and then when I say,

77   you're sure, they do nine, so it's obviously not a very good question

78   is it, that one

79 EMMA: They didn't explain it properly.

80 BC: Oh, which bit do you think was most confusing, do you know?

81 EMMA: This bit where they say find all the possible ways that boys and

82   girls can be paired, write the pairs below, one pair is already

83   shown. Rob and Katy, they probably think, Oh, we'll write those

84   two down so that's three are paired, they're paired up with a

85   person, and then write the way, so it can be paired, like pick it

86   out of a bag or something like that,

87 BC: Yeah.

88 EMMA: Because they're not explaining it properly, they're just

89 BC: No.

90 EMMA: saying that, that can mean anything.

91 BC: Right, OK, that's very helpful, That was 19, number 13.

Finally, she produces an account of why there are nine pairs to be found, and a critique of the item's construction (lines 75–90). As in the case of Charlie, when she arrived at the die/pin item, she had no difficulty in constructing the require 'goal' and answer. She wrote:

1 and top	1 + side
2 + top	2 + side
3 + top	3 + side
4 + top	4 + side
5 + top	5 + side
6 + top	6 + side

Her understanding of what is required here is demonstrated in the discussion:

EMMA: Do I have to write 'and' or can I just … ?

BC: No leave it out if you like then we might get in a couple more quickly.

EMMA: [she writes]

BC: You're using up that last one, 6 and side, OK, how many of those are there all together are there? [Interviewer has covered responses with his hand.]

EMMA: Twelve.

BC: How do you know that?

EMMA: Because there's six on the dice and there's six ways you can go with that, so that's twelve.

BC: OK, right even though it's covered up, you know it's twelve, good. Number 17.

We will look briefly at one last child from amongst those who recovered from three pairs to produce nine. Mike, a working-class boy, did write something for the tennis item in the group test:

Rob and Katy
David and Gita
Rashid and Ann

He received, of course, no mark. In the interview, he initially wrote the same three pairs, with one reversed:

Rob and Katy
Gita and David
Rashid and Ann

In this case, almost immediately the interviewer began to probe, Mike recognised what the required 'goal' of the problem was (line 6), and produced a further six different pairs (not shown here). There is a suggestion later in the interview that he found three pairs an appropriate response for the incorrect 'goal' he had formulated (lines 16–20).

```
 1 MD:   Finished?
 2 MIKE: Yeah.
 3 MD:   OK so how did you work that out?
 4 MIKE: Easy, I just looked at that and just paired them up.
 5 MD:   See it says here it says find all the possible.
 6 MIKE: Oh all the possible, oh yeah.
 7 MD:   OK let's do that and you carry on. [child works]
 8 MIKE: That's another one.
 9 MD:   Is that all of them? [He now has nine different pairs.]
10 MIKE: Done it.
11 MD:   OK so how did you do that then?
12 MIKE: It's just don't know really, I just looked at that and just paired
13        them up in different places.
14 MD:   And was that easy or?
15 MIKE: Yeah easy.
16 MD:   So if it was like a real competition, how do you think they would
17        have done it?
18 MIKE: They would have just
19 MD:   What like you did in the first place?
```

20 MIKE: Yeah.
21 MD: Yeah so they would have stopped there, have you seen competitions
22   done like that before? No, you don't. OK, that's 19 good,
23   13 now.

Conclusion

In this paper we have discussed children's responses to a 'realistic' maths test item. We have shown that, at both 10–11 and 13–14 years of age, a considerable minority of children experience difficulty in reading the intentions of the test designers in a way which enables them to show their 'mathematical' skills and understanding in their best light. These children, at both ages, are more likely to be from intermediate- and working-class backgrounds than from the service class. However, the older children are less likely than the younger children to misread the demands of the item, suggesting that between the ages of 10–11 and 13–14, children do succeed in gaining a better understanding of the peculiar 'rules of the game' which characterise much of school maths. Of course, we must be aware of the danger of overgeneralising from this case – though much can be learned from it. However, elsewhere, in an analysis of performance on more than one hundred National Curriculum maths items, we have shown more generally that there are greater social class differences at age 10–11 in children's performance on 'realistic' items than on 'esoteric' items (Cooper and Dunne, 2000). It is of course likely that some part of this difference is due to problems in the design of 'realistic' items. No doubt some of the ambiguity of meaning children experienced in the wording of the tennis item could be removed. Notwithstanding such remedial action, there will nevertheless remain an underlying problem for children to tackle before they can attend to the 'mathematical' operation embedded in the noise of the everyday context. Should they or should they not import 'everyday' considerations? Does the appearance of children's names, in the context of tennis, imply that these are not merely tokens to be arranged as elements of abstract sets? Test designers need to give further careful thought to just what it is that they are testing. An examination of recent test papers suggests that it seems to have been decided, for the moment at least, that the testing of maths in the English National Curriculum will be via the use of mainly 'realistic' items. Given the interpretative problems that these items can produce – especially for children from intermediate- and working-class social class backgrounds – we would urge that further thought be given to their unintended consequences for both the validity and the fairness of the assessment of what children know and, in some contexts at least, can do.

Appendix: Social class groups

(Combined from Goldthorpe and Heath (1992) and Erikson and Goldthorpe (1993).)

1 service class, higher grade: higher grade professionals, administrators and officials; managers in large industrial establishments; large proprietors
2 service class, lower grade: lower grade professionals, administrators and officials; higher grade technicians; managers in small industrial establishments; supervisors of non-manual employees
3 routine non-manual employees
4 personal service workers
5 small proprietors with employees
6 small proprietors without employees
7 farmers and smallholders
8 foremen and technicians
9 skilled manual workers
10 semi- and unskilled manual workers
11 agricultural workers

We have collapsed 1 and 2 into a service class, 3–8 into an intermediate class, and 9–11 into a working class.

Notes

1 Funded by the ESRC via grants R000235863 and R000222315.
2 It should be noted that these younger and older children are not matched samples. In particular, the older children have lower mean 'ability' scores.

References

Bernstein, B. (1996). *Pedagogy, Symbolic Control and Identity: Theory, Research, Critique*, Taylor and Francis, London.

Boaler, J. (1994). When do girls prefer football to fashion? An analysis of female underachievement in relation to 'realistic' mathematics contexts. *British Educational Research Journal*, **20**(5), 551–564.

Bourdieu, P. (1974). The school as a conservative force. In J. Eggleston (ed.) *Contemporary Research in the Sociology of Education*, Methuen, London, 32–46.

Bourdieu, P. (1986). *Distinction: A Social Critique of the Judgement of Taste*, Routledge and Kegan Paul, London.

Bourdieu, P. (1990). *The Logic of Practice*, Blackwell, Oxford.

Bowles, S. and Gintis, H. (1976). *Schooling In Capitalist America*, Routledge and Kegan Paul, London.

Cooper, B. (1985). *Renegotiating Secondary School Mathematics: A Study of Curriculum Change and Stability*, Falmer Press, Basingstoke.

Cooper, B. (1992). Testing National Curriculum mathematics: Some critical comments on the treatment of 'real' contexts for mathematics. *The Curriculum Journal*, **3**(3), 231–243.

Cooper, B. (1994). Authentic testing in mathematics? The boundary between everyday and mathematical knowledge in National Curriculum testing in English schools. *Assessment in Education: Principles, Policy and Practice*, 1(2), 143–166.

Cooper, B. (1998a). Assessing National Curriculum mathematics in England: Exploring children's interpretation of Key Stage 2 tests in clinical interviews. *Educational Studies in Mathematics*, 35(1), 19–49.

Cooper, B. (1998b). Using Bernstein and Bourdieu to understand children's difficulties with 'realistic' mathematics testing: An exploratory study. *International Journal of Qualitative Studies in Education*, 11(4), 511–532.

Cooper, B. and Dunne, M. (1998). Anyone for tennis? Social class differences in children's responses to National Curriculum mathematics testing. *The Sociological Review*, 46(1), 115–148.

Cooper, B. and Dunne, M. (2000). *Assessing Children's Mathematical Knowledge: Social Class, Sex and Problem-Solving*, Open University Press, Buckingham.

Dunne, M. (1994). The construction of ability: A critical examination of teachers' accounts. D.Phil. thesis, University of Birmingham.

Erikson, R. and Goldthorpe, J. H. (1993). *The Constant Flux: A Study of Class Mobility in Industrial Societies*, Clarendon, Oxford.

Goldthorpe, J. and Heath, A. (1992). *Revised class schema 1992. Working Paper 13*, Nuffield College, Oxford.

Holland, J. (1981). Social class and changes in orientation to meaning. *Sociology*, 15(1), 1–18.

Lave, J. (1988). *Cognition in Practice: Mind, Mathematics and Culture in Everyday Life*, Cambridge University Press.

Mehan, H. (1973). Assessing children's school performance. In H. P. Dreitzel (ed.) *Childhood and Socialisation*, Collier-Macmillan, London, 240–264.

Newman, D., Griffin, P. and Cole, M. (1989). *The Construction Zone*, Cambridge University Press.

Nunes, T., Schliemann, A. D. and Carraher, D. W. (1993). *Street Mathematics and School Mathematics*, Cambridge University Press.

Popper, K. (1963). *Conjectures and Refutations*, Routledge and Kegan Paul, London.

Säljö, R. (1991). Learning and mediation: Fitting reality into a table. *Learning and Instruction*, 1, 261–272.

SCAA (1994). Schools Curriculum and Assessment Authority (1994). *Mathematics Test: Teacher's Pack, Key Stage 2 1994*, SCAA.

SCAA (1996). Schools Curriculum and Assessment Authority (1996). *Key Stage 2 Tests 1996*, London, Dept. for Education and Employment.

SEAC (1993): Schools Examination and Assessment Council (1993). *Pilot Standard Tests: Key Stage 2: Mathematics*, SEAC/University of Leeds.

6 Establishing a community of practice in a secondary mathematics classroom

Merrilyn Goos, Peter Galbraith and Peter Renshaw

skimmed 19.7.04

Introduction

We have been developing a research programme in mathematics education based on key concepts from socio-cultural theory that foreground the interactive and communicative conditions for learning, and the inherently social and cultural nature of cognition itself (Goos, Galbraith and Renshaw, 1994; Goos, Galbraith and Renshaw, 1996; Renshaw, 1996). The socio-cultural perspective is one of a number of contemporary models of learning that is attempting to reform classroom practices by promoting less hierarchical, more interactive, more networked forms of communication within the classroom, and more explicit consideration of the connection between classrooms and the cultural and institutional practices of related communities, specifically in this context, knowledge communities where mathematics is an important cultural tool. The centrality of community in socio-cultural theory reflects the view that knowledge acquisition should be seen as progress to more complete participation in the practices, beliefs, conventions and values of communities of practitioners, and not primarily as the acquisition of mental structures *per se.*

In this chapter we focus on how a particular type of mathematics classroom can be created, a classroom that enables the practices, values, conventions and beliefs characteristic of the wider communities of mathematicians to be progressively enacted and gradually appropriated by students. One case – a mathematics classroom at the upper secondary school level – is analysed in detail in order to reveal the working assumptions, the tacit classroom culture, that underlie the interaction patterns between the teacher and the students. Leone Burton (1999) presents a view of mathematics learning as a narrative process in which mathematical knowledge is validated by the community of knowers, and outlined the different agendas for teachers and different responsibilities of learners that this position presents. Our own analysis highlights changes to the roles of teachers and students that are required for this local community of practice to take hold and thrive.

The current research programme has taken shape in various partnerships with teachers, where our suggestions about possible classroom practices consistent with socio-cultural theory, have been taken up selectively by the teachers and implemented in ways that they considered were feasible, and compatible with the complex conditions of their particular schools. The research programme, therefore, should not be considered as theory applied to practice, or practice derived in some principled way from theory, but rather as a research partnership in which key theoretical ideas become better understood in the context of classroom practice, and possibilities for changing classroom practices are created by theoretical insights.

In the majority of contemporary classrooms, learning mathematics is seen as mastering a predetermined body of knowledge and procedures. The teacher's job involves presenting the subject matter in small, easily manageable pieces and demonstrating the correct procedure or algorithm, after which students work individually on practice exercises. However reasonable this approach may appear, numerous research studies (e.g. Schoenfeld, 1988) have shown that such mathematics instruction can leave students with imperfect understanding and flawed beliefs about mathematics. When students' activity is limited to imitating the technique prescribed by the teacher, they can create the appearance of mathematical competence by simply memorising and reproducing the correct way to manipulate symbols, and may even come to believe that producing the correct form is more important than making sense of what they are doing (Cobb, 1986; Cobb and Bauersfeld, 1995).

Associating competence with symbol manipulation is but one of many undesirable consequences of the traditional approach to teaching mathematics. As Hilary Povey and Leone Burton point out in Chapter 3, this epistemology of *external authority* silences learners and leaves them dependent on authoritative others for validation of their knowing. Reliance on the teacher or text as the source of knowledge reduces students to a passive, accepting role, and leads them to expect that there must be a readily available method or rule for every kind of problem. The term 'problem' is itself problematic, as students know that the practice exercises on which they work constrain them to use the algorithm most recently taught, a situation that is not only highly contrived, but also leaves them helpless when faced with genuine problems where the solution method is not immediately obvious (Schoenfeld, 1992). As a result of school experiences such as these, students equate mathematics with meaningless practice on routine exercises, and learn that mathematics is not meant to make sense.

The last decade has seen the emergence of an international reform movement in mathematics education that has promoted notions of communication, collaborative interaction and group problem-solving – goals and practices that stand in contrast to those of traditional instruction. In the United States, for example, the National Council of Teachers of Mathematics (NCTM) has set new goals for students' learning, including the need to develop reasoning and problem-solving skills, to learn to communicate mathematically, and to work collaboratively as well as individually (NCTM, 1989, 1991). A similar shift in priorities has occurred in Australia, where the intent of the NCTM documents is echoed in the *National Statement on Mathematics for Australian Schools* (Australian Education Council, 1991). Like the NCTM agenda, the reformist goals for school mathematics in Australia are concerned with the development of collaborative learning and communication skills, the development of problem-solving capacities and the experience of the actual processes (e.g. conjecture, generalisation, proof, refutation) through which mathematics develops. In part, this reform agenda is consistent with the interests of employers who have criticised schools for the perceived communication and problem-solving skills of graduating students.

In part, it reflects the changing circumstances of contemporary society where mathematics has become a crucial tool for anyone wishing to participate in public discussion of current social, ecological, technological and economic issues. It is important that the reform agenda reflects, in addition, specifically educational concerns about the nature of mathematical thinking, and classroom conditions that will help students to learn to think mathematically. Research into mathematical education is no longer limited to studies of knowledge resources and heuristics (concerns more in keeping with the traditional approach to instruction outlined above), but also examines the role of metacognitive monitoring and control, beliefs and affects, and classroom practices that promote constructive engagement in mathematical communities (Schoenfeld, 1992). To provide such an educational perspective on recent efforts to reform mathematics teaching and learning we have employed socio-cultural theory. In the next section of the paper we summarise the key concepts from the theory and illustrate how we have made use of these concepts to guide out classroom research. Unlike Booth *et al.* (1999), our aim is not to juxtapose different theoretical perspectives; however, it is worthwhile noting again that our appreciation of socio-cultural theory itself has grown through the research project.

The socio-cultural perspective

Cognition is a social and cultural phenomenon

A key theoretical claim of socio-cultural theory is that human action is mediated by tools, and that such mediation not only changes the relationship of people to the world by extending their capacity to transform it for their own purposes, but tool use also transforms the individual, incorporating the individual into new functional systems of action and interaction that are culturally and historically situated. Cognition is not located purely within the individual, therefore, but in the functional system – it is stretched across the individual, the cultural tools, the activity and its context (Lave and Wenger, 1991).

Cultural tools do not simply amplify cognitive processes – they fundamentally change the nature of the task and the requirements to complete the task. The rapid development of computer technology and its application to classrooms provide numerous examples of how cultural tools transform the task and the cognitive requirements (Crook, 1991). For instance, students can use either graphics calculators or computer spreadsheet and graphing programs to rapidly solve the cubic equation $x^3 + 4 = x$, a task for which there is no ready algorithm if one is working 'by hand' (Kemp, Kissane and Bradley, 1996). Similarly, graphics calculators can lead to less tedious and more efficient execution of calculus problems (Berger, 1996). However, the most powerful use of technology is in enabling students to explore ideas and tackle problems that would otherwise be beyond them. From this perspective, therefore, learning should not be considered simply as the accumulation of internal mental processes and structures, but as a process of appropriating cultural tools that transform tasks, and the relationship of individuals to the tasks as well as to the other members of their community. How does such appropriation occur?

The ZPD as scaffolding

To understand how learning occurs, how people come to appropriate the cultural tools that transform their relationship to each other and the world, we need to appreciate what Vygotsky meant by the zone of proximal development – the ZPD. He formulated it in different ways depending on the particular problem he was analysing (see Lave and Wenger, 1991; Minick, 1987; Valsiner and van der Veer, 1992). The most widely quoted definition describes the ZPD as the distance between what a child can achieve alone, and what a child can achieve with the assistance of a more advanced partner. In our research programme this notion of the ZPD has highlighted the productive role peer tutors can play in scaffolding the learning of their fellow students. It also places the teacher in a pivotal role in the classroom, particularly to support students in becoming more self-regulating participants in classroom activities. Initially, the teacher and peer tutors act as the guides, who scaffold and support the performance of the less expert partners by directing their attention to key aspects of the task, simplifying the task, monitoring ongoing performance and adjusting the degree of assistance depending on the partner's competence in completing the task. The movement towards self-regulation requires the more expert partner to withdraw support as competence grows, and to provide opportunities for independent task completion. The students receiving help, however, should not be considered as passive or compliant in the situation. We have observed many instances in classrooms where students actively create their own supportive scaffolds – formal tutoring arrangements don't need to be organised, because students become accustomed to looking around for assistance from peers and the teacher where a culture of collaboration has been established.[1]

The ZPD in egalitarian partnerships – distributed complementary (in)competence

The second context in which Vygotsky analysed the notion of the ZPD was in relation to children's play. Vygotsky noted that when children played together they acted above their normal level of development and were able to regulate their own and their partners' behaviour according to more general social scripts, and take the perspective of others. Unlike the scaffolding notion, which is based on differential levels of expertise between partners, this view of the ZPD involves egalitarian relationships. Applied to our interest in mathematics education, we see learning potential in peer groups where there is incomplete but relatively equal expertise – each partner possessing some knowledge and skill but requiring the others' contribution in order to make progress. In the classrooms that we have been studying, we have identified such egalitarian groups as contexts where uncertainty leads to exploration and speculation. Such situations approximate the actual practices of mathematicians striving to go beyond the established boundaries of their knowledge, and so provide a more authentic experience of doing mathematics under conditions of uncertainty. Another advantage of these groups is that, removed from the direct influence of the teacher, the students take personal responsibility for the ideas that they are constructing, so the authorship of mathematical knowledge is vested in themselves and their partners. (The notions of *authorship* and *authority* are further elaborated by Leone Burton and Hilary Povey in Chapters 3.) One memorable incidental comment from a student highlighted the issue of authorship for us – after working together on a problem and making progress the student turned to his partner and said, 'That was really good thinking X'. It is unusual for students in most classrooms to compliment each other in this way – except in a mocking tone – so the comment stood out as representing something novel and suggested that these students had begun to see each other as real contributors to knowledge construction.

Nevertheless, it is important to recognise that social validation of knowledge by students themselves is a necessary but not a sufficient condition for a successful learning community to operate within the mathematics classroom. This is because the concept of what is acceptable as knowledge varies with the maturity and experience of the learner. For example, in relation to proof, research shows that in the early years a simple reassertion of a statement may be deemed adequate by the student. At a later stage there is appeal to evidence, driven by the awareness of a need to write supporting arguments. Even at the secondary level, however, the base of this evidence is empirical for many students, with a sequence of numerical checks tendered as conclusive proof of a generalisation. Only at advanced levels is the need for cogent reasoning from initial assumptions recognised, an appreciation that requires an understanding of the public status of discipline knowledge and the importance of public verification or falsification. Consequently, social validation in classrooms will not be sufficient when personal perceptions of learners allow the acceptance of mathematically inadequate forms. This serves to emphasise the essential role of the teacher in a classroom community of enquiry as the one who facilitates vigorous mathematical debate and who simultaneously ensures that the substantive arguments of students are tested against disciplinary knowledge. Not all constructions are equally valid; however, all are equally legitimate as a basis from which to proceed towards greater understanding. Indeed, the presence of a variety of incomplete constructions provides a rich environment for the exercise of critical collaborative approaches to the establishment and defence of authenticated knowledge.

The ZPD as the interweaving of everyday and scientific knowledge

The third context in which Vygotsky theorised the notion of the ZPD was in relation to schools and the access that schools provide to more organised and systematised forms of knowledge. He proposed two broad types of knowledge – everyday or local knowledge that is based on the experiences and cultural tools available in the child's immediate community, and scientific knowledge, which has a coherent organisation and a history of development that gives it greater consistency and generality than everyday knowledge. In terms of the ZPD, the child's everyday knowledge represents their established competencies, whereas the challenge presented by using and understanding the scientific knowledge defines the upper limits of the ZPD. Scientific concepts do not simply replace everyday concepts during the process of learning and development – that would produce only an empty formalism, and reduce the notion of the ZPD to a transmission model of teaching. Rather, to ensure the development of personal understanding, scientific concepts must be linked to the fabric of the children's existing concepts. In the

ZPD the teacher and the students need to weave together the two conceptual forms so that the everyday, or previously acquired, concepts are transformed by the more general and abstract concepts, while the scientific concepts are tested and made accessible by being applied to the students' experiences and represented in a way that is relevant to them. For example, in the context of senior secondary school mathematics this inter-weaving may occur when constructing mathematical models of real world phenomena, or when students' previously developed knowledge of real number systems and opera-tions is connected to the algebra of complex numbers or matrices.[2]

This notion of the ZPD places the teacher in a pivotal role in the classroom because it is the teacher who needs to have an expert grasp of the discipline of mathematics, and the capacity to see in the students' ideas the link to the more general forms and conventions of mathematics. The teacher's own beliefs, about the nature of mathe-matics and how it is learned will also determine whether such opportunities are recog-nised and exploited (Fennema and Loef-Franke, 1992; Thompson, 1992). Limitations of the effectiveness of transmissive teaching have often been documented, but the significance of the outlook of the teacher in providing alternatives has been less frequently addressed in depth. Some time ago Howson (1975) lamented:

> The major concern for worry was that teachers in many cases never learned to learn – their university and college preparation had turned them into absorbers of predigested information, but they had not been encouraged or trained to learn or create mathematics by themselves. They had been trained to accept what was offered to them, but not to question the criteria underlying the selection and methods of presentation of the material, they had not learned to view mathe-matics as an ongoing activity.

However, by emphasising the role of the teacher and the significance of disciplinary knowledge, we are not advocating a return to a transmission model of teaching; nor in our own study are we merely concerned with a change of instructional mode for students as consumers. The teacher is an integral part of the community of learners, and the actions of the teacher in our study display features illustrating that the approach we take is incompatible with the characteristics described by Howson. Instead, the teacher has to establish the conditions in the classroom where students become engaged in the process of enquiry and are willing to share their insights initially using familiar forms of representation and language. Thus the interweaving of concepts at differing levels of abstraction renders the separation of teacher from learner, and knowledge from individual, an impossibility.

There is another aspect of this weaving metaphor for the ZPD that requires clarifi-cation. The notion of scientific knowledge implies a compendium of handed-down wisdom, as if scientific knowledge were a product and not a process. Knowing is not an inert accumulation but an active process, a way of speaking and acting in various communities of practice. Thus, as students appropriate knowledge from a particular community of practitioners, they become participants in ongoing social and institu-tional practices, even if they are only peripherally engaged at first.

This interpretation of the ZPD is consistent with the view that learning to think mathematically involves more than acquiring skills, strategies and declarative knowledge. It involves the development of habits and dispositions of interpretation, and meaning construction, that is, a mathematical point of view (Schoenfeld, 1994). When students adopt the epistemological values of the discipline they 'come to see mathematics as a vehicle for sense-making' (Schoenfeld, 1989, p. 81), rather than a collection of arbitrary rules for symbol manipulation. Our goal, therefore, is not to recreate in the classroom some idealised image of the professional mathematical community, but to foster a local hybrid culture, where the mathematical point of view is constantly being applied to students' experiences and concerns. In this sense authentic knowledge is not simply the students' personal constructions *per se,* or formal mathematics *per se,* but the combination of both.

The ZPD – created by the challenge of participating in the classroom culture

The ZPD is normally applied to individuals, but recently it has been applied to whole groups, and it seems to us that this is both consistent with socio-cultural theory, and of practical significance in removing the implication that effective teaching in the ZPD requires sensitive diagnosis of the diverse levels of development of students, followed by one-to-one instruction. Ann Brown and her colleagues (Brown, A, 1994; Brown and Campione, 1995) consider the class a *community of learners* where children are inducted into more disciplined and scientific modes of thinking that involve exploration, speculation, conjecture, gathering evidence and providing proof. Students are viewed as having partially overlapping zones that provide a changing mix of levels of expertise that enables many different productive partnerships and activities to be orchestrated. Through the establishment of participation frameworks such as peer tutoring sessions, reciprocal teaching episodes, teacher-led lessons, individual and collaborative problem-solving sessions, students become enculturated into taken-for-granted aspects of classroom life that promote a shared knowledge base, a shared system of beliefs, and accepted conventions for communicating and verifying knowledge claims. The lived culture of the classroom becomes, in itself, a challenge for students to move beyond their established competencies, and to enter more fully into disciplined and scientific modes of enquiry and values.

[This final version of the ZPD subsumes the other three notions that we identified above.] Included in a community of learners are episodes of scaffolding, peer-initiated exploration and speculation, as well as weaving together informal and scientific perspectives during teacher-led and peer-directed activities. Only a handful of studies have documented the formation of such classrooms (e.g. Alibert, 1988; Borasi, 1992; Brown, R. A. J., 1994; Brown and Renshaw, 1995; Elbers, Derks and Streefland, 1995; Lampert, 1990). In each case, the participating teachers worked from the premise that mathematics is learned through engagement in social and communicative activity, and they organised an environment in which students were actively engaged in mathematical sense-making. However, since models of practice derived from the literature can appear unrealistic to teachers, we decided not to list particular practices for teachers to follow, but indicated in general terms the type of classroom activities we were interested in documenting. In particular, we indicated a special interest in videotaping or audiotaping peer group discussion whenever it might occur in their classrooms.

In the second section of this chapter we report a case study of one classroom where a culture consistent with our guiding theoretical principles appears to be taking hold, and we provide our view of the conditions and practices that have enabled this to occur.

The classroom study

The study reported here is part of a two-year research project investigating patterns of classroom social interactions that improve senior secondary school students' mathematical understanding, and lead to the communal construction of mathematical knowledge. Four mathematics classes (three Year 11 and one Year 12) and their teachers participated in the first year of the study; three of the teachers, each with a new Year 11 class, continued their involvement in the project's second year. Multiple methods were used to gather data on features of classroom interaction and students' individual thinking. At the beginning of each year questionnaires and associated written tasks were administered to obtain information on students' beliefs about mathematics, perceptions of classroom practices, and metacognitive knowledge. From March until September one mathematics lesson per week was observed for each class to record teacher–student and student–student interactions. At least 10 lessons were videotaped in each classroom in the first year of the project. The research plan for the second year included an additional two-week period of intensive observation, during which every lesson in a unit of work nominated by the teacher was videotaped. Stimulated recall interviews (Leder, 1990) have been conducted with teachers and students on a number of occasions to seek their interpretations of selected videotape excerpts, and students' views about learning mathematics have been elicited in individual and whole-class interviews, and in reflective writing.

Categories of teacher–student interaction were identified from our observations that were consistent with the theoretical principles outlined earlier in this chapter. Table 6.1 shows the list of categories for both the teacher and students. Although the categories of interaction were derived from observations of all four classrooms participating in the first year of the study, they were exemplified to varying degrees in each of the classrooms. Evidence from field notes and videotapes indicated that one classroom, more than the other three, approximated a community of enquiry. The material in the remainder of the chapter is based on data gathered from this teacher and his Year 12 and Year 11 classes over the two years of the study.

The categories of teacher–student interaction tell only part of the story. Taken together they reveal the emerging culture of the classroom as a community of practice. The teacher's actions were crucial in establishing the culture, but it is impossible to describe the actions of the teacher without considering the corresponding actions of the students. The teacher's invitations or challenges to students can be resisted, rejected or subverted. (Some signs of resistant behaviour are described later in the chapter.) That almost all students accepted these invitations to participate in new ways in the classroom indicates the teacher's high level of professional expertise, but also a certain entering competence on the part of the students – as if they were now

Table 6.1 Assumptions about and learning mathematics implicit in teacher–student interactions

Assumptions	Teacher actions	Student actions
Mathematical thinking is an act of sense-making, and rests on the processes of specialising, generalising, conjecturing and convincing.	The teacher models mathematical thinking using a dialogic format to invite students to participate. The teacher invites students to take responsibility for the lesson content by providing intermediate or final steps in solutions or arguments initiated by the teacher. The teacher withholds judgement on students' suggestions while inviting comment or critique from other students.	Students begin to offer conjectures and justificatons without the teacher's prompting. During whole class discussion students initiate argumentation between themselves, without teacher mediation.
The processes of mathematical inquiry are accompanied by habits of individual reflection and self-monitoring.	The teacher asks questions that encourage students to question their assumptions and locate their errors. The teacher presents 'what if?' scenarios.	Students begin to point out and correct their own and each other's errors, and those made by the teacher. Students ask their own 'what if?' questions.
Mathematical thinking develops through teacher scaffolding of the processes of inquiry.	The teacher calls on students to clarify, elaborate, critique and justify their assertions. The teacher structures students' thinking by asking questions that lead them through strategic steps.	Students spontaneously provide clarification, elaboration, critiques, and justifications. Students take increasing responsibility for suggesting strategic steps.
Mathematical thinking can be generated and tested by students through participation in equal-status peer partnerships.	The teacher structures social interactions between students, by asking them to explain and justify ideas and strategies to each other.	Students form informal groups to monitor their progress, seek feedback on ideas, and explain ideas to each other.
Interweaving of familiar and formal knowledge helps students to adopt the conventions of mathematical communication.	The teacher makes explicit reference to mathematical language, onventions and symbolism, labelling conventions as traditions that permit communication. The teacher links technical terms to commonsense meanings, and uses multiple representations of new terms and concepts.	Students begin to debate the appropriateness and relative advantages of different symbol conventions.

ready to take up the challenge to be more active in classroom activities and to extend their thinking. The culture of the classroom, therefore, represents the joint production of the teacher and the students.

In Table 6.1 we have listed the five assumptions about doing and learning mathematics that appear crucial to creating the culture of the community of mathematical inquiry. The assumptions were derived over time from our observations of classrooms, dialogues with teachers, and reflections on these experiences drawing on the theoretical and research literature reviewed above. The assumptions are:

1   Mathematical thinking is an act of sense-making, and rests on the processes of specialising and generalising, conjecturing and justifying;
2   The processes of mathematical enquiry are accompanied by habits of individual reflection and self-monitoring;
3   Mathematical thinking develops through teacher scaffolding of the processes of enquiry;
4   Mathematical thinking can be generated and tested by students through participation in equal-status peer partnerships;
5   Interweaving of familiar and formal knowledge helps students to adopt the conventions of mathematical communication.

Illustrative classroom episodes

An annotated observation record of two sequential lessons with the Year 11 class is provided in Tables 6.2 and 6.3. These lessons have been chosen because it is during the early stages of Year 11 (the first year of students' senior secondary schooling) that the teacher plays a crucial role in *establishing* the classroom community of enquiry. The annotations refer to the previously developed categories shown in Table 6.1. In these records the abbreviations T and S refer to the teacher and unidentified students, while other letters of the alphabet are used to identify specific students. Following the presentation of the classroom episodes we draw together specific incidents that illustrate how the culture of the classroom was being formed through teacher–student interaction.

Specifying the teacher's role in creating the tacit culture of mathematical inquiry

The classroom culture should be considered as an interrelated system that has been built through the actions of both the teacher and the students. By highlighting the teacher's role here we do not disregard the contributions of the students in responding to the teacher's challenge to enter into the community of inquiry. (Further elaboration of the students' response is left to a later section of the chapter.) It follows also that we are not presenting here a list of prescriptive actions – as if there were a recipe that any teacher could follow to create a community of enquiry. Instead we acknowledge the complexities of educational settings in which teachers and learners find themselves (see Burton, 1999), and view the underlying assumptions of the classroom culture as providing goals for teachers, guides to

Table 6.2 Year 11 maths lesson 1: Finding the inverse of a 2 × 2 matrix

Annotation	Interaction	Blackboard
Structures Ss' thinking (backward)	T reminds Ss of procedure for finding inverse of a 2 × 2 matrix using simultaneous equations. Asks Ss to solve the resulting equations. Ss provide equations and solution. T: So the inverse of $\begin{pmatrix} 3 & 1 \\ 5 & 2 \end{pmatrix}$ is $\begin{pmatrix} 2 & -1 \\ -5 & 3 \end{pmatrix}$	$\begin{pmatrix} 3 & 1 \\ 5 & 2 \end{pmatrix}\begin{pmatrix} a & b \\ c & d \end{pmatrix} = \begin{pmatrix} 1 & 0 \\ 0 & 1 \end{pmatrix}$ $3a + c = 1$ $5a + 2c = 0$ $3b + d = 0$ $5b + 2d = 1$ $a = 2, b = -1, c = -5, d = 3$
Encourages self-checking	T: Can you check via matrix multiplication that you do get the identity matrix? Ss confirm this is so. T: Is it inefficient to do this every time?	
Models mathematical thinking Authorship Sense-making	Ss concur. T: Could we find a shortcut? L suggests reversing the position of *a* and *d*, and placing minus signs in front of *b* and *c*. T elicits symbolic representation and writes on blackboard.	Inverse of $\begin{pmatrix} a & b \\ c & d \end{pmatrix}$ is $\begin{pmatrix} d & -b \\ -c & a \end{pmatrix}$?
Models mathematical thinking	T: How could we verify this? Ss suggest doing another one. T provides another example; asks students to use 'L's conjecture' to write down the hypothetical inverse and check via matrix multiplication. Ss do so – they are convinced the method works.	$\begin{pmatrix} 2 & 1 \\ 1 & 1 \end{pmatrix} \xrightarrow{inverse} \begin{pmatrix} 1 & -1 \\ -1 & 2 \end{pmatrix}$ $\begin{pmatrix} 4 & 1 \\ 3 & 2 \end{pmatrix} \xrightarrow{inverse} \begin{pmatrix} 2 & -1 \\ -3 & 4 \end{pmatrix}$?
Structures Ss' thinking (forward)	T gives another example for Ss to try. Gradual increase in S talk as they realise L's conjecture doesn't work' for this one (matrix multiplication does not yield the identity matrix).	$\begin{pmatrix} 4 & 1 \\ 3 & 2 \end{pmatrix}\begin{pmatrix} 2 & -1 \\ -3 & 4 \end{pmatrix} = \begin{pmatrix} 5 & 0 \\ 0 & 5 \end{pmatrix}$
Structures Ss' thinking (backward) *Structures Ss' thinking (forward)*	T reminds Ss they can still find the inverse by solving simultaneous equations. Ss do so and verify via matrix multiplication. T: How is this related to L's conjecture? (which is half right). Ss reply that the first attempt is too big by a factor of 5, so they need to divide by 5.	Inverse is $\begin{pmatrix} \dfrac{2}{5} & \dfrac{-1}{5} \\ \dfrac{-3}{5} & \dfrac{4}{5} \end{pmatrix}$
Structures Ss' thinking (consolidation) *Models mathematical thinking* *Sense-making and authorship*	T: What did you divide by in the previous example? Ss realise they could divide by 1. T: So the new method (dividing by something) works. But how do you know what to divide by? Homework: Find a rule that works for these two cases. Test it on another matrix of your choice	$\begin{pmatrix} 2 & 1 \\ 1 & 1 \end{pmatrix} \xrightarrow{inverse} \begin{pmatrix} \dfrac{1}{1} & \dfrac{-1}{1} \\ \dfrac{-1}{1} & \dfrac{2}{1} \end{pmatrix}$

Table 6.3 Year 11 maths lesson 2: Inverse and determinant of a 2 × 2 matrix

Annotation	Interaction	Blackboard
	T asks Ss to remind him of the matrix worked on last lesson (homework). The first try gave $\begin{pmatrix} 5 & 0 \\ 0 & 5 \end{pmatrix}$: you had to adjust by dividing by five. (Ss were to find a rule for the divisor). T: What was the divisor?	$\begin{pmatrix} 4 & 1 \\ 3 & 2 \end{pmatrix}\begin{pmatrix} 2 & -1 \\ -3 & 4 \end{pmatrix} = \begin{pmatrix} 5 & 0 \\ 0 & 5 \end{pmatrix}$ $\downarrow$ $\begin{pmatrix} \frac{2}{5} & \frac{-1}{5} \\ \frac{-3}{5} & \frac{4}{5} \end{pmatrix}$
Sense-making	D: $ad - bc$. T: Did you invent your own matrix and test it? Ss: Yes, it worked. T names 'this thing' ($ad - bc$) as the *determinant*.	
Mathematical conventions and symbolism	T: Let's formalise what you've found. What would 1 write as the inverse of $\begin{pmatrix} a & b \\ c & d \end{pmatrix}$?	
	AV volunteers the formula, which T writes on blackboard. L: Would the inverse of a 3 × 3 matrix be similar? T: Yes, but it's messy – you can use your graphics calculator to do it. You need to be able to find the inverse of a 2 × 2 matrix longhand. R: What part of that is the determinant? T labels $ad - bc$ and writes the symbol and name 'del' on blackboard.	$\frac{1}{ad - bc}\begin{pmatrix} d & -b \\ -c & a \end{pmatrix}$ $\nabla = ad - bc$ *del*
Models mathematical thinking (test conjecture with another example)	T puts another example on blackboard and asks Ss to find the inverse. After working for a short time Ss begin to murmur 'zero'. They find that $ad - bc$, the determinant of the matrix, is zero, therefore the inverse cannot be calculated. R: Is our method *still* wrong?	$Find \begin{pmatrix} 3 & 6 \\ 2 & 4 \end{pmatrix}^{-1}$
Authorship of knowing	T: No. Remember, some elements of the real number system have no inverse. So what is the test to find if a matrix is non-invertible? L: The determinant is zero. T: A non-invertible matrix is called a *singular* matrix. What happens if you try to invert this matrix using your graphics calculator? Ss try it: see 'error' message.	

Annotation	Interaction	Blackboard
Structures Ss' thinking (consolidation)	T: We can think about this another way. Remember how to use simultaneous equation method to find the inverse ... What happens if the matrix is singular? First find the inverse of this matrix, using simultaneous equations. Ss work on solving the simultaneous equations.	$\begin{pmatrix} 2 & 1 \\ 1 & 1 \end{pmatrix}\begin{pmatrix} a & b \\ c & d \end{pmatrix} = \begin{pmatrix} 1 & 0 \\ 0 & 1 \end{pmatrix}$ $2a + c = 1$ $2b + d = 0$ $a + c = 0$ $b + d = 1$ $a = 1, c = -1, b = -1, d = 2$
Structures Ss' social interaction	T tours the room. Asks AG 'Have you done it?' AG: No. T: Then ask AR (sitting beside him) to explain it.	
Structures Ss' thinking (backward)	Ss finish finding solutions. T: What is this related to, from Junior maths? Ss: Finding the intersection of two lines. T: These are all linear equations so we could solve them by graphing. Ss use graphics calculators to find graphical solutions. T: So one way to find the inverse is to set up simultaneous equations and solve (algebraically or graphically). Now try to find the inverse of $\begin{pmatrix} 3 & 6 \\ 2 & 4 \end{pmatrix}$ (which we just found is singular) by solving simultaneous equations graphically	
Structures Ss' thinking (forward)	Ss find parallel lines – no solution. T: Another interesting thing ... you know how to turn a matrix equation into simultaneous equations ... (Ss do the conversion and solve the equations) T: Can we do the reverse? What if I gave you the simultaneous equations – how would you make a matrix equation?	$\begin{pmatrix} 4 & 2 \\ 1 & 1 \end{pmatrix}\begin{pmatrix} a \\ b \end{pmatrix} = \begin{pmatrix} 10 \\ 3 \end{pmatrix}$ $4a + 2b = 10$ $a + b = 3$ $a = 2, b = 1$
Structures Ss' thinking (backward)	AR explains how the numbers and the letters are arranged in matrix formation. T: What was the reason we wanted to find matrix inverses in the first place? R: We couldn't divide by a matrix! T reminds Ss where they left off previous work on solving a problem that required division of one matrix by another (like the equation on blackboard).	$\begin{pmatrix} 4 & 2 \\ 1 & 1 \end{pmatrix}\begin{pmatrix} a \\ b \end{pmatrix} = \begin{pmatrix} 10 \\ 3 \end{pmatrix}$ $3x = 6$
Sense-making and authorship	T: Recall the parallel with the real number system ... to solve this algebraic equation you'd multiply both sides by the multiplicative inverse of 3. Homework: Solve the matrix equation (by 'inventing' matrix algebra).	

the direction of their actions. In each local context, the teacher will need to creatively devise means to move towards the goals.

Mathematical thinking is an act of sense-making, and rests on the processes of specialising and generalising, conjecturing and justifying

Although the teacher had a specific agenda during the lessons he did not merely demonstrate how to do the mathematics – even though it would have been a simple task to show the students how to find the inverse of a 2×2 matrix. Instead. he involved the students in the processes of mathematical enquiry by:

1   presenting a problem for them to work on. For example, the teacher first chose the matrix $\begin{pmatrix} 3 & 1 \\ 5 & 2 \end{pmatrix}$ and asked the students to find the inverse by using their existing knowledge of the simultaneous equation method. Because this matrix has a determinant of one, it represented a simple case which would allow the students to see part of the pattern linking the matrix to its inverse;
2   eliciting students' conjectures about the general form of the inverse matrix, based on the specific case they had examined;
3   withholding judgement to maintain an authentic state of uncertainty regarding the validity of conjectures. Thus the students' initial conjecture of $\begin{pmatrix} d & -b \\ -c & a \end{pmatrix}$ as the inverse (which, although incorrect, did satisfy the conditions of the specific case) was treated as an hypothesis, rather than an error;
4   asking students to test conjectures and justify them to their peers. Rather than rejecting students' initial conjecture, the teacher offered a counter-example, $\begin{pmatrix} 4 & 1 \\ 3 & 2 \end{pmatrix}$, whose inverse the students found to have the form $n\begin{pmatrix} d & -b \\ -c & a \end{pmatrix}$. Students were then asked to find a formula for n, and test their new conjecture on another matrix of their own choice.

In the lessons illustrated above, it is the students who 'invent' and test an algorithm for inverting a 2×2 matrix – although the teacher's guidance certainly facilitated their process of invention. The teacher acknowledged and validated their authorship by labelling one student's initial suggestion as 'L's conjecture' (see Table 6.2). Students also asserted their author/ity, as demonstrated by the student's question as to whether their discovery of non-invertible matrices makes 'our method' wrong (see Table 6.3). The teacher interactively explicated the nature of mathematical thinking, rather than presenting himself as a model to be observed.

The processes of mathematic enquiry are accompanied by habits of individual reflection and self-monitoring

Self-directed thinking is initially prompted by teacher questions ('Can you check via matrix multiplication that you do get the identity matrix?'). As the students become accustomed to the teacher's expectations (particularly in Year 12), more subtle interventions are used to promote reflection; for example, allowing time for students to read textbook explanations and examples in order to provide substance for a whole-class discussion. Here, the teacher acts in the role of 'reviewer' of students' work, in much the same way as a journal referee.

Mathematical thinking develops through teacher scaffolding of the processes of enquiry

The teacher helped the students make sense of the mathematics by asking questions that prompted the students to clarify, elaborate, justify and critique their own and each other's assertions. These interventions can move students' thinking either *forwards* towards new ideas ('Could we find a shortcut?', 'How is this related to L's conjecture?') or *backwards* towards previously developed knowledge or a previously identified goal ('What is this related to from Junior maths?', 'What was the reason we wanted to find matrix inverses in the first place?'); or they can serve to *consolidate* students' thinking by drawing together ideas developed during the lesson ('What did you divide by in the previous example?').

Mathematical thinking can be generated and tested by students through participation in equal-status peer partnerships

The teacher also signalled that social interaction with peers was valued in working on mathematical problems. This was particularly noticeable during the early weeks of Year 11, when classroom norms were being established. (For example, in the lessons illustrated above, the teacher asked students to explain their solutions to each other.) Later in the year, and particularly in Year 12, these forms of argumentation and social interaction appeared in both small-group and whole-class discussion without explicit support from the teacher, their appropriation by the students a sign that certain patterns of interaction could be taken for granted. While some of these episodes involved peer scaffolding or tutoring, the main purpose was to demonstrate the process of socially validating knowledge claims in a community of enquiry,

Interweaving of familiar and formal knowledge helps students to adopt the conventions of mathematical communication

The teacher avoided using technical terms until students had developed an understanding of the underlying mathematical ideas ('This thing is called the determinant.' 'Let's formalise what you've found.'). The availability of precise language then helped the students to make their thinking visible while discussing ideas with their peers.

The teacher's beliefs about learning and teaching mathematics

We pointed out earlier that teachers' beliefs about learning and teaching mathematics influence the features of the classroom environment they create. These beliefs can be inferred from the actual practices of the classroom, but we acknowledge that classroom constraints and institutional pressures often prevent teachers from acting according to their beliefs. The stimulus for the teacher to elaborate his beliefs was a videotape of a lesson with his Year 12 class. As the videotape was played, the teacher was asked to comment on the interaction, explain what he was doing and why (as in Meade and McMeniman, 1992). From the interview we identified three core beliefs, which are illustrated below with excerpts from the transcript.

Students learn mathematics by making sense of it for themselves

I want to try as much as possible to get them to work it out for themselves.

(Having the students reconstruct a mathematical argument developed in a previous lesson), you're getting them to try to build some sense into it, by getting them to reconstruct it themselves they have to be able to make some sense out of it even if it's only internal consistency with the mathematics ... you hope that way that's building in a more robust cognitive structure they can use later on.

The other important thing about it as well, by doing it this way you've got a degree of ownership involved ... the kids are engaged, and I really think that's because they're owning what's going on, it's not just sitting there, listen to this and away you go.

If you never gave them the opportunity, if you just told them, then they're expecting you – or it's easy enough to wait to be told again. I don't think, long term, that's a great advantage.

The teacher's strategy of engaging the students actively in the lesson is related to beliefs about personal responsibility and sense-making. The teacher is also looking forward in the students' development rather than focusing on the present situation – noting the advantage of 'robust cognitive structures' that the students can use later on, and justifying the push to independence by considering the 'long-term' perspective. The teacher's beliefs here are entirely consistent with the notion of the ZPD: he wants them to appropriate the mathematics, and be prepared for independent engagement in the future. It is worth noting also that there is no preoccupation with examinations or covering the syllabus – concerns that normally justify greater teacher control, and less emphasis on in-depth understanding.

Teachers should model mathematical thinking and encourage students to make and evaluate conjectures

There's an element of attempting to model the problem-solving process in this as well ... at the beginning of Year 11 they do a unit on it and I attempt to keep coming back to these things.

…they won't always offer information and it's important they're encouraged to guess and just have a go. So then other people can criticise it, or they can criticise themselves once they've had a guess.

Having taught the class in Year 11, the teacher is himself a part of the history of experiences of these students, and is able to make connections across time, reminding them of related prior knowledge and helping them compose the required mathematical knowledge for the present task. Thus modelling mathematical thinking involves demonstrating how one searches for related prior knowledge and tests its relevance to the current situation. The teacher more than anyone else in the classroom is able to provide this continuity – connecting the past with the present and anticipating future developments.

Nevertheless, the students show resistance to some of the practices required in a community of enquiry – not always offering information, or being prepared to guess. The teacher's comments here suggest he accepts this type of resistance, and sees his role as challenging them out of their reticence.

Communication between students should be encouraged so they can learn from each other, sharpen their understanding, and practise using the specialist language of mathematics

I do think it's important that they're able to communicate with other people and their peers. They will learn at least as much from each other as they will with me. To be able to do that they have to talk to each other. It's also a part, one of the reasons I often force them to say things because they need to be able to use the language because the language itself carries very specific meanings; and unless they have the language they probably don't have the meanings properly either. They need the language to be able to obviously communicate, but I think it also has something to do with their understanding as well.

Again the teacher sees himself as pushing against the students' resistance to communicating with clarity and precision – 'I often force them to say things'. This has two aspects – to promote peer interaction, which is seen in itself as a learning experience of at least equal importance to teacher-led sessions, and to give the students the experience of using conventional mathematical language.

All of these features of the teacher's beliefs correspond to key aspects of the ZPD – notably the importance of weaving the language of the everyday with mathematical language, and the potential of peer interaction to promote development – and are consistent with the cultural assumptions of the classroom we had inferred from the teacher–student interaction patterns.

Students' emerging beliefs

Students' responses to interview questions and reflective writing tasks showed that they were remarkably well attuned to the teacher's goals, and were aware that their classroom operated differently from others they had experienced. They also felt that there were benefits in the approach practised by their teacher. Below we use excerpts from transcripts to illustrate their emerging beliefs.

Knowledge claims have to be validated by convincing one's peers. This process involves proof that is acceptable to peers, not mere assertion

Stimulated recall interview with three Year 12 students, based on a videotaped lesson segment capturing their discussion about a problem (I is the interviewer, R is a student).

> I: One of the interesting things is that you don't just accept what each other says.
> R: We always assume everyone else is wrong about it!
> I: But it's not just saying, 'No it isn't', 'Yes it is'.
> R: Yeah, we've got to be proven beyond all doubt!

Explaining to peers is a context that promotes self-evaluation, and consolidation of understanding. Without such opportunities, learning becomes rote transmission

Whole class interview with the Year 12 class.

> D: So many times I find myself trying to explain something to other people, and you find something you've kind of missed yourself … Even if they don't really know what they're doing, explaining it to them imprints it to your mind.
> E: Yeah, and if you can explain it to someone else it means you know.
> B: In other subjects like (names a non-mathematics subject), the teacher doesn't give you much time to talk to other students. Most of the time, she's (i.e. the teacher) talking. When I talk to D (another student) about something, we get in trouble for talking.
> D: It's more like learning parrot fashion.
> B: It's mostly pure learning, so what do you discuss? It's already all proven …

Learning involves engagement in activities – doing – during which peer interaction and teacher guidance enable personal understandings to develop

Reflective writing (Year 11 class). Responses to the questions: How did the teacher help you to learn this topic? How did your classmates help you to learn?

> AV: The teacher mainly guided us – we learned most things by ourselves. Classmate discussion was very important in this unit, i.e. comparing answers, discussing and explaining things to each other.

Whole class interview with the Year 11 class.

> L: In other subjects the teacher asks the questions; here we do.

It is clear from the above examples that the students' beliefs about mathematics learning and teaching were consistent with those of their teacher, and compatible with socio-cultural theory. In the next section we show how the students' beliefs were manifested in their classroom interactions with each other, and with the teacher.

Students' participation in the community of enquiry

Earlier we noted that a classroom community of enquiry is interactively constituted as teacher and students respond and adapt to each other's challenges, questions, and beliefs, and we presented detailed observations of two lessons to illustrate the teacher's role in establishing such a community with a Year 11 class. We now draw on our observations of the mature community that operated within the Year 12 class in order to demonstrate how students eventually appropriated both the modes of reasoning and the patterns of social interaction valued by the teacher. Here we describe two contexts within which students asserted their author/ity: whole-class discussion, and individual practice on problems.

Student–student talk during whole-class discussion

During whole-class discussion, the teacher expects students to clarify and justify the ideas they contribute, as well as critique the contributions of other students. In contrast with traditional classrooms where such public talk must be channelled through the teacher, students in this classroom frequently directed their comments to each other without the teacher's mediation, thus sparking the kind of argumentation that was previously orchestrated through the teacher's intervention. The following instance comes from a lesson introducing Hooke's Law.

The class had again interrogated a worked example demonstrating how to describe the motion of a mass executing simple harmonic motion while suspended from a spring. During the, ensuing whole-class discussion, some students the change of notation from $x = r \cos \omega t$ (as used in the lesson mentioned above) to $x = a \cos nt$ (a more general form that applies to all kinds of simple harmonic motion, not just that derived from a projection of uniform circular motion on a diameter of the circle). Rather than providing a rationale, the teacher withdrew from the discussion to allow students to resolve the issue for themselves:

ROB: Why did they suddenly skip to a?

BELINDA: Because x is equal to $a \cos nt$.

BEN: Why use a and n, when we have the exact same formula with r and ω? Does it refer to ω involving radians?

ROB: On this side [referring to the handout containing the example – also used in the lesson mentioned earlier] they said $x = r \cos \omega t$, on the other side $x = a \cos nt$.

BELINDA: Excuse me, I have a point to make here! You can't always use r because – (to teacher) Oh, sorry! (Teacher indicates she should continue.) I don't know if anyone will agree with me – because you're not always using a circle, it's not always going to be the radius.

ROB: Radius, yeah.

BELINDA: So the amplitude's not always the radius.

By ceding control of the debate the teacher provided another opportunity for students to engage in the processes of mathematical thinking, and to deal explicitly with symbol conventions.

Informal discussion while working on problems

Students rarely worked individually on textbook problems, but clustered into informal groups so that they could discuss their progress with each other. Although such interactions sometimes involved little more than periodic checking of results and procedures, the discussion reached a deeper level if a student was unable to resolve a difficulty or if a disagreement arose. One such instance occurred towards the end of the Hooke's Law lesson mentioned above. Rob, Ben and Duncan had been working together on the task shown in Figure 6.1.

After the trio had completed parts (a) to (c), Ben noticed the unusual conditions for part (d), in which the initial displacement of the mass is negative rather than positive ($d = -0.1$). In the discussion that followed the boys clarified their understanding of 'amplitude' and agreed that it would be unchanged from part (c). Then, instead of simply carrying out the calculations for (d), they compared the problem conditions for (c) and (d) in order to decide which aspects of the motion would be the same and which would be different in these two situations. A mutually agreed representation of the problem was established only after vigorous debate in which the boys challenged each other to justify their conjectures, as the following edited transcript shows:

> ROB: Oh, the same – it's the same: k equals, let me guess …
>
> BEN: (pause) No … no.
>
> DUNCAN: The only thing that's going to change is the amplitude.
>
> BEN: It doesn't change the amplitude.
>
> DUNCAN: Yes it does!
>
> BEN: (after a slight pause) How?
>
> ROB: Because that's all that changes – the acceleration's the same, because it's the mass that –
>
> BEN: The amplitude doesn't change –
>
> DUNCAN: Yes it does!
>
> BEN: How?
>
> DUNCAN: See, if you pull it down, it depends on how much you pull it down. You pull it down a little bit –
>
> ROB: – it'll be a small amplitude.
>
> BEN: No, no, but isn't the amplitude the amount away, either up or down, from the stationary point? (uses hands to demonstrate).
>
> DUNCAN: Yeah –
>
> BEN: If it goes up point one it's not going to go down point one.
>
> DUNCAN: No, I know, but it *should* be. If it was a perfect system.
>
> BEN: (expression of sudden understanding on his face) No, it's going to be exactly the same as the last – !
>
> DUNCAN: (pause, thinks) Oh, of course, that's just negative (pointing to $d = -0.1$).

A mass M is attached to the end of an elastic of natural length a and reaches its equilibrium position when the string is extended by l. The mass is then displaced downwards a further distance d and released. Find the period and amplitude of the motion for each set of data:

(a) $M = 6\,\text{kg}, l = 1\,\text{m}, d = 0.5\,\text{m}$
(b) $M = 1\,\text{kg}, l = 0.4\,\text{m}, d = 0.3\,\text{m}$
(c) $M = 10\,\text{kg}, l = 0.5\,\text{m}, d = 0.1\,\text{m}$
(d) $M = 10\,\text{kg}, l = 0.5\,\text{m}, d = -0.1\,\text{m}$

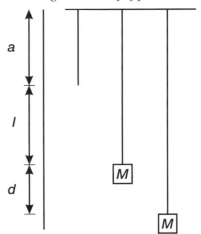

Figure 6.1 The elastic problem

> ROB: Why are we doing it? But the, the other thing, the period's going to be the same.
>
> BEN: (confident now) The period's going to be the same. Everything's going to be the same.

Perhaps the most crucial contributions to the discussion were made by Ben, whose insistence on asking 'How?' caused all three boys to critically examine their and each other's explanations. Booth *et al.* (1999) examined the diverse interpretations that students bring to mathematics tasks. What the above discussion shows is the productive potential of this diversity in promoting dialogue and the development of shared understanding.

Student resistance

Although the results of our study are encouraging and enlightening, we do not wish to imply that all students have accepted their teacher's goals for learning and doing mathematics. In both the Year 11 and Year 12 classes there were a few students who preferred to work alone, and rarely joined in whole-class discussions. One instance will serve to illustrate this point. The Year 11 students completed a written task that asked them to reflect on their learning during a self-paced, computer-based unit of work. Most students commented favourably on the opportunities for engagement with each other, the teacher, and the mathematics (see the earlier section on students' emerging beliefs). Nevertheless, the resistance of one student is clear in his answers to some of the questions that were used to structure students' writing.

> How did the teacher help you learn this topic?
> Making us do the work.

> How did your classmates help you learn this topic?

Ignored me.

What kind of help was the most effective for you?
Teacher. He paid some attention to me.

Clearly, this student perceives himself as isolated from his classmates, and somewhat marginal even to the concerns of the teacher. Students in these marginal positions may be unwilling to move from their comfort zones and expend the effort that participation in a community of mathematical enquiry entails. Others may lack the maturity to interact effectively with peers. The challenge for the teacher is to find ways for such students to live on the fringe of the community, in the hope that they might benefit through vicarious, rather than actual, participation.

Discussion

This chapter has been concerned with explicating a socio-cultural approach to the reform of mathematics education that is consistent with the changing conceptions of mathematics teaching and learning expressed in both new curriculum documents and the mathematics education research literature. These changes represent a move towards regarding mathematics as a discipline of humanistic enquiry, rather than of certainty and objective truth, and they pose a significant challenge to teachers to develop classroom practices in keeping with new goals for learning that emphasise reasoning and communication skills, and the social origins of mathematical knowledge and values.

Possibilities for new approaches to mathematics teaching are suggested by the concept of the classroom as a community of practice, within which students learn to think mathematically by participating in the intellectual and social practices that characterise the wider mathematical communities outside the classroom. This chapter has described how one teacher created such a community. Of central importance were the teacher's beliefs about mathematics, which were the source of both the learning goals he held for his students and the teaching practices he sought to implement in the classroom. To achieve his goals of sense-making and communal authorship of ideas the teacher modelled mathematical thinking processes, provided scaffolding to support students' appropriation of cognitive and metacognitive strategies and the language of mathematics, and through consistent everyday patterns of interaction with the students communicated the values of the discipline.

Despite the success of this teacher in socialising his students into mathematical practice, the widespread adoption of the classroom culture that we have documented here remains unlikely. The first, and most obvious, barrier is that raised by teacher beliefs. As beliefs appear to be formed as a consequence of teachers' own experiences of schooling, it is difficult to see how the cycle of teacher beliefs → student beliefs → teacher beliefs can be broken without substantial and long-term in-service education.

School structures and philosophies represent a second barrier to change, especially since in community of practice classrooms teachers need to adopt new roles and move out of their traditional position as the dispensers of knowledge. Students also need to be flexible and adaptable in taking up the challenges and new responsibilities that membership of the classroom community entails. The problem may be less serious in primary schools, where teachers work with the same class all day and students' learning experiences therefore have some consistency and continuity. Secondary school teachers face greater difficulties in establishing a sense of community in their classrooms, first, because they teach many classes, and second, because their students are also members of many other classroom communities, whose values may not coincide with those of the mathematics teacher. The task of the teacher who participated in the research study described in this chapter was made easier by his school's espoused philosophy of encouraging negotiation and collaboration between teachers and students.

Finally, it is important to realise that changes to teaching practices can be resisted by students, whose views about mathematics have been formed through long experience with prescriptive teaching methods (Nickson, 1992). Participation in a community of enquiry makes unfamiliar demands on students as well as teachers, and it is unreasonable to expect students to quickly embrace changes that challenge their ideas about what mathematics is, and how it is best learned. However, the positive responses of the students in the present study suggest that a teacher's patience and persistence will eventually be rewarded.

Although the study described in this chapter has identified actions that teachers might take to bring about changes in their classrooms, perhaps the most difficult task confronting the teacher is to learn what *not* to do, that is, to resist the urge to do the mathematics for the students, and to let them grapple directly with ideas in what might appear to be a messy and inefficient fashion. However, it should be clear from the results presented here that such a teacher is far from being an irresponsible or passive participant in the classroom; rather, he or she is the representative of the culture into which students seek entry, and is responsible for structuring the cognitive and social opportunities for students to experience mathematics in a meaningful way.

Notes

1 Ultimately an individual might extend the limits of existing mathematical knowledge and understanding. In his celebrated essay on mathematical creativity, Henri Poincaré describes several examples of the way in which he was challenged to develop new understandings and new knowledge without social mediation or the direct involvement of peers. These creative insights were achieved during periods of reflective inner dialogue on challenging dilemmas presented by the existing discipline, and involved the systematic selection, testing and verification of emergent ideas against the corpus of discipline knowledge previously attained as a member of the mathematical community. Poincaré played both the role of tutor and learner during these inner dialogues, with insights being generated and guided by previously acquired cognitive resources, themselves the product of prior learning socially validated within a community of practice.

2 Here, it is worth pointing out that the power associated with such disciplined mathematical reasoning comes from its universality. A mathematician ascribes the same significance to necessary and sufficient conditions or strategies of proof

whatever the domain of mathematical discourse. As teachers, we assume this portability property each time we apply reasoning to a new area, each time we argue by analogy, each time we generalise across contexts. The Piagetian tradition has supported various 'concrete' approaches to teaching mathematics, including the use of manipulatives, use of numbers rather than letters, and a range of enactive and iconic supports for formal learning. However, the concreteness is defined with respect to one particular type of mathematical 'object', and the rules by which these 'objects' are manipulated, and according to which conclusions are drawn, are seldom treated as problematic. That is, a common pedagogical assumption is that while students may be ignorant of the specific concept or result that is the object of the forthcoming lesson, they share a common understanding with the teacher concerning other mathematical concepts and practices that are used in the lesson, such as the modes of reasoning employed.

In pointing out a counter-example to a proposition, the teacher may assume that the students share a common perception of what has been achieved. Similarly, if a student agrees with each individual component of a chain of reasoning it tends to be assumed that the student will comprehend inferences deduced from a proof as a whole. However, past research (e.g. Galbraith, 1986) has shown that such assumptions are ill-founded. Regarding counter-examples, for instance, it was common for students to require several, and in some cases to even vary the number required across contexts. Such evidence demonstrates that many students bring notions about mathematical reasoning that do not reflect a shared meaning with their teachers or the world of mathematics, The constructivist view argues that no matter how clear and precise are a teacher's examples and explanations, students will take these notions, couple them with their existing beliefs and understandings, and fashion some version of the intent at a personal and subjective level. The notion of the ZPD as a community of learners is squared directly at this problem. In such a classroom community it is the discourse and processes of mathematics that are elevated to the central role, and the meanings and significance of mathematical reasoning and concepts are generated and stabilised through social dialogue mediated by rigorous appeal to the canons of the discipline.

References

Alibert, D. (1988). Towards new customs in the classroom. *For the Learning of Mathematics*, **8**, 2, pp. 31–35.

Australian Education Council. (1991). *A National Statement on Mathematics for Australian Schools*, Australian Education Council and Curriculum Corporation, Carlton, Victoria.

Berger, M. (1996). The graphic calculator as a tool in the ZPD. Short presentation delivered at *The 8th International Congress on Mathematical Education*, Seville, 14–21 July 1996, (Poster 322).

Booth, S., Wistedt, W., Hallden, O., Martinsson, M. and Marton, F. (1999). Paths of Learning – the Joint Constitution of Insights. In L. Burton (ed.) *Learning Mathematics: From Hierarchies to Networks*, Falmer Press, London.

Borasi, R. (1992). *Learning Mathematics Through Inquiry*, Heinemann, Portsmouth.

Brown, A. (1994). The advancement of learning. *Educational Researcher*, **23**, 8, pp. 4–12.

Brown, A. and Campione, J. C. (1995). Guided discovery in a community of learners. In

K. McGilly (ed.) *Classroom Lessons: Integrating Cognitive Theory and Classroom Practice*, Massachusetts Institute of Technology Press, Cambridge, MA.

Brown, R. A. J. (1994). Collective mathematical thinking in the primary classroom: A conceptual and empirical analysis within a socio-cultural framework. B.Ed. Thesis, The University of Queensland, Australia.

Brown, R. A. J. and Renshaw, P. (1995). Developing collective mathematical thinking within the primary classroom. In B. Atweh and S. Flavel (eds) *Proceedings of the 18th Annual Conference of the Mathematics Education Research Group of Australasia*, Mathematics Education Research Group of Australasia, Darwin, Australia.

Burton, L. (1999). The Implications of a Narrative Approach to the Learning of Mathematics. In L. Burton (ed.) *Learning Mathematics: From Hierarchies to Networks*, Falmer Press, London.

Cobb, P. (1986). Contexts, goals, beliefs and learning mathematics. *For the Learning of Mathematics*, **6**, 2, pp. 2–9.

Cobb, P. and Bauersfeld, H. (1995). Introduction: The coordination of psychological and sociological perspectives in mathematics education. In P. Cobb and H. Bauersfeld (eds) *The Emergence of Mathematical Meaning: Interaction in Classroom Cultures*, Lawrence Erlbaum, Hillsdale, NJ.

Crook, C. (1991). Computers in the zone of proximal development: Implications for evaluation. *Computers and Education*, **17**, pp. 81–91.

Elbers, E., Derks, A. and Streefland, L. (1995). Learning in a community of inquiry: Teacher's strategies and children's participation in the construction of mathematical knowledge. Paper presented at *The 6th European Conference for Learning and Instruction*, Nijmegen, The Netherlands, August.

Fennema, E. and Loef-Franke, M. (1992). Teachers' knowledge and its impact. In D. Grouws (ed.) *Handbook of Research on Mathematics Teaching and Learning*, Macmillan, New York.

Goos, M., Galbraith, P. and Renshaw, P. (1994). Collaboration, dialogue and metacognition: The mathematics classroom as a 'community of practice'. In G. Bell, R. Wright, N. Leeson and J. Geake (eds) *Proceedings of the 17th Annual Conference of the Mathematics Education Research Group of Australasia*, Mathematics Education Research Group of Australasia, Lismore, Australia.

Goos, M., Galbraith, P. and Renshaw, P. (1996). When does student talk become collaborative mathematical discussion? In P. Clarkson (ed.) *Proceedings of the 19th Annual Conference of the Mathematics Education Research Group of Australasia*, Mathematics Education Research Group of Australasia, Melbourne, Australia.

Howson, A. G. (1975). University courses for future teachers. *Educational Studies in Mathematics*, **6**, pp. 273–292.

Kemp, M., Kissane, B. and Bradley, J. (1996). Graphics calculator use in examinations: Accident or design?' *Australia Senior Mathematics Journal*, **10**, 1, pp. 36–50.

Lampert, M. (1990). Connecting inventions with conventions. In L. P. Steffe and T. Wood (eds) *Transforming Children's Mathematics Education: International Perspectives*, Lawrence Erlbaum, Hillsdale, NJ.

Lave, J. and Wenger, E. (1991). *Situated Learning: Legitimate Peripheral Participation*, Cambridge University Press.

Leder, G. (1990). Talking about mathematics. *Australian Educational Researcher*, **17**, pp. 17–27.

Meade, P. and McMeniman, M. (1992). Stimulated recall – An effective methodology for examining successful teaching in science. *Australian Educational Researcher*, **19**, 3, pp. 1–18.

Minick, N. (1987). The development of Vygotsky's thought: An introduction. In R. W. Rieber and A. S. Carton (eds) *The Collected Works of L. S. Vygotsky, Volume 1: Problems of General Psychology*, Plenum Press, New York.

National Council of Teachers of Mathematics (NCTM). (1989). *Curriculum and Evaluation Standards for School Mathematics*, NCTM, Reston, VA.

National Council of Teachers of Mathematics (NCTM). (1991). *Professional Standards for Teaching Mathematics*, NCTM, Reston, VA.

Nickson, M. (1992). The culture of the mathematics classroom: An unknown quantity? In D. A. Grouws (ed.) *Handbook of Research on Mathematics Teaching and Learning*, Macmillan, New York.

Renshaw, P. (1996). A socio-cultural view of the mathematics education of young children. In H. Mansfield *et al.* (eds) *Mathematics for Tomorrow's Young Children*, Kluwer Academic, Dordrecht.

Schoenfeld, A. H. (1988). When good teaching leads to bad results: The disasters of well-taught mathematics courses. *Educational Psychologist*, **23**, pp. 145–166.

Schoenfeld, A. H. (1989). Ideas in the air: Speculations on small group learning, environmental influences on cognition, and epistemology. *International Journal of Educational Research*, **13**, pp. 71–87.

Schoenfeld, A. H. (1992). Learning to think mathematically: Problem solving, metacognition and sense making in mathematics. In D. A. Grouws (ed.) *Handbook of Research on Mathematics Teaching and Learning*, Macmillan, New York.

Schoenfeld A. H. (1994). Reflections on doing and teaching mathematics. In A. H. Schoenfeld (ed.) *Mathematical Thinking and Problem-Solving*, Lawrence Erlbaum, Hillsdale, NJ.

Thompson, A. (1992). Teachers' beliefs and conceptions: A synthesis of the research. In D. A. Grouws (ed.) *Handbook of Research on Mathematics Teaching and Learning*, Macmillan, New York.

Valsiner, J. and van der Veer, R. (1992). The encoding of distance: The concept of the 'zone of proximal development' and its interpretations. In R. R. Cocking and K. A. Renninger (eds) *The Development and Meaning of Psychological Distance*, Lawrence Erlbaum, Hillsdale, NJ.

Section 2

Communication in mathematics classrooms

Communication in mathematics classrooms includes teacher–pupil dialogue, the role of diagrams, pupil–pupil dialogue that is often missed in the classroom and the interaction between pupils and technology. Some forms of communication adopted in classrooms militate against some students being able to display mathematical skills in favour of other students. While some students have strong preferences for oral or written communication, others find written or diagrammatic communication more effective. Not all of these forms of communication are valued in the same way by teachers even though teachers may claim that they are. Pupils appear to cope differentially with apparent inconsistencies and hidden messages, when a teacher says one thing and means another.

In Chapter 7, Robyn Zevenbergen argues that pedagogical practices can be socially biased and may contribute to a learner's success or failure to participate in classroom dialogue. She looks particularly at the social context of mathematics and how this is implicated in social disadvantage. Her interest is in the 'linguistic habitus' of primary children, the ways they interact and talk in classrooms, and how this affects the way they are recognised or marginalised as learners.

She found the patterns of interactions in middle-class families are most similar to the discourse of primary classrooms. This means that pupils whose linguistic habitus matches that of the formal school setting will have greater access to knowledge through the pedagogic practices. For example, the statement 'Will you get out your mathematics books' can be interpreted as a question or an instruction. If pupils interpret an intended instruction as a question then they are immediately disadvantaged.

Zevenbergen describes the type of talk that goes on in classrooms as 'triadic' dialogue where the teacher remains in control and the interactions are highly ritualised. In this form of dialogue the teacher maintains control over the structure and content of the lesson and over the behaviour of the pupils. She argues that the 'triadic' dialogue precludes a community of practice where the pupils have control over their learning. This suggestion has an impact on the notion of a three-part lesson currently being recommended by government agencies in England – the first part often being entirely in the form of a triadic dialogue. This begs the question whether it is possible for teachers to create a community of practice when starting lessons with a triadic dialogue.

The use of diagrams can show pupils' ability to communicate in a variety of forms and use of a diagram can be helpful in solving problems. In Chapter 8, Candia

Morgan raises the issue of inequity again when she talks about the role of diagrams in mathematics classrooms and the values that teachers place on them. Even though she found that teachers encourage pupils to draw diagrams, they tended to approve of some forms and not of others. Although teachers saw diagrams out of context as valuable, once they viewed them in context then a value was attached to particular forms of diagrams. For example, teachers often view an analytic diagram as evidence of thinking and a naturalistic diagram as evidence of low mathematical attainment by a pupil. She argues that if pupils follow a teacher's advice to draw a diagram this might result in a lower teacher assessment of their achievement.

Jenny Houssart's article (Chapter 9) is about informal classroom communication between pupils and she presents evidence of communication between pupils that is hidden from their teachers. This communication in the form of 'whispering' is part of the unofficial culture within the classroom, where the discourse is different from the official one. The key point in the article is that the whisperers, low attaining pupils, show evidence of an enquiring mathematical perspective that is normally attributed to competent adults. The type of comments the whisperers make do not match the teacher's perception of their attainment. Houssart identifies that the whisperers tend to speak for one of three reasons: when making a discovery, when extending or supplementing an idea or when pointing to errors.

In this article, Houssart shows that whisperers possess high order skills but they are not accurate at completing worksheets. If the school mathematics culture is one where the accurate completion of worksheets is valued then the achievements of the whisperers may not be recognised. This appears to be another example of the way in which the practice of relying on communication in the form of written mathematics may be discriminatory and lead to inequity in classrooms.

In Chapter 10, Celia Hoyles' research shows how interaction with a computer can offer a window onto possibilities and a way of illuminating pupil meaning and interpretation. A teacher can use computers as a medium for pupils' communication using mathematics. Hoyles is concerned about how pupils can become better learners of mathematics through the use of technology. She finds that by using the computer technology pupils can, for example, see through particular cases to a general case. Whilst computers can give pupils a tool for communicating their thinking, Hoyles identified that pupil beliefs about mathematics may impact on their interaction with technology. If pupils believe that mathematics is only a collection of sums with right and wrong answers, then the interaction with any form of technology will be less effective than it might otherwise be.

Further reading

Mercer, N. (1995). *The Guided Construction of Knowledge: Talk amongst Teachers and Learners*, Multilingual Matters Ltd, Clevedon.

Morgan, C. (1998). *Writing Mathematically: The Discourse of Investigation*, Falmer, London.

Pimm, D. (1987). *Speaking Mathematically: Communication in Mathematics Classrooms*, Routledge and Kegan Paul, London.

7 Mathematics, social class and linguistic capital

An analysis of mathematics classroom interactions

Robyn Zevenbergen

Introduction

The role of classroom interactions in the construction of mathematical meaning has been well documented, particularly by those working in the area of constructivism. This body of literature has been powerful in illuminating the role and importance of interaction in the negotiation and development of mathematical meaning. What is less researched is the political dimension of such interactions whereby the competencies needed to participate effectively, as determined by the hegemonic culture embedded with such interactional practices, are closely aligned to the social background of the students. This chapter seeks to explore one aspect of interactional patterns in mathematics classrooms in terms of the social milieu within which such interactions occur and the subsequent potential for students to participate effectively within such contexts. In so doing, my purpose is to raise awareness of how some pedagogical practices can be socially biased in order that they may be identified as contributing to the successful (or failed) participation in classroom dialogue. As a consequence of this analysis, some of the apolitical assumptions that have been built into the constructivist writings may also be challenged.

Using the theoretical constructs offered by Pierre Bourdieu, this chapter critically analyses the three-phase interactional practices offered by ethnomethodologists in order to understand how the social context of mathematics is implicated in the construction of social disadvantage. In so doing, the purpose of the chapter seeks to raise awareness of how some students are (further) disadvantaged through the practices of classroom interactions that are often taken as normal within the everyday life of the classroom. The focus of this chapter is on practices within the primary school setting and draws on the theoretical constructs of habitus, cultural capital, and field.

It is argued that students enter the school context with a linguistic habitus that predisposes students to interact and talk in ways that will be recognised or marginalised in and through the pedagogic practices of the classroom. Where students enter the classroom with a linguistic habitus congruous with the legitimate linguistic practices of the classroom, such habitus becomes a form of capital that can be exchanged for academic success.

Theoretical constructs

The notions of habitus and field are integral to this analysis of classroom talk. For Bourdieu, habitus is the embodiment of culture and provides the lens through which the world is interpreted. Habitus predisposes (but does not determine) thoughts, actions, and behaviours. Harker (1984) argued persuasively that habitus can alter over time, thereby challenging those (such as Jenkins, 1982) who suggest that habitus is deterministic. In some contexts, such as the classroom, some habitus may have the effect of conveying more power and status than in other contexts. For example, where a child has been socialised within the familial context to have particular attributes, likes, dislikes, and language forms, she or he may be able to exchange such dispositions for power within that context. The student whose language is that of the middle-class register may be positioned as a more authoritative voice within that community and hence may be positioned as having more power and status than her or his peers whose linguistic register is that of the working class. The embodiment of such characteristics of tastes, dispositions, and language can be seen to be the constitution of habitus, that is, more simplistically, the embodiment of culture.

A range of studies of home–school differences has shown that the patterns of interactions are substantially different for many students. In her comprehensive study, Brice Heath (Heath, 1982, 1983) has shown that students from socially disadvantaged backgrounds are more likely to be exposed to declarative statements when they are expected to undertake tasks. In contrast, middle-class parents are more likely to pose a pseudoquestion when requesting their children to undertake tasks. Such practices come to be embodied in the habitus so that the student perceives task requesting within this framework. When entering the formal school context, their habitus predisposes them to frame tasks within their pre-existing habitus so that when a teacher poses the task as 'Could you get out your maths books' it is interpreted quite differently depending on the previous experiences. For the purposes of this chapter, it is important to note that the patterns of interactions within middle-class families are most similar to those of the formal school setting, whereas the converse is the case for working-class students. In this way, it can be argued that middle-class students are more likely to have a habitus that has embodied such patterns of interactions than their working-class peers. However, as Harker (1984) suggested, the habitus can be reconstituted so that, for students whose habitus is different from that of the formal school context, there is potential for it to be brought closer to that which is legitimated through school practices, thus suggesting a transformative component of pedagogy rather than a deterministic reading. However, such reconstitution must be undertaken with considerable effort.

In concert with habitus is the construct of field. Habitus can be seen to be the subjective component of analysis, whereas field can be thought to be the more objective aspect of analysis. For aspects of habitus to have more power than others – such as the familiarity with pseudoquestions over declarative statements – there must be some external, or objective, factors that determine the importance of some things over others. Such power and status are conveyed through the structuring practices of the field. Within the context of the schools and classrooms, certain practices are seen to be more legitimate than others, and those students who are able to display or assimilate those practices within their own repertoire of behaviours are positioned more favourably. For example, students who are able to display effective use of the mathematics register, test-taking skills, and the like, are more likely to be positioned as effective learners of mathematics than their peers who do not demonstrate such characteristics. The skills that are seen to hold status and power within the field of mathematics may be very different from another context. This is borne out in the ethnomathematics studies where students who display the street talk and skills within street selling may be positioned as marginal within the field of education. For these students, the dispositions that have become embodied within their habitus and predispose them to be effective in bartering due to the structuring practices of the market place are positioned less favourably within mathematics education where the structuring practices do not legitimate the practices of the market place. The practices within these two divergent fields differentially convey power on the participants. Mathematics education, as a field, values and conveys power and status on those who display the characteristics, attributes, and dispositions seen as desirable within the field at any given point in time. As a field, the characteristics seen as desirable are transitory and change over time as can be readily observed through changes in what is seen as valuable knowledge within mathematics education research and publications. An example of such changes is the emergence, and later dominance, of constructivist writings.

When considering the objective structuring practices of the field in concert with the subjective components of the habitus, it can be seen that some forms of habitus are more empowering than others depending on the field within which one is operating. Within the field of mathematics education, there are particular forms of habitus that are more likely to be recognised as legitimate and valued. In terms of this chapter, it is argued that the patterns of interaction with which the student has familiarity due to familial contexts are more likely to facilitate the construction of a habitus that has greater or lesser synergy with the interactional patterns of the classroom depending on the types of interactions within a family. The structuring practices of the field of mathematics value particular practices over others so that those students for whom there is a greater synergy between the home practices and the school practices, and hence habitus, the greater the chance of being constructed as an effective participant and learner of mathematics. To this end, various characteristics embodied within the habitus have the potential to be of greater or lesser worth depending on the field. As such, such cultural characteristics can be seen to have greater or lesser value and subsequently can be exchanged for differing positions within the field. For example, the students whose habitus is more congruent with those aspects valued within the field of mathematics are more likely to be positioned as effective learners of mathematics and as a consequence reap the rewards associated with such positioning. In this way, aspects of culture can be seen to be forms of capital that, when embodied in the habitus and legitimated through the field, can be exchanged for other gains, including success in mathematics.

Language as a form of capital

In considering aspects of culture that can be exchanged for other rewards, the importance of language needs to be considered, particularly in relation to mathematics education. In appropriating Bourdieu's constructs, his premise that language is not just words for the expression of ideas, but rather is generated through and within social hierarchies, is central to the chapter. Linguistic exchanges are not simple exchanges of language but bring into play complex relationships of power between the student(s) and teachers.

Linguistic competence – or incompetence – reveals itself through daily interactions. Within the mathematics classrooms, legitimate participation is acquired and achieved through a competence in the classroom dialogic interactions. Students must be able to display a discursive competence that incorporates a linguistic competence, an interactional competence along with a discursive competence, if they are to be seen as competent learners of mathematics. Classroom interactions are imbued with cultural components that facilitate or inhibit access to the mathematical content. To gain access to this knowledge, students must be able to render visible the cultural and political aspects of the interactions. Bourdieu, in response to questions posed by Wacquant (Bourdieu and Wacquant, 1992) argued that:

> Linguistic competence is not a simple technical ability, but a statutory ability. … what goes in verbal communication, even the content of the message itself, remains unintelligible as long as one does not take into account the totality of the structure of the power positions that is present, yet invisible, in the exchange.
>
> (p. 146)

As noted earlier, from their early years, students are located within familial structures and practices that will facilitate the development and embodiment of particular cultural features, the least of which is language. For these students, the embodiment of their cultural background into what Bourdieu referred to as the habitus predisposes them to think and act in particular ways. This embodiment of culture includes a linguistic component. Students whose linguistic habitus is congruent with that of the discursive practices represented in mathematics classrooms are more likely to have greater access to the knowledge represented in and through such practices.

From this perspective, language must be understood as the linguistic component of a universe of practices that are composited within a class habitus. Hence, language should be seen to be considered as another cultural product – in much the same ways as patterns of consumption, housing, marriage, and so forth (Bourdieu, 1979). When considered in this way, language is the expression of the class habitus that is realised through the linguistic habitus and is evidenced in the following comment:

> Of all the cultural obstacles, those which arise from the language spoken within the family setting are unquestionably the most serious and insidious. For, especially during the first years of school, comprehension and manipulation of language are the first points of teacher judgement. But the influence of a child's original language setting never ceases to operate. Richness and style of expression are continually taken into account, whether implicitly or explicitly and to different degrees.
>
> (Bourdieu, Passeron and de saint Martin, 1994a, p. 40)

To this end, the linguistic habitus of the student will have substantial impact on his or her capacity to make sense of the discursive practices of the mathematics classroom and hence their subsequent capacity to gain access to legitimate mathematical knowledge along with the power and status associated with that knowledge. The processes through which the schooling procedures are able to value one language and devalue others must be systematically understood. Through this process, we can better understand how mathematical pedagogy both inculcates mathematical knowledge and imposes domination.

Pedagogic discourse

The study of language within the pedagogic situation can be identified within two quite distinct areas – quantitative linguistics, which is seen to embrace the objectivity associated with sociolinguistics, and the subjectivist position identifiable through interactional linguistics (Collins, 1993). Greenfell (1998) suggested that to this coupling social psychology also should be added to include those writings that address feelings, attitudes, and motivations. Bourdieu's work seeks to unite this objective–subjective dualism.

In considering the more specific language of classrooms, three principle approaches have been identified by Edwards and Mercer (1987) – linguistic, social, and anthropological. It is the linguistic approach that is of particular importance to this chapter. Within the linguistic approach, the ethnomethodological approaches of Sinclair and Couthourd (1975), Lemke (1990), and Mehan (1982) identified particular ritualised practices within the classroom interactions through which classroom knowledge is structured and built. The interactions occurring within the classroom have been found to have highly ritualised components with clearly identifiable discursive practices (Lemke, 1990; Mehan, 1982). They argue that these components are not explicitly taught but are embedded within the culture of the classroom. The highly ritualised practices of classroom interactions can be seen in the types of interactions that occur across the various phases of the lesson. For example, the most common form of interaction consists of a practice in that the teacher asks a question, the students respond, and the teacher evaluates that response that Lemke (1990) referred to as 'triadic dialogue'. This interactional practice can be observed in the following:

T: What does area mean?
S: The outside of the square.
T: Not quite, someone else? Tom?
S: When you cover the whole surface, that's area.
T: That's good.

Lemke (1990) argued that this practice allows teachers to keep control of the content and flow of this phase of the lesson. Although Lemke focused on the science classroom, the style and purpose of this interaction can be just as readily applied to the mathematics classroom and are aptly summed up as follows:

Triadic dialogue is an activity structure whose greatest virtue is that it gives the teachers almost total control of the classroom dialogue and social interactions. It leads to brief answers from students and lack of student initiative in using scientific language. It is a form that is overused in most classrooms because of a mistaken belief that it encourages maximum student participation. The level of participation it achieves is illusory, high in quantity, low in quality.

(Lemke, 1990, p.168)

v. good ✱

✱ This practice is not made explicit to students; rather it must be learned through implicit means. To participate in the classroom interactions effectively, students must have knowledge – either intuitive or explicit – of these unspoken rules of interaction.

Mehan (1982) identified three key phases of a lesson – the introduction, the work phase, and the concluding/revision phase. In each of these phases there is a shift in the power relations between the students and teacher. Such shifts permit different forms of interactions to occur (Mehan, 1982; Schultz, Florio and Erickson, 1982). For the purposes of this chapter, I discuss the introductory phase only for this is the phase where triadic dialogue is most common. Mehan (1982) argued that, during the introductory phase of the lesson, the teacher maintains tight control over the students, initially to ensure that the students are ready for the content of the lesson. Once control has been established and attention gained, the lesson can then proceed. Triadic dialogue is commonly observed in this phase in order to keep control of the academic content of the lesson and the control of the students. Dialogue between students and between teacher and students is not generally part of this phase. If the teacher initiates a question but the student is not able to respond, it is not appropriate for students to express their lack of understanding because this will interrupt the flow of the phase, If there is a misunderstanding or lack of understanding, it is more appropriate for this to be voiced in the work phase of the lesson (Lemke, 1990).

What is not apparent from the above corpus of knowledge of classroom interaction is the recognition that these interactions recognise a particular linguistic form that will be more accessible to some students than others. Social and anthropological studies (such as Bernstein, 1986; Heath, 1983; Willis, 1977) focused on how social background is implicated in academic achievement. Heath's (1983) and Walkerdine's (1988) work with parents and children have found the forms of interactions very class-oriented. Using Bernsteinian notions of register and relay, it is understood that the content of the mathematics lessons is embedded within discursive practices that, at the level of register, are more likely to be those of the middle class. For example, the common practice of asking pseudoquestions such as 'Would you like to get the Lego blocks?' is typically a middle-class register. For working-class students to then enter the classroom, there needs to be some reconstruction of the linguistic habitus if the students are to be able to participate effectively in classroom interactions. In this sense, the interactions within the classroom can be considered another cultural product that is more familiar and hence accessible to some students and not others. The linguistic habitus of the students will facilitate or hinder a student's capacity to render visible the mathematical content embedded in the pedagogic action. As Collins (1993) argued:

… such cues [triadic dialogue] are not necessarily *understood* by all participants, but they are certainly part of the *functional conflict* between dominant and dominated languages in (and out of) educational settings.

(p. 131)

In the preceding sections, I have drawn on the work from a number of traditions – theoretical and methodological – and have proposed that the social background of the student will facilitate the construction of a particular linguistic habitus. The field of mathematics, having its own regulatory discourses and discursive practices, will recognise and value some linguistic practices and not others.

The study

A year-long ethnographic study of two classrooms was undertaken. The two classrooms were located in socially divergent sites – one an independent school that serves a middle to upper class clientele (Angahook). Parents typically were high-income professionals. The other classroom was in a state school serving a predominantly working-class clientele (Connewarre) where parents were typically low income, engaged either in manual occupations or in receipt of government welfare. The classrooms were in the second last year of primary school and most students were approximately 10 to 11 years old. Mathematics lessons were videotaped and later transcribed noting the language used and annotated with student actions. The videotapes and transcriptions were supported with classroom observations, field notes, and interviews. The transcripts were then analysed using a variety of discursive analyses. For the purposes of this chapter, the analysis was on the use of triadic dialogue in the introductory phase of the lesson and how the students responded to the practice.

As an ethnographic study, the data used in this chapter seek to demonstrate a commonality that becomes apparent over a sustained period in the field. Over the year, aspects of the lessons would vary, but a consistency in interactional patterns was apparent, and it is these patterns that are the focus of this chapter. The data used for the following analysis could be analysed from a number of perspectives, but this would deny the repetitiveness that could be observed across the sustained period of observation and videotape data. For example, the teacher at Angahook may be seen to be using a technique in which students are asked to define the term *degrees of difficulty*, whereas the extract from Connewarre is more of a funnelling technique in which the students are required to guess the word (prism). These forms of analysis are substantively different in intent from that of this chapter. Rather, what is clear across the sustained research period is that both teachers engage in the patterns of triadic dialogue, and the transcripts used in this chapter are representing this aspect of teaching rather than other forms of analysis. Although such alternative analyses would be valid, they would represent the immediacy of the two transcripts, rather than seeing the transcripts more holistically within the context of the prolonged study. As such, the transcripts included in this chapter should be seen to be representative of the year-long study in terms of the means through which teachers introduced concepts rather than isolated events.

Angahook

In the lesson extract presented here, the students were undertaking an activity in the calculation of diving scores at the Olympic Games. Prior to the extract shown, the teacher (T) used a number of short mental arithmetic tasks. The following is the introduction to the lesson.

1 T: You are asked to judge the diving for the Olympics, you will need to know the degree of difficulty because what if someone did just a plain dive and did it perfectly and got full marks for it and what if someone else did a triple somersault, back flip, side swinger double pike and knocker banger and only got half marks for it because they entered the water and made a bit of a splash. Is that fair?

2 C: No.

3 T: So we have to talk about degrees of difficulty. What do you think that means? What does that actually mean? Robert?

4 ROBERT: You have to add a bit more to the score because of the degrees of difficulty.

5 T: Good boy. Yes, good. Daniel?

6 DANIEL: Well the performance of their dive, how they dive, and well like they might have a very good dive and make a very big splash and may even get off.

7 T: Right, good. OK you are on the right track. What do you want to say about degree of difficulty Cate?

8 CATE: How hard it is?

9 T: How hard it is. Tom what would you like to say about degree of difficulty? That's not a word we use much in our everyday language … degree of difficulty.

10 TOM: The percentage of how hard it is.

11 T: Good. Because you're focusing on the word degree though, aren't you? So, a really hard dive. Now you can see on this sheet they're talking about DD, which is short for degree of difficulty and a really hard dive. What would be a really hard dive? What would be the highest number for a degree of difficulty be? Have a look at your sheet. Try and work out the degree of difficulty. Vicky?

12 VICKY: 8.

From this extract it can be seen that the teacher follows the triadic dialogue identified by Lemke and others. The teacher retains control of the content and interactions through the use of the three phases of interactions. Using this approach she is able to control the flow of the lesson as can be seen in the last interaction where Tom has mentioned 'percentages', which she then takes as a cue for linking percentage and degree in a way that suits her purposes. She is very focused in what she is seeking from the students and, through the use of the triadic dialogue, is able to control the content of the lesson in a manner congruent to these goals. In this extract from the introductory phase, she is seeking from the students some definition as to the meaning of 'degree of difficulty'. In the subsequent transcript, she then applies this definition to an example, again using the triadic dialogue to elicit responses as to how the students would use the construct in the worked example. The work phase consisted of the students working through a number of examples on a worksheet. The conclusion employed the triadic dialogue to elicit 'correct' responses to the worked examples.

Examining the flow of the interactions indicates that there is a complicit agreement between the teacher and students to participate in the interactions. There are no transgressions or challenges to the teacher's authority. This allows for the content to be covered as the teacher desires.

The teacher is able to maintain control over both the form and content of the lesson and over the students through a mutual compliance with the implicit rules by both the students and the teacher. She has used triadic dialogue to structure the interactions and students infrequently transgress the rules. This allows her to retain the focus of the lesson and, in so doing, the students are exposed to a significant amount of mathematical knowledge that is embedded in that dialogue. In this extract, the students are exposed to the mathematical signifier degrees of difficulty. Similar examples are found in the other mathematics lessons. In this way, the use of the triadic dialogue acts as conduit for the relay of mathematical language and concepts. The complicity of the students in this linguistic exchange enables the teacher to expose the students to this language thereby creating an environment that is potentially rich in mathematical language.

The work of Heath (1982), for example, has shown that middle-class students are more likely to be familiar with these forms of school interactions due to their similarity with the linguistic patterns of the home environment. Similarly, Bernstein's notion of elaborated codes suggests that the linguistic patterns of middle-class families prepare the children for the language used in the schools. The complicity evident here suggests a familiarity with the discursive practice of triadic dialogue.

The methodological approach derived from Bourdieu's work has as its central focus the notion of habitus and field. The field of mathematics education has as one of its central features the specificity of the mathematical discourses so that it is expected that students will be conversant with the language of the field. From this extract, the teacher has an important role in the induction of the students into this discourse. One of her roles is supporting and extending student learning such that they are able to learn or assimilate the appropriate modes of expression. Her leading of students as they come to express what they understand to be degrees of difficulty indicates a process through which students come to learn the accepted forms of language within the field of mathematics education. The way in which she achieves this is through the pedagogical relay, which in this case was triadic dialogue. Students' familiarity and complicity with the implicit rules of interaction allow them to gain access to the concept of degrees of difficulty.

The capacity of the students to participate in this form of interaction is due, in part, to their prior experiences at home and earlier years of schooling. The patterns of interaction they have come to see as part of typical school procedures have become embodied into a habitus – this may be seen to be a middle-class habitus as well as a school habitus.

This embodiment of legitimate school interactions offers greater access to legitimate school knowledge such that this habitus can be seen to be an empowering aspect of the repertoire of potential behaviours. To this end, such familiarity can be quite useful in gaining access to knowledge but equally in teachers' interpretations of performance and subsequent positioning within the classroom hierarchy.

Connewarre

Connewarre is a large government school that is located within a large housing commission estate. The clientele of the school is predominantly working class with many of the parents receiving government support. The classrooms are smaller than Angahook with approximately 25 to 30 students in each class. The mathematics curriculum is generally more open and hands-on at this school. The teacher introduces mathematics lessons with problem-solving activities undertaken in small groups. Students are physically involved in the activities, and it is not uncommon for the students to draw on the carpet with chalk to represent the task or physically construct the problem. The following transcript extract is the introduction to a lesson in which the teacher has drawn a net on the board that the students have to draw onto a card and then construct. Students are then required to develop a number of nets for nominated prisms.

1 T: So if I put those together we start talking more about a shape I am talking about. It's sort of a rectangle on the sides, all the way round but you don't call it is a rectangle, because a rectangle is just the flat surface. What do you call the whole thing if that was one whole solid shape. What do you call that?
2 C: A cube.
3 [calling out]
4 T: He said a cube. Don't call out please.
5 C: A rectangular rectangle.
6 T: You're on the right track.
7 C: A 3D rectangle.
8 T: Three dimensions, technically I suppose you're right.
9 C: A rectangular.
10 T: It's a rectangular something. Does anyone know what it is called?
11 C: A parallelogram.
12 T: Put your hand up please.
13 C: [unclear]
14 T: No.
15 [more calling out]
16 T: I guess you could have a rectangular parallelogram, but no. A rectangle is a special parallelogram.
17 C: A rectangular oblong.
18 T: The word we are looking for is prism.
19 C: Yeah, that's what I said.
20 T: Say the word, please.

21   C: Prism.
22   T: Not like you go to jail, *prison*, that's prison. Excuse me, could you return those, please.
23   [calling out]
24   T: So one thing that we think about with rectangular prisms and that this shape on here is, excuse me … Now you can leave them down, please. You need a little bit of practice at lunch because you can't stop fiddling. This shape here is drawn out on the graph, this grid here [net for a rectangular prism]. We're going to try and do the same thing. Draw the shape and then cut it out. If you look at the shape, it's made up of rectangles and squares.

In this extract, the triadic dialogue does not function effectively for the teacher to control the class or the content. The challenges to the teacher's authority can be observed throughout the extract, thereby distracting from the flow of content. In lines 10 and 11 of the extract, it is apparent that a student has violated the more explicit interactional rule of indicating willingness to answer by putting up a hand. In this line the student has violated this rule by calling out, and his response is ignored and his violation of the rule acknowledged. A similar violation occurs in line 18 where the student calls out that he has said this, but this response is ignored by the teacher. In both cases, the responses made by the students are rendered silent by the teacher's actions.

In this extract, it is apparent that the teacher had as his purpose the need to introduce students to the term 'Prism'. He attempted this through a guided approach after the students did not recall the correct response (line 1). Using the responses offered by students, he evaluated and extended on their responses, attempting to lead them to the response he desired. Throughout the text, his reliance on triadic dialogue can be observed, although often fragmented by the challenges made by the students. Some of the challenges are at the level of explicit challenges, whereas others are transgressions of the triadic dialogue.

In line 10 he asks a question as to the name of the solid, yet in spite of earlier responses leading to the name, and with evaluations of responses suggesting that the term rectangular is a component of the name, a student suggests (improperly and incorrectly) that the solid is a parallelogram.

By line 18, it becomes necessary for him to introduce the term himself whereupon he asks the students to repeat the name. This is not an uncommon strategy. In this case, a number of the students say the word 'prison' rather than prism. In line with notions of linguistic registers, it is likely that many working-class students would not be exposed to this mathematically signifier in their non-school contexts so that they misread the word to be prison – a far more common word. The teacher attempts to correct this misreading of the word and reiterates the word with emphasis on the ending of the word so that the students can hear the subtle difference. This example indicates the difference in linguistic registers that may be apparent in working-class schools and the need for teachers to be aware of such differences.

Unlike the interactions at Angahook, the students here are not as complicit in the patterns of triadic dialogue being attempted by the teacher. The reasons for this non-complicity cannot be ascertained from the existing data. The transgressions made by the students could be seen to be resistance to the imposition of a dominant culture as has been noted in the studies of Willis (1977). Alternatively, the non-compliance with the triadic dialogue of classroom interactions may be a result of the students' lack of familiarity with such practices due to the differences in the home–school discursive practices. These differences have been noted by Heath (1982, 1983) and Bernstein (1986). The discursive practice of triadic dialogue is not found within the home practices of working-class families so that the students have not had the opportunity to incorporate this practice into their repertoire of interactional skills. As such, the interactional practices of the home environment have facilitated the construction of a primary habitus that is incongruent with that of the school. In order for students to be complicit in this practice within the school context, they must reconstruct their primary habitus. However, as Lemke (1990) is at pains to recognise, these practices are not explicitly taught, so that working-class students are potentially excluded from this practice unless they can 'crack the code' of classroom interactions. In order to be an effective participant in these interactions, working-class students must be able to identify and assimilate such practices into their school habitus.

Where the students have been able to reconstitute their primary habitus and have recognised the implicit rules of classroom interactions but continue to challenge the teacher's authority – as may be the case in this classroom – the outcome is still the same. Effectively such action excludes them from the mathematical content and their positionings are marginal within the dominant practices of school mathematics. However, in this case, there is a suggestion of agency on behalf of the student.

The linguistic habitus of the student implies a propensity to speak in particular ways that, as can be observed in the case of the interactions in this extract, work to exclude students from the mathematical content. The students are not as competent in the linguistic exchanges of the mathematical interactions as their middle-class peers, thereby marginalising them in the process of learning. The teaching of mathematics in this way tacitly presupposes that the students will have the discursive knowledge and dispositions of particular social groups, namely, the middle class. The students are not as complicit in the classroom practices and in so doing are being excluded from active and full participation in the mathematics of the interactions. In this way, students have been exposed to the symbolic violence of formal education.

Conclusion

The data support Voigt's (1985, p. 81) claim that 'the hidden regularities, the interaction patterns and routines allow the participants to behave in an orderly fashion without having to keep up visible order'. The data, of which the transcripts used here are representative samples, confirmed the use of triadic dialogue in the mathematics classroom. The transcripts from both classrooms confirm a low level of questioning aimed at the students guessing the outcome desired by the teacher. In the instances cited here, these were both focused on guessing a particular word – degree of difficulty and prism. These do not constitute high levels of mathematical reasoning. The use of triadic dialogue in these classrooms confirms Lemke's concerns that the participation encouraged through this strategy appears to involve many students, but it is low in quality. This, in itself, raises questions about the usefulness of this practice in mathematics teaching and learning but is outside the realm of this chapter.

What appears to occur across the classrooms in this study, as represented in these two transcripts, is that the middle-class students comply with and participate in the triadic dialogue. In contrast, the working-class students appear to either resist or fail to recognise the structure of the interactions. In identifying the socio-cultural norms of the classrooms, in this case, triadic dialogue, I have sought to identify a way in which some students are able to gain access to mathematical content and processes more readily than others. The compliance of the middle-class students allowed the teacher to progress through the introductory phase more easily and in so doing is able to expose the students to more mathematical content. Compliance with such practices also positions the students more favourably with the patterns of interaction most likely to occur in the secondary school context. Conversely, the non-compliance of the working-class students positions them as marginal and excludes them content while simultaneously failing to prepare them for the interactional patterns most common in the secondary school context. As such, I propose that one subtle and coercive way that some students are advantaged and others excluded in and through the practices of mathematics is through the dis/continuities between the linguistic habitus of the students and the practices of classroom interactions. Some students enter the formal mathematics classroom with a habitus that is akin to that which is valorised within that context. These students will be able to participate more effectively and efficiently than their peers for whom the patterns of interaction are foreign to their habitus. The practice of triadic dialogue becomes a form of symbolic violence for those students whose linguistic habitus is different from that valorised within the school context. It is symbolic in that most educators are not aware of the subtle differences in patterns of language use between the home and school contexts for working-class students.

The modes of expression within classrooms are rarely explicitly taught, yet it is expected that students should participate and comply within such practices. As I have shown in this chapter, triadic dialogue is one such mode of interaction. Mathematics is embedded within these interactions, and students need to be able to crack the code of the unspoken rules of classroom interaction in order that they gain access to the mathematics. In contrast to models that suggest that violations of cultural norms within a classroom may be due to a deficit in understanding how language works as a medium for conversation, there is a need to recognise that such patterns of interaction are an integral component of school and classroom cultures. Accordingly, classroom interactional styles may be socially biased and as a consequence exclude or embrace students, depending on the interactional styles that they may bring to the classroom.

> Pedagogies that tacitly select the privileged and exclude the under-prepared are not regrettable lapses; they are systemic aspects of schooling systems serving class-divided societies.
>
> (Collins, 1993, p. 121)

Triadic dialogue may be implicated in the stratification of student outcomes. As a component of the culture of mathematics classrooms, and for that matter most classrooms, triadic dialogue as a practice facilitates or hinders effective participation in classroom interactions.

Quite clearly, the patterns of interaction that have been the focus of this chapter are dominant in mathematics classrooms. What is less well known are other patterns of interactions that may be found in classrooms and are influential in hindering or supporting learning of mathematics. Further studies are needed to identify and document patterns of interactions within homes and schools. These will be useful in developing a greater understanding and awareness of how schools and mathematics are implicated in the construction of advantage and disadvantage in mathematics education.

For students whose habitus is dissimilar to that valorised within the context of the classroom, in this case the working-class students, changes need to be made in order that such students can gain access to the mathematical content more readily. In most cases, such changes would be seen to be the reconstitution of the habitus whereby the students would need to learn the new codes of the classroom interactions in order to be able to participate effectively. However, it could be argued that, as educators become aware of the cultural norms of classroom practice that effectively exclude some students, it could well be the classroom practice that needs to be reconstituted. Such change may involve a radical reconstruction of classroom practice, or more simply, the making explicit of such cultural norms – in this case, triadic dialogue.

Habitus becomes a form of capital that can be exchanged for academic success within this context. The linguistic habitus of the middle-class students predisposes them to act in ways congruous with the goals of the teacher so that their possession of knowledge of what constitutes *appropriate* classroom linguistic exchanges is similar to that which the system values. This allows them to participate in effective classroom practice. Alternatively, the linguistic habitus facilitates the appropriation of what the system offers. The dispositions, as per the linguistic habitus, of each of the classes has facilitated or hindered their acquisition of mathematics. The linguistic habitus is differentially valued within the mathematics classroom. The linguistic code with which students are familiar and use within the classroom becomes a form of capital that can be exchanged for other culturally recognised goods – in this case, grades and the subsequent academic success conveyed to the individual.

> The more distant the social group from scholastic language, the higher the rate of scholastic mortality.
>
> (Bourdieu, Passeron and de saint Martin, 1994b, p. 41)

References

Bernstein, B. (1986). On pedagogic discourse. In J. Richardson (ed). *Handbook of theory and research in sociology of education,* Greenwood Press, Weston, CT.

Bourdieu, P. (1979). *Distinction: A social critique of the judgement of taste.* Harvard University Press, Cambridge, MA.

Bourdieu, P., Passeron, J. C. and de saint Martin, M. (1994a). *Academic discourse: Linguistic misunderstanding and professorial power* (R. Teese, trans.). Stanford University Press, Stanford, USA.

Bourdieu, P., Passeron, J. C. and de saint Martin, M. (1994b). Students and the language of teaching. In P. Bourdieu, J. C. Passeron and M. de saint Martin (eds) *Academic discourse: Linguistic misunderstanding and professorial power*, Stanford University Press, Stanford, USA, pp. 35–79.

Bourdieu, P. and Wacquant, L. (1992). *Responses*. Seuil, Paris.

Bourdieu, P. and Wacquant, L. J. D. (1992). *An invitation to reflexive sociology*. Polity Press, Cambridge.

Collins, J. (1993). Determination and contradiction: An appreciation and critique of the work of Pierre Bourdieu on language and education. In C. Calhoun, E. LiPuma and M. Postone (eds) *Bourdieu: Critical perspectives*, Polity Press, Cambridge, pp. 116–138.

Edwards, D. and Mercer, N, (1987). *Common knowledge*. Routledge, London.

Greenfell, M. (1998). Language and the classroom. In M. Greenfell and D. James (eds) *Bourdieu and education: Acts of practical theory*, Falmer Press, London, pp. 72–88.

Harker, R. K. (1984). On reproduction, habitus and education. *British Journal of Sociology of Education,* 5(2), 117–127.

Heath, S. B. (1982). Questioning at home and at school: A comparative study. In G. D. Spindler (ed.) *Doing the ethnography of schooling*, Holt, Rinehart and Winston, New York.

Heath, S. Brice. (1983). *Ways with words: Language, life and work in communities and classrooms*, University of Cambridge.

Jenkins, R. (1982). Pierre Bourdieu and the reproduction of determinism. *Sociology,* **16**(2), 270–281.

Lemke, J. L. (1990). *Talking science: Language, learning and values*, Ablex, Norwood.

Mehan, H. (1982). The structure of classroom events and their consequences for student performance. In P. Gilmore and A. A. Glatthorn (eds) *Children in and out of school: Ethnography and education*, Center for Applied Linguistics, Washington, DC, pp. 59–87.

Schultz, J. J., Florio, S. and Erickson, F. (1982). Where's the floor? Aspects of the cultural organisation of social relationships in communication at home and in school. In P. Gilmore and A. A. Glatthorn (eds) *Children in and out of school: Ethnography and education*, Center for Applied Linguistics, Washington, DC, pp. 88–123.

Sinclair, J. and Couthourd, M. (1975). *Towards an analysis of discourse*. Blackwell, Oxford.

Voigt, J. (1985). Patterns and routines in classroom interaction. *Researches en Didactique de Mathematiques*, **6**(1), 69–118.

Walkerdine, V. (1988). *The Mastery of Reason*. Routledge, London.

Willis, P. (1977). *Learning to labour*. Kogan Paul, London.

8 What is the role of diagrams in communication of mathematical activity?

Candia Morgan

Introduction

In investigating the ways in which teachers assess pupils' texts, 11 experienced teachers were asked to read and assess three piece of student's coursework on tasks set by LEAG (LEAG, 1991). Six of the teachers read work on the 'Inner Triangle' task (investigating the relationship between the dimensions and the area of trapezia drawn on isometric paper) while the rest read work on the 'Topples' task (investigating the point at which piles of Cuisenaire rods starting with a small rod and adding successively larger rods will topple over). All of the children's texts on both tasks contained diagrams of one sort or another. It is the ways in which teachers read these diagrams and the values that they placed on them that I intend to address in this paper.

Diagrams as a 'good thing'

The first point to note is that all the teachers at some point expressed approval of diagrams. This approval was several times expressed in general terms, suggesting that diagrams are valued in their own right, regardless of their contribution to the solution or communication of the particular mathematical problem. Charles described his approach to assessment in these terms:

> Well, shall I say we would do the thing like this, OK? Have a look for children being systematic in their approach, I've got a couple of things written down here … putting down, tabulating results, perhaps drawing diagrams, putting down ideas, putting forward hypotheses, testing out ideas, um what else? … perhaps coming up again eventually at the other end with algebraic formulas, things like that …
>
> (Charles: 4–8)

Such lists of features are typical of the descriptions teachers gave of their practice. There is little distinction drawn between items related to the act of solving the problem (like hypotheses, testing ideas) and those to do with the form in which the work is presented. According to Charles' self reports of his practice, tables and diagrams, like ideas and hypotheses, do not need any context in order to justify their existence.

While actually reading the children's texts, individual diagrams were, on the whole, ascribed meanings and sometimes values within their contexts; when considering the whole text, however, the mere presence of diagrams in the text appears to be significant in coming to an overall evaluation. Thus, in summing up their evaluations of complete pieces of coursework, some teachers summarised by listing an inventory of 'bits', including diagrams, which appear to form part of a list of context-free criteria.

> He's got some patterns here and he's done a few diagrams … no algebra, oh he's found, yes he has done a formula, he hasn't done an extension.
>
> (Fiona: 288–290 Craig)

> … used a variety of forms … a results chart. I wonder if it would have been possible to do a graph for it – I don't know without working it through.
>
> (Joan: 118–119 Sam)

Reading as a teacher/adviser (see Morgan, 1993), Joan's suggestion that it might have been possible to do a graph seems to be related only to the fulfilment of this criterion in order to gain a higher grade rather than to the quality of the mathematical solution of the problem. One of the few general justifications for this valuing of diagrams was given by Charles:

> Umm yeah, I mean I think erm there definitely is a need for diagrams. One thing the pupils don't usually draw themselves decent diagrams to help them with problems definitely. But I think given the fact that this is actually a practical thing, you're actually doing that practically, I think there's probably less need for a diagram. Umm, well quite a lot of things you do, I mean, diagrams do count obviously and to actually get them, one of the big problems they've got even with like in the sixth form is that they don't draw diagrams to help themselves work things out. They try and do it all in their head … they never do … It's all right but I mean it's not, it's not that valuable. It actually, it doesn't help the problem. No, that's one thing I would look for actually is if they are actually using sensible diagrams to help them with problems and things like that. That's one thing I would look for in assessment.
>
> (Charles: 248–259)

He has some difficulty here in reconciling his knowledge of the specific 'Topples' task as one in which physical objects are manipulated (hence lessening the need for diagrams to help solve the problem) with the general principle that there is 'a need for diagrams'. This difficulty is manifested in the repeated shifting between the specific and the general. In spite of his admission that, in this case, drawing a diagram 'doesn't help the problem', Charles concludes this passage by restating the fact that 'That's one thing I would look for in assessment', resolving his difficulties by reaffirming the non-contextualised performance indicator. The absolute value given by these teachers to the drawing of diagrams may have been influenced by their perception that this is something that pupils (even those in the sixth form) do not generally do.

Diagrams as signs of 'low ability'

In spite of the value ascribed to diagrams described in the previous section, there were also a number of indications given in the interviews that in some cases diagrams might not be appropriate or might even be a sign of work done by a 'less able' child. Too many diagrams or diagrams which are not arranged according to an easily recognisable system may be taken as evidence that the child was working at a more concrete, practical level. Thus Dan, having described a boy he remembered who had very quickly 'seen' a formula as a solution to the 'Inner Triangles' task, went on to describe in general terms the characteristics of work by other groups of children:

> But if they don't see that [the formula] then I think I'd be looking for somebody who would be quite carefully and systematically looking at some diagrams that they could make that had 8 units and then sort of transferring those ideas into 32 triangles. I can't remember … as this was offered as an Intermediate/Higher level piece of work I don't remember anybody having enormous difficulties. If it was offered lower down, maybe children might get a little bit, might find it a bit difficult, might try varying kinds of diagrams before they actually come up with some answers to that.
>
> (Dan: 20–27)

He has identified a hierarchy of types of children in terms of the way in which they make use of diagrams in attempting to solve the problem. The highest level of abstraction is characterised by an absence of the practical activity which is embodied in the drawing of diagrams. Thus Andy states as one of the things he would look for when assessing that the child should be able to:

> calculate the area of a triangle [*sic*] just by looking at the dimensions given for any particular trapezium without drawing them and counting.
>
> (Andy: 27–29)

There comes a point in the assessment of a solution to the problem at which the *absence* of a diagram becomes a positive performance indicator. Similarly, while 'good presentation' is valued, it is also possible that a teacher may interpret some forms of presentation as detracting from the mathematical content of the work. Thus Harry, reading Sally's 'Topples' text, begins by praising her presentation:

> Three dimension illustrations to start with, very nice, nicely presented.
>
> (Harry: 190 Sally)

but quickly moved on to criticise the form of the presentation:

> Oh, she's colour coded anyway. She's used some sort of key. Um, not really necessary. She could have just put the numbers on, …
>
> (Harry: 195–196 Sally)

There is a suggestion here that the use of colour is an unnecessary elaboration. Using numbers to label her diagrams would not only have saved her time but might also be interpreted as a more abstract, and hence more highly valued, way of thinking about the problem.

These qualifications of teachers' reactions to the presence of diagrams and elaborate presentation in children's texts imply that the context-free approval of diagrams described above does not reflect the way in which the teachers actually read. Their advice to their pupils to 'draw diagrams' may not be helpful to pupils as it does not provide any means of distinguishing between those uses of diagrams which will be approved and those which will be taken as signs of a low level of mathematical achievement or will be judged to have been a waste of time.

Some examples of readings of specific diagrams

I shall now move on from general issues to consider teachers' readings of some specific diagrams, attempting to make some connections between the forms of the diagrams and the understandings that the teachers appear to have constructed from them and the value's ascribed to them. It is interesting to note that there were in several cases contrasting readings made by different teachers.

An analytic diagram as evidence of thinking

Richard's 'Inner Triangles' text contains a hexagon with a diagonal drawn in, dividing it into two trapezia Figure 8.1.

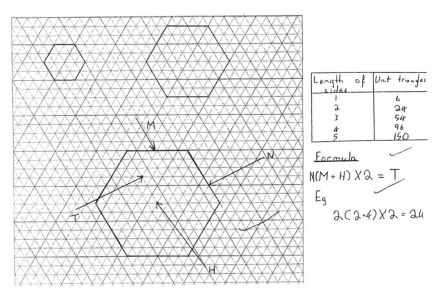

Figure 8.1 Richard's 'Inner Triangles'

The structure of this diagram is analytic and, having no numeric labelling, appears to represent a 'general' hexagon. It may thus be interpreted as making a statement like 'A hexagon consists of two congruent trapezia'. This led Joan to comment:

> I wonder ... the fact that he's drawn that dotted line across the middle makes me

think he was looking at it in terms of two trapezia but he hasn't said that here, yet anyway unless it's further on, so that seems like a very sensible idea … , but it would have been a good idea perhaps if he's written in there

(Joan: 143–147 Richard)

While the diagram is enough to make Joan think she knows how Richard was approaching the problem, she is not satisfied that the diagram can stand by itself. Her suggestion that 'it would have been a good idea' to provide the same information in words may indicate her own uncertainty about the inference she has made but the impersonal construction suggests that her criticism is based on a more general criterion about what she considers to be appropriate methods for communicating such ideas. Similarly, Dan commented on the same diagram:

D: He's moved into hexagons which he's seen as being two trapeziums and therefore fairly simply got

I: How do you know he's seen them as two trapeziums?

D: Cos he's drawn it on there. He's taken basically the same formula and multiplied by two, and my guess is that […] that's how he saw it. But again there's no writing whatsoever.

(Dan: 157–162 Richard)

Here Dan makes a connection between the form of the diagram and the formula on the page next to it; this corroboration surely contributes to his greater confidence in the inference he has made. Nevertheless, like Joan, he remarks 'on the absence of writing'. In this case, given Dan's confidence in his 'guess', the criticism of the lack of writing appears to be being made from the position of an examiner concerned with fulfilment of criteria rather than with understanding the student's thinking. In contrast to Dan's use of Richard's diagram to deduce the way in which the hexagon formula was derived, Andy completely ignores the diagrams on this page:

Now he's probably got enough evidence there to sh … to produce that formula. He's produced what appear to be five pieces of data and … because of his experience with the trapezia in the first part I would be confident that he could produce that formula for the second part. Although it's not apparent just from looking again, it look as if the formula has been produced …

(Andy: 211–216 Richard)

The five pieces of data he refers to must be the entries in the table (as there are only three diagrams altogether) and it is assumed that the formula has been achieved by pattern spotting using the table. Much of Richard's text consists of a series of pages with very similar structures (diagrams, table, formula) for each of the shapes he has considered. This structure may be influencing the way in which Andy is reading each individual page. From Andy's reference to the earlier 'experience' on trapezia it appears that he has constructed a picture of Richard's text as a series of self-contained pieces of work, each of which independently follows the same pattern of working. Any changes in Richard's achievement in later parts of the work may be explained by a greater facility gained through repeating and practising the same set of techniques rather than by the use of earlier work to derive later results in a new way.

Dynamic counting diagrams

Craig's response to the first part of the 'Inner Triangles' task is presented using roughly drawn diagrams on isometric paper, cut out and pasted onto lined paper so that they are embedded within the written answers to the questions Figure 8.2.

Question

2 Give the dimensions of a trapezium containing

    a) 8 unit triangles   b) 32 unit triangles

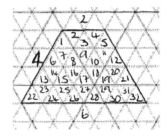

        = top length 1
          bottom length 3
          slant length 2

                 = top length 2
                   bottom length 6

Figure 8.2 Craig's response

The small triangles in each of the trapezia are marked in sequence with numbers, indicating a systematic counting process. This is taken as evidence that this is the way that Craig himself has found the number of triangles in each of the trapezia:

> Um he's immediately got into that and shown that he is actually working it out and then he's showing clearly that he's got an 8 unit triangle and a 32 unit triangle it can be no, even without writing, there's no doubt in your mind that he's done it, he's worked it out, he's got the answer … Now again, he's used the same technique in investigating it. He's shown that he's gone from one trapezium to another and he's counted and it's not the same trapezium that he's used, he's used a separate one, although it's a bit small he's actually shown what's happened.
>
> (Dan: 263–270 Craig)

The numbering, together with the 'roughness' of the diagrams suggests for Dan not only that Craig has counted in a particular way, but also that he has done the work himself rather than copying answers. While several other teachers also read Craig's diagrams in a similar way, Joan appears to see them as a method of communication with the reader rather than as a tool for solving the problem:

> He's started off in quite a nice way with the diagrams next to the working out which is useful.

(Joan: 166–167 Craig)

While Dan has read Craig's diagrams as self-contained messages, apparently ignoring the verbal and symbolic part of the text or seeing it as merely a label for the diagram, Joan is integrating her reading of the whole page. The positioning of the diagrams offset to the right of the questions and answers may suggest that they are re-presentations of that information rather than working out that might have preceded the answers.

A dynamic diagram as 'explanation'

Richard's diagram of a trapezium has a number of features which mark it as a form of explanation rather than as a piece of data Figure 8.3.

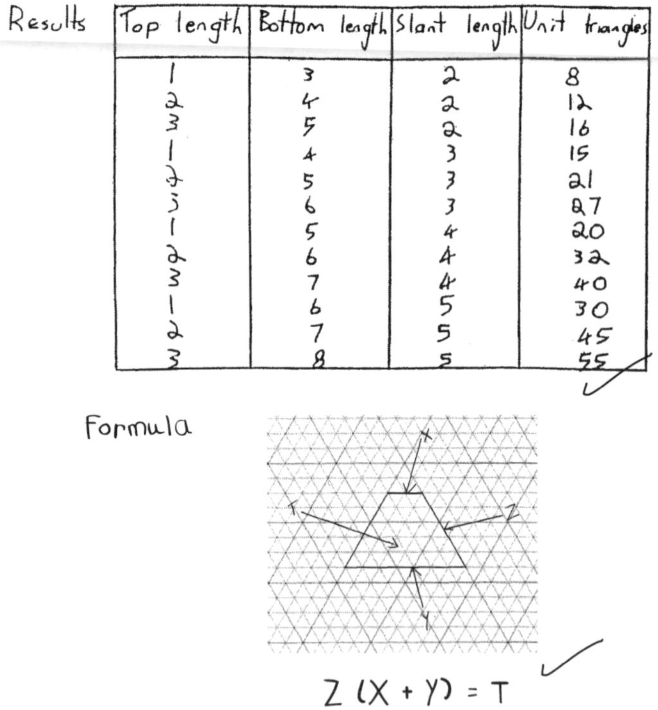

Results

Top length	Bottom length	Slant length	Unit triangles
1	3	2	8
2	4	2	12
3	5	2	16
1	4	3	15
2	5	3	21
3	6	3	27
1	5	4	20
2	6	4	32
3	7	4	40
1	6	5	30
2	7	5	45
3	8	5	55

Formula

$$Z (X + Y) = T$$

Figure 8.3 Richard's trapezium

Firstly, its position on the page after the table of results for the number of inner triangles in a trapezium means that, even if the page is read as a narrative of the author's method of solution, the diagram cannot be taken as chronologically prior to the table. It is also labelled with variable names rather than with numbers; it must, therefore, be read as a generic trapezium rather than a specific example. The arrows which connect the variable names to the corresponding parts of the diagram stress the importance of these labels; they may be read as instructions to the reader to pay attention to the way in which the diagram is labelled. This interpretation appears to coincide with the readings by Andy:

> He's indicated on a diagram what the variables stand for and that's fine
> (Andy: 187–188 Richard)

and by Joan, although she is initially less specific about the diagram's role:

> And he's explained it quite nicely with the diagram.
> (Joan: 136–137 Richard)

In contrast, Fiona, looking for evidence of working out, did not even recognise the existence of the diagram:

> This is a major problem because he's got these results but unless one is there in the class and you're a teacher you don't know whether this is his results or somebody else's. He hasn't shown any diagrams of where these results have come from. He hasn't done any drawings as far as I can see. He's come up with a formula which is z equals. z must be the slant height. Is equal to x plus y equals t.
> (Fiona: 57–61 Richard)

Fiona is looking for diagrams as evidence of data generation. Because this diagram does not fulfil Fiona's expectations about the functions of diagrams within the genre, its existence is not even acknowledged. In spite of the arrow joining the variable name z to the slant height of the diagram, she appears to have to construct this correspondence for herself using her existing knowledge of the problem rather than reading it from the diagram.

Dan, on the other hand, accepted this diagram as evidence of working out by constructing a story about how Richard might have made use of the single diagram to generate several pieces of data:

> He's written out a table and although there's not a great deal of, there doesn't appear to be a great number of diagrams he could have used the diagrams as he was going along, in other words he could have blanked off some of them to get his ... to get his table [*demonstrates how to use a single diagram to represent many trapezia by covering part with his hand*]. It's a little bit difficult to see where he got perhaps all of these but he might well have done them from as he was working along the shape. He's trying a systematic system of working by doing the one two three one two three making the top length, looking at the top length, extending the top length and that's why I'm suggesting that you don't necessarily have to

draw simple diagrams all the time. Children <u>do</u> but it wasn't actually necessary in this piece of work.

(Dan: 105–115 Richard)

In this case, the very lack of diagrams has led Dan to hypothesise about the method Richard might have used. He had previously identified Richard as of 'high ability', which may have influenced the way in which he has interpreted this minimalist diagram.

The multiplicity of readings of this single diagram is indicative of the variety of expectations that teachers bring to their reading and of the influence of these pre-existing expectations on the meanings that they construct from the text.

Naturalistic diagrams as signs of practical activity

In her response to the 'Topples' task, Sally drew a large number of diagrams showing three-dimensional representations of the piles of rods Figure 8.4.

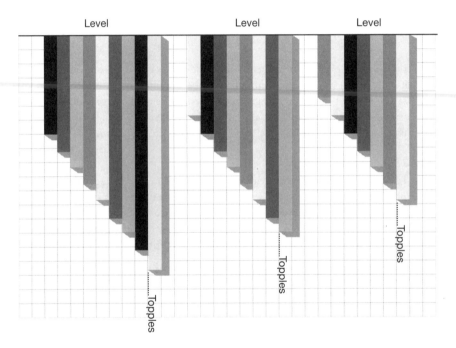

Figure 8.1 Sally's response to the 'Topples' task

The naturalism of these diagrams is enhanced in two ways: firstly each rod is coloured (using the same colour scheme as the original Cuisenaire rods used for the practical activity) rather than labelled with numbers; secondly, where the length of a rod in a pile is greater than 12 units it is drawn as a combination of two smaller rods. This again corresponds to the structure of the concrete materials used by all the pupils whose work was read and by the teachers in preparing for their interviews. Although the other pieces of work on this task also contained the results for piles that must have been built in this way, neither included diagrams for any but the smallest piles.

As shown earlier, Sally's presentation was appreciated aesthetically by the teacher-readers but was simultaneously devalued as over-elaborate and a waste of time. The naturalism of her diagrams, however, seems also to have contributed to the way in which Harry made sense of her mathematical activity. Whereas in the case of the other two texts, the activity was presented and read as being largely about abstract patterns of numbers, Harry questions the validity of Sally's results based on the story that he has constructed about her practical activity.

> H: Now one of her illustrations here shows I think that she's used, she's actually using split rods. We haven't actually tried that but I'm sure that would have an influence on the result.
> I: Probably the rods only go up as far as twelve don't they?
> H: Yeah [laughs] I wonder what she makes of that. One that – I'd be interested to see if the results show anything different.
>
> (Harry: 198–203 Sally)

Although the constraints of the materials used mean that the other pupils and Harry himself must also have used split rods, the effects of this on the results generated by the practical activity are only considered in Sally's case. The naturalistic form of her diagram creates a story about the nature of her activity:

> [Diagrams] … represent events taking place over time as <u>spatial</u> <u>configurations</u> and so turn 'process' into 'system' – or into something ambiguously in between. … Diagrams are therefore akin to expository writing, while naturalistic images … are akin to story writing.
>
> (Kress and Van Leeuwen, 1993)

This story is used to explain why her results are different from those produced by the others:

> I: Yeah but she actually came up with different answers there as well in her original data.
> H: Mmm, I think this is just going to go back to what was said about the blocks being split. So I think that's had an effect there. Um … when it's five at the bottom … yeah she's got twelve um I'm not convinced that would make it topple. But in her illustration, is that is that I can't see which one.
> I: This is the one with five on the bottom. That isn't split.
> H: Right. So I'm not sure that that's – I'm not sure that it would topple then. But if she's convinced that it did topple – again we said about the accuracy of the actual modelling of it the setting up of it. If it toppled it may be something to do with it but she's convinced that it toppled. Then we have to accept that. Um but it's the six one the next one I think where the problem may be.

Because she feels that she's gone, she's extended it to one next level and she's spotted that it's still two extra um that I think that's what's made her convinced that that is the correct solution. Um, but it would be this, and I would I would – post investigation again I would try to see if can get any – go down to CDT or whatever and get some blocks of wood and chop them up and see you know if it does make a difference. I would get actually longer lengths um to try and eradicate this. So that's what's done it I think. That's what's caused the damage.

(Harry: 213–229 Sally)

Although he suggests alternative sources for Sally's errors – general inaccuracy in building the piles even when they are not split or blindly continuing a pattern of numbers – the remedy he prescribes for her difficulties is still based on the persistent idea that the split rods are causing the errors. The naturalistic form of Sally's diagrams so strongly presents her work as being of a very concrete nature that this overrides all the other possible interpretations that Harry had identified.

Summary

When considered out of context, diagrams are seen by teachers to be valuable in their own right. This value seems to be ascribed to them either because they are seen as a demonstration that a pupil has the ability to use a variety of forms of mathematical communication or because they are believed to be helpful in solving problems. Within the context of a particular problem, however, the use of a diagram to help solve the problem may be given a low value by being seen as a sign of a concrete, practical approach rather than a more prestigious abstract approach to the problem. Naturalistic diagrams in particular may give rise to a reading of the author's activity as concrete; such a reading may affect the ways in which the rest of such a text is interpreted.

From the variations in the interpretations of the same diagram by different teachers, it is clear that diagrams are not 'transparent' unambiguous forms of communication. Readers' expectations about the nature of the text that they are reading and about generically appropriate functions of the diagrams within that text are influential in shaping the meanings that they construct from a diagram and the values that they place upon it. Indeed, if the form of a diagram diverges too far from the reader's expectations, it may be ignored or passed over with little effort to incorporate it into a coherent reading of the whole text.

The variability in the teachers' readings of diagrams in the children's texts calls into question the general advice to draw diagrams that many of them give to their pupils. While the mere presence of a diagram in the text may be taken as a positive performance indicator the meanings ascribed to that diagram seem to be more important in contributing to the teacher's evaluation of the text as a whole and of its author. Where the diagram does not conform to the teacher's expectations of the genre it may be passed over without making a significant contribution to the meanings constructed by the reader; where it is taken to indicate a concrete way of working it may lower the teacher's judgement of the whole text. The teachers' general approval of diagrams when expressed out of context shows little conscious account being taken of the variability of the ways in which diagrams may be used or of the variability in their own judgements about specific diagrams read in context. In this general form, it cannot therefore be useful to pupils. Indeed, by following the advice to draw a diagram, it is actually possible that a pupil may lower the teacher's evaluation of their achievement. In order to be useful, such advice needs to form part of a more general awareness of the features of the coursework genre as a whole and of the functions that diagrams may play in teacher's constructions of meanings within this genre.

References

Kress, G. and Van Leeuwen, T. (1993). *Reading Images: The Design of Visual Communication*, Routledge, London.

LEAG. (1991). *Mathematics Coursework and Performance Indicators 1988–1991*, London and East Anglian Group.

Morgan, C. (1993). Teachers assessing coursework: Themes and tensions. *Proceedings of the British Society for Research in Mathematics Learning*, Manchester Metropolitan University, pp. 64–69.

Teachers'
perception

9 'The whisperers'

Rival classroom discourses and inquiry mathematics

Jenny Houssart

Introduction

> A class of nine- and ten-year-old children was working on fractions of shapes. Two worksheets were given out and the children were asked to look first at the one starting with a rectangle. This caused some confusion as one sheet started with a circle and one with a square. In response to this, the teacher asked, 'Do you know what a rectangle is?' He pointed to the sheet in question and one of the children said, 'But it's a square'. The teacher looked again at the sheet, admitted that it was a square and apologised for calling it a rectangle. As the teacher started to explain the sheet, one of the children sighed slightly and said in a whisper, 'Well, anyway, it is a rectangle'.

The last remark uttered in the above was one of many unsolicited comments heard during a year of participant-observation research in a mathematics classroom with myself in the role of a classroom helper. This article will focus on these remarks and those who made them.

The class in question comprised nine- and ten-year-olds in a British primary school. They were a 'bottom set': in other words, they were all considered to be 'less able' as far as mathematics was concerned. There were four children in the class who regularly made unsolicited comments about the mathematics being considered. I call them 'the whisperers', as many of the comments were made as whispered asides without apparent expectation of a response. Sometimes the contributions were louder and represented a challenge to official classroom discussion.

The whisperers formed an unofficial culture within the classroom, with a discourse which differed from the official classroom one. Comparing the two discourses and the two cultures which they represent shows that the whisperers adopted an inquiry mathematics perspective, whilst their teacher followed a school mathematics tradition. The two cultures failed to interact successfully and the whisperers continued to be considered as relatively unsuccessful at mathematics.

This study contrasts with existing work which suggests that inquiry mathematics is something introduced by teachers and often met with resistance by children. It also highlights the difficulties of categorising children according to 'mathematical ability'.

Background

Examination of the literature confirms that the discourse style favoured by the teacher in this study follows a familiar pattern[Discourse in primary mathematics classrooms can be limited and follow predictable patterns (Brissenden, 1988). Instruction and explanation can be dominant features of classroom talk, often driven by the need to maintain institutional norms (Bauersfeld, 1995).] Also familiar in classrooms are 'question–answer–evaluation' sequences (Sinclair and Coulthard, 1975). The final part of this sequence is often used by the teacher to comment on the pupil's answer as it compares with the teacher's own 'ideal response' (Brissenden, 1988).

Pimm (1987) points out that pupils do not speak only in response to the teacher and he distinguishes between them talking for others and talking for themselves. Studies of the culture of mathematics classrooms assert that pupils generally become familiar with the unwritten rules controlling classroom discourse. Such rules are part of the customs and practices which develop in classrooms and become taken-as-shared by the participants (Voigt, 1998; Cobb and Yackel, 1998).

The idea of mathematical discourse reflecting classroom culture is further explored by Richards (1991), who identifies four domains of discourse associated with different cultures. He asserts that these cultures have different assumptions, goals and methodologies and that each is associated not only with a different linguistic domain, but with a different mathematics. The 'school math' culture identified by Richards and the associated discourse of the standard mathematics classroom matches the assumptions and dominant discourse of the particular classroom under discussion.

However, many of the unsolicited comments made by the whisperers seem more reminiscent of the 'inquiry math' culture Richards associates with mathematically literate adults. Closer analysis suggests that the whisperers also differ from the teacher in their assumptions, goals and methodologies and can therefore be seen as comprising a separate, unofficial culture within the classroom. Richards suggests that in linguistic exchanges between different cultures using different discourses there is often an exchange of words without communication taking place. It is only when consensual domains are established that the exchange of words can become *communication*.

I use Richards' distinctions to examine the culture and discourse of the whisperers, attending both to the nature of the discourse and to the shifting and complex interplay between the whisperers' marginal culture and the dominant classroom culture.

Context, cultures and domains of discourse

I gathered information about the class and the teacher by means of participant-observation in one lesson each week for an entire school year. Supporting information came from interviews and discussions with the teacher and from examining documents such as lesson plans and children's work. The teacher was very experienced and had worked in both primary and special schools. He was used to working with bottom sets and often emphasised repetition of simple ideas in order to ensure success for all children. He demonstrated considerable patience in assisting children who had difficulty in grasping new ideas. He was also concerned about the children's performance in written assessments carried out at the end of the year and was under some pressure to make this a priority.

The teacher therefore emphasised the need to complete written tasks correctly. He was not a mathematics specialist, but felt the subject could be made 'fun'. This was sometimes done by emphasising non-mathematical contexts or diversions. He was helped by classroom assistants, a role I assumed while researching. Assistants sat at the tables with groups of children and were therefore in a good position to hear children's comments.

The classroom operated with familiar rules. Discussion was usually initiated and controlled by the teacher, while pupils spoke mostly in response to teacher questions and were expected to put their hands up and be given permission to speak. Generally such rules were observed and the classroom was relatively orderly without being totally silent. I use the term 'official talk' to refer to the open discussions which were in accordance with these unwritten classroom rules. Such talk was either initiated by the teacher or acknowledged by him, either by giving children permission to speak or by commenting on what they had said. Official talk was carried out in normal voices so that everyone could hear and the teacher expected everyone in the room to listen to the official talk.

There was a certain amount of low-level talk on occasions, sometimes caused by several pupils wanting to answer questions at once, sometimes caused by them seeking help from the other adults in the room. Although it is not possible to say how much of this talk was audible to the teacher, it seems likely that he was aware of and tolerated it, though he sometimes reminded children to put their hands up. I will refer to this talk as 'unofficial'. It was often carried out in whispers, was not aimed at everyone in the room and was usually not acknowledged by the teacher.

Listening to this unofficial talk revealed that some pupils regularly made unsolicited comments about the mathematics being considered. Throughout the course of the year, I recorded such comments, or whispers, in all but two lessons. These whisper-free lessons focused almost entirely on the completion of worksheets under test conditions. Most lessons contained several whispers, with 11 being the most I recorded in a single lesson. My notes suggest that about four whispers per lesson was the mean over the year, though this is likely to be an underestimate as I was not always near enough to the whisperers to hear everything they said. Although the comments are referred to as 'whispers', there is evidence that about a third of them were eventually heard by the teacher, sometimes as a result of repetition.

There were four children, out of 20 in the class, who regularly made such comments, though a few others made similar contributions on occasions. All four whisperers were boys, all from relatively disadvantaged backgrounds. Two, Pedro and Wesley, were African-Caribbean and two, Sean and Darren, were white. Although discussion of gender, race and class are beyond the scope of this article, it is worth noting that when the study was carried out there was concern about the performance within British schools of boys (Arnot *et al.*, 1998) and African-Caribbean children (Commission on the Future of Multi-Ethnic Britain, 2000). There are also many studies which show that the process of organising pupils into sets by 'ability' disadvantages black and working-class children (Sukhnandan with Lee, 1998).

I consider the whisperers as a group for the purposes of this article primarily because of their regular, unsolicited comments. They also had many other features in common. However, they did not all sit together and were therefore not always in a position to hear each other's comments. Seating in the classroom, both of children and adult helpers, was determined by the teacher and frequently changed. Children felt to be working at a similar level tended to be grouped together, with adults sitting with those judged to need help.

I tended to be asked to sit with those judged to be about 'middle' of the set as far as their attainment was concerned. Sean worked on my table for most of the year, Wesley for about one term and Darren for a few weeks. On the other weeks, these boys were usually at a table near me (as was Pedro), though occasionally individuals were too far away for me to hear unless they raised their voices.

Wesley and Darren preferred to sit together and were sometimes allowed to. Sean and Wesley also sometimes sat on the same table, as did Pedro and Darren. The whisperers sometimes showed awareness of each other's comments when they were close enough to hear them. Occasionally, one of the other whisperers responded to a comment, though this was not usually the case. Comments were primarily one-off, editorialising asides, apparently made for the benefit of those making them, rather than to elicit a response from others.

A striking common feature of the whisperers is that all made only modest mathematical progress over the year, failing to realise the potential shown in their whispered comments. Although the teacher sometimes acknowledged their positive oral and mental performance, they were never among those he discussed as possible high performers in the end-of-year test, or as candidates for moving to a higher set. All four boys seemed to have some non-mathematical difficulties, including problems with reading and recording, which hampered their performance in written tasks. On the positive side, they all did reasonably well in mental arithmetic tests which required them to write answers only. Sean, in particular, achieved success in more extended oral or practical tasks which required little or no recording (Houssart, 2000a).

Another common feature of the whisperers is that their preferred approach to calculation differed from that encouraged by the teacher. This can be seen in some of the examples given in the next section. Other incidents throughout the year confirmed that the boys were reluctant to use the procedures and algorithms introduced by the teacher. They showed a preference for working mentally and for using methods which dealt with numbers holistically, rather than digit by digit. The comments of the whisperers also suggest that they were able to link work introduced to ideas they had met before. They also showed an enthusiasm for extending ideas and saying what they noticed, even if this meant going beyond what the teacher had planned for the lesson.

Thus, the whisperers had many things in common regarding their approach to mathematics. In many respects, their approach differed from that of the teacher, with the result that they had things to say which he was unlikely to ask for. This may begin to explain why these four boys whispered and others in the class, who accepted the teacher's approach to mathematics, did not. Another factor is their attitude to the teacher and to authority. Although not seriously badly behaved in any of the lessons I observed, these boys did have a slightly 'laddish' reputation. They were certainly prepared to question the teacher's authority, albeit in a fairly mild way, and they did not totally accept the unwritten rules of classroom behaviour which may have deterred others from whispering.

Like most of the children in the class, the whisperers sometimes responded to the teacher's questions to the whole class. Sometimes they did this openly as part of the official discussion, sometimes they were not called upon to answer, but did so anyway in a whisper. Their answers were usually correct. The whisperers were also similar to other children in the class in that they sometimes made comments concerning the work set. Such comments from the whisperers usually referred either to the ease of the work itself or the difficulties they had with the reading and recording involved.

In addition to the two types of comments above, which were made by many children, the remaining comments made by the whisperers were all unsolicited comments about the mathematics being considered. Closer examination suggests that these remarks fall into three main categories. The first occurred when they had noticed or discovered something. The second was when they had something to add and the third was when something had been said which they did not like or disagreed with.

The discourse initiated by the whisperers therefore differed from that initiated by the teacher. This is a reflection of the difference between the unofficial culture of the whisperers and the dominant classroom culture, which is based on acceptance of the goals, assumptions and methodologies of the teacher. A summary of the nature of the dominant culture in the classroom and that of the whisperers appears in Table 9.1, together with their associated domains of discourse. In the sections which follow, I examine more closely the discourse initiated by the whisperers, paying particular attention to what happens when their remarks are loud enough to be heard and hence to represent a threat to the presumptions of the dominant culture.

The whisperers make discoveries

Comments arose when the whisperers had noticed something, sometimes involving generalisations, such as asserting that all multiples of six are even or that all rectangles have four right angles. On other occasions, the comments were about ways of reaching answers, such as 'it's two more' when forming a sequence of odd numbers. Sometimes a more complex discovery was made, such as Darren's realisation that three distinct digits could be arranged to make six different numbers.

The majority of such discoveries remained as whispers and thus the teacher had no opportunity to comment. Sometimes, however, the teacher became aware that the whisperers had noticed something. Two contrasting examples of this are given below. In the first example, Sean and Darren started by whispering their discoveries, but then repeated them and were heard by the teacher. He was impressed and invited them to share their discoveries with the class.

> The children were drawing round plane shapes, then cutting out the shapes, folding them and marking on the lines of symmetry. A few children showed particular interest in how many ways a circle could be folded. Darren said the

Table 9.1 Comparison of cultures and domains of discourse

Teacher: assumptions, goals, methodololgies	Teacher-initiated discourse	Whisperers: assumptions, goals, methodologies	Discourse initiated by the whisperers
Work needs to be kept simple	Clear and simple explanations	Much of the mathematies considered is too easy for them	Say what they have noticed or discovered
Introduce one idea at a time	Ideas often repeated		Try to extend or supplement ideas
Master ideas before moving on	Harder ideas introduced only when the teacher thinks children are 'ready'	Work introduced can be linked to ideas they have met before	Take issue with things they do not like or disagree with
Written work is important and needs to be completed correctly	Closed questions asked and answers evaluated	Completing written tasks can be problematic	
Standard procedures for calculation need to be taught and mastered	More open questions sometimes asked, teacher knows the answers	Formal procedures imposed by the teachers are rarely used	
	Instructions given about completing written tasks	Prefer to calculate mentally, using non-standard methods	
	Standard procedures introduced and reinforced		

circle could be folded ' … in any way'. Sean said, ' … it can go anywhere through the middle, any line on the circle'. They were later invited to tell the rest of the class what they had discovered.

In the example above, the discoveries had been made as a result of working on the task set by the teacher. In the next example, however, the discovery arose when the child had abandoned the official task because he had noticed something interesting.

The teacher asked the children to do $101 - 79$ using a calculator and then gave the correct answer. Wesley became interested in the incorrect answer obtained by the boy behind him who sometimes had difficulty with the calculator due to poor hand control. The teacher moved on to discuss the next task, but Wesley continued to press buttons on his calculator. At one point, he appeared to copy down a number from the calculator on the back of a digit card.

The teacher started to introduce the written task which was to do a page of subtractions using a standard written method before checking the results using a calculator. The teacher admonished Wesley for turning round and talking to the boy behind him. Wesley said, 'I was telling him something about maths', but the teacher did not reply. As the books were given out later, Wesley told me what he had been whispering about. He showed me that repeatedly pressing the equals symbol changes the answer. I asked what was happening and he explained by clearing the calculator, entering 3 and repeatedly pressing equals to generate the three times table. I asked, 'So can you do any table?' And he replied that 'you can do the twenty-four times table.'

In this example, Wesley seemed to be offering the teacher the opportunity to discuss his discovery by saying that he was 'telling him something about maths'. Wesley may have felt that his action was justifiable and a contribution to the lesson. However, the teacher did not seem interested in what Wesley had to say, but was more concerned about him being off-task.

These two contrasting examples are supported by similar incidents of both types. They suggest that if the whisperers drew the teacher's attention to the fact that they had noticed something, he sometimes responded positively with the result that the whisperers' discourse merged with the official classroom discourse. This usually occurred when they were working on a task set by the teacher. Sometimes, it seemed that the task was set up with the hope of them noticing something, perhaps the teacher had even decided what this might be. Noticing something not on the agenda, such as Wesley's discovery about the constant function on the calculator, provoked a different reaction. In such cases, the whisperers were ignored and did not persist.

Occasionally, comments about noticing something met with a reaction from one of the other whisperers, rather than from the teacher. One such occasion was when Darren made a comment about the digits in multiples of nine being 'turned round'. Darren was actually talking about odd and even digits, but his comment may have influenced Pedro who soon made a comment about 81 being 18 'turned round'. There was a similar incident between Sean and Wesley on another occasion, concerning fractions. On neither of these occasions did real discussion ensue, but rather, one whisper led to another.

There is other evidence that the whisperers were sometimes aware of each other's comments. Analysis of the whispers in any given lesson shows there were often similarities in the whispers which suggests that the boys may have been influenced by each other. When I was on the same table as two whisperers, I also felt that their body language and facial expressions suggested that they listened to each other.

The whisperers extend or supplement ideas

Sometimes the whisperers added something to an answer which had been given, or to what the teacher was saying. In many cases, this involved simply moving on to the next question or part of the question, but it could also involve continuing apparent patterns or predicting what would happen next. For example, in a task which involved colouring answers on a hundred square, the numbers coloured already were 6, 12, 24, 18, 36. Sean whispered that he thought the next answer would be 30. In a place-value task, the teacher asked for the next odd number after 319. Pedro answered 321 in a normal voice, but then continued the sequence 323, 325, … in a whisper.

Another example of a child taking an idea further than the teacher suggested is given below. In this case, Sean related the idea being introduced by the teacher to something which had been done in a previous session.

> The teacher was introducing the idea of converting metres to centimetres, though a previous session had involved converting centimetres to millimetres. When the teacher said that one metre is a hundred centimetres, Sean whispered, 'A hundred centimetres is a thousand millimetres'. The teacher moved on to talking about a piece of string, which he said was just under a metre long. Sean said in a whisper, 'nine hundred and ninety nine millimetres perhaps'.

In all the examples above, the whisperers were content to make these additions quietly. They made no attempt to break into the 'official' classroom discussion and did not seem concerned that their comments were not acknowledged. However, there were exceptions to this. Of the three categories of whisper, it was the extensions which appeared to be heard most frequently, though with limited effect.

An example of this occurred during a block of work on fractions. For some weeks, the teacher had been dealing with simple fractions via folding, cutting and colouring. He seemed to be avoiding discussion of equivalence and this was raised by the whisperers on several occasions. An example of this is given below.

> The teacher was going through a sheet on fractions which the children had just completed and was giving them the answers. The sheet consisted of shapes which were partly coloured. The instruction read, 'Write the fraction that is coloured', but actually three alternatives were given for each shape and children had to put a ring round the correct answer. For one shape, the teacher gave the correct answer as 2/4 (the alternatives offered on the sheet were 1/4 and 3/4). Pedro added, 'That's a half'.

Pedro made this contribution in a normal voice rather than a whisper, though it was not acknowledged by the teacher and Pedro did not persist. There were occasions when the teacher acknowledged such remarks with responses such as 'We're not doing that yet' or 'We're doing that next week'. There was one occasion on which a whisperer persisted and was allowed to share his idea with the class. Darren wanted to go beyond checking the answers to a mental arithmetic test and to discuss how the answers were reached.

> The teacher was reading out answers to the mental arithmetic test. Darren wanted to explain how he had done one of the questions (from 26 take away 11). The teacher seemed to ignore this for a while and continued to give answers. However, Darren persisted and was eventually allowed to explain how he had reached the answer. Darren said, 'Take away 1, 25 are left. Take away 10 leaves 15'. The teacher moved on to the next question. Darren's comment was not used or praised.

Although the whisperers' attempts to extend ideas were made in a normal voice more frequently than other comments, this was to little effect. The teacher had a range of responses which effectively neutralised their comments. One response was to ignore their comments and often they did not persist. If their ideas were acknowledged, it could be with a polite reminder that they were not doing that yet, thus potential discussion was effectively closed down by the teacher. A final possibility was to allow the child to share what they had to say, but then move on without embracing or engaging with the comment. Thus, the whisperers attempts to extend ideas were excluded from the official discourse. The two types of discourse coexisted and impinged on each other, but had not merged.

The whisperers point to errors or things they do not like

Sometimes, comments were made about errors made by other children. This usually arose when children were asked to write or draw on the board or to give answers to completed work. Usually, the whisperers merely pointed out errors and inaccuracies under their breath, though sometimes they did this in a normal voice. In all of the instances I recorded, the whisperers were correct in their identification of errors.

On occasion, the whisperers went beyond identification of errors and exhibited a feel for what is important and correct in mathematics.

> The teacher had written ½ and ¼ on the board and was talking about which is bigger. He pointed out that although 4 is bigger than 2, ¼ isn't bigger than ½. He speculated about why this is and a girl put her hand up and said, 'Size doesn't matter'. Sean said in a whisper, 'Size *does* matter'.

> The teacher was drawing the children's attention to the line in a fraction which he said is like the division symbol except for the dots. A child said, 'Dots aren't that important'. Sean whispered, 'They is'.

Comments were also made disagreeing with the teacher rather than other children. Sometimes this was about checking answers, but occasionally the whisperers took issue with him on more fundamental issues.

> The teacher wrote a 5 on the board with a 9 underneath it and asked if it could be a 'take away'. The teacher was leading to the point that it must be an addition because 'you can't take nine away from five'. Although no one disputed this openly, Sean did say in a whisper, 'You'd go below zero, it would have to be a minus'.

In this incident, Sean was content to whisper and this was the case for the majority of comments involving dissent. However, there were some occasions when the whisperers were more open in their disagreement. This sometimes led to exchanges with the teacher in which both sides defended their point of view. The first incident I give below arose when the teacher was trying to introduce non-mathematical humour. It suggests, like the dots remark above, that the whisperers were unhappy with un-mathematical comments.

In what seemed to be an attempt to reinforce the words 'numerator' and 'denominator', the teacher pointed to the parts of a fraction and suggested giving them names such as Anne. Pedro appeared not to like this and said to the teacher, 'It's a number'. The teacher replied, 'Why can't it have a name?' Pedro responded, 'It's got a name'.

The second incident is chosen as it demonstrates differing views on calculation. This was perhaps the most important difference between the whisperers and their teacher and one which apparently caused frustration on both sides.

The teacher was discussing economical methods of calculation. He was encouraging a formal written method for halving or dividing by two, on the grounds that other methods could not be used with larger numbers. To prove his point, he said, 'What would you do if it was a half of two hundred and eighty six?' Sean seemed to want to take issue with the teacher's assertion that you cannot use subtraction as the numbers get bigger and he answered, 'Take away'. The teacher used a challenging tone and asked, 'Take away what?' and Sean responded 'One hundred … and … forty … three'. Sean's ability to answer this seemed to surprise the teacher.

In these last two examples, the two types of classroom discourse are no longer separate. They have clashed rather than merged. The issue of calculation in particular was one on which neither the whisperers nor the teacher shifted throughout the year. Often they coexisted, occasionally they clashed, but they never appeared to reconsider their views.

Discussion

Why did these boys continue to make whispered comments, despite their apparently having little effect? Were they talking for others or for themselves? In most cases, they seemed unconcerned that their comments were not heard by the teacher, though it is possible that they were still talking for 'others' in the room, but not the teacher. They may have been whispering for each other.

Responses to comments from the other whisperers were infrequent, but suggest they were able to see the value of each other's comments. It is also possible that Sean, who often sat next to me, was whispering to me in my role as a helper. He may have perceived me as less likely to judge than the teacher, as well as knowing that I was unlikely to respond because the teacher was talking. Another possibility is that the whisperers were talking for themselves, trying to formulate their ideas.

Whether the boys were making comments for themselves or others, the comments provided evidence of unofficial mathematical activity in which the boys were engaging. It showed that they were taking opportunities to do some mathematics which matched their own view of the subject. Whispering may have aided their thought processes. It also meant they were able to register their understanding and sometimes their dissent. Thus, the whispering can be seen as having a dual function, partly for the benefit of the person making the comment and partly for any potential

Table 9.2 Outcome when whisperer's discourse is audible

Type of discourse	Circumstances	Teacher response	Outcome
Making discoveries	Discovery based on official task, possibly anticipated by teacher	Teacher responds positively: discussion ensues	Communication based on agreement
Making discoveries	Discover based on off-task activity	Teacher ignores	Whisperers neutralised: no communication
Extending ideas	Child does not persist	Teacher ignores	Whisperers neutralised: no communication
Extending ideas	Child does not persist	Teacher acknowledges: 'closes down'	Whisperers neutralised: words exchanged, but no true communication
Extending ideas	Child persists	Teacher acknowledges: allows comment, moves on	Whisperers neutralised: words exchanged, but no true communication
Disagreeing	Child takes issue directly with teacher	Teacher engages: disagreement ensues	Communication based on disagreement

audience. The whisperers got ideas 'off their chest' by expressing them in a whisper, with the possibility that someone with a similar view might hear.)

The whisperers' discourse reflected their cultural assumptions and differed from the teacher-initiated discourse. Returning to the model proposed by Richards (1991), these observations confirm that the dominant classroom culture was reminiscent of 'school mathematics'. The whisperers had more in common with 'inquiry mathematics': for example, they asked questions, solved problems and proposed conjectures.

Even when the whisperers were heard, discussion did not necessarily result, and when it did, it could take the form of disagreement. In fact, the most common outcome when the whisperers were heard was that their comments were neutralised by the teacher (see Table 9.2). These findings are in line with those of Richards, in that the different assumptions of the teacher and the whisperers meant that words could be exchanged or acknowledged without genuine communication taking place.

Where these findings differ from some of the examples given by Richards is in the relative positions of the teacher and the pupils. Richards associates the inquiry culture with mathematics as it is used by mathematically literate adults. It is ironic that while the teacher adopted the discourse associated with 'school mathematics', the whisperers' discourse was close to that of the 'inquiry mathematics' culture. However, the whisperers were nine- and ten-year-olds judged to be in the bottom 25 per cent of their year group and not expected to pass the formal tests they were due to sit the following year.

Other perspectives also encourage the view that the whisperers were acting like mathematicians rather than mathematical failures. In their oral contributions, the whisperers demonstrated features which some teachers associate with 'able mathematicians', such as trying to generalise and showing an interest in pattern (Watson, 1996; Allebone, 1998).

In fact, the spontaneous behaviour of the whisperers was similar to that many mathematics educators see as desirable but difficult to elicit. For example, the art of asking questions is highly regarded in mathematics, with emphasis placed on the type of questions likely to promote mathematical thinking (Watson and Mason, 1998; Martino and Maher, 1999).

However, it seems that in the case of this particular group of children, mathematical statements were made without questions being asked. Some of the most interesting comments by the whisperers arose when the teacher simplified matters to the point of saying things which were not, strictly speaking, mathematically correct. His claiming that you cannot subtract 9 from 5, that a square is not a rectangle and that large numbers can only be divided using a standard method all provoked the whisperers into dissent.

Despite their demonstration of mathematical understanding and occasionally mathematical knowledge in advance of that expected by the teacher, the whisperers consistently performed at a level well below that expected for their age in formal work. They were considered by the teacher to be correctly placed within this low-ability set.

One approach to this contradiction might be to suggest that there are obstacles preventing these children from showing their 'true ability'. Certainly, there is some evidence that non-mathematical difficulties hampered the completion of written tasks on which they were judged. Such difficulties included poor reading skills, slow recording skills and difficulty with organisation of work and materials (Houssart, 2000b).

Another possibility is that the idea of 'mathematical ability' is a vast oversimplification. In particular, the experiences of the whisperers suggest that it is perfectly possible to possess supposed 'higher-order' skills, such as the ability to generalise or extend ideas, without being accurate in the completion of worksheets.

A further possibility is that the differences between the cultural assumptions of the whisperers and those of their teacher contributed to their 'failure'. For example, the priority given to written tasks in terms of assessment meant that these boys were not considered to be doing well and were not seen as needing extension work. Assessment based on oral contributions might have reached the opposite conclusion. The provision of worksheets designed to help children carry out calculations in standard ways was also a hindrance, as it forced them into a method of recording which was unhelpful and did not relate to their own methods of calculation.

The failure of the two cultures to engage with each other created discontent on both sides and tended to emphasise their compartmentalisation. For the teacher, there was disappointment that children who sometimes made promising comments consistently failed to perform on formal tasks. For the whisperers, there was discontent at lack of recognition, coupled with boredom when the harder work they sought did not materialise. It seemed that, despite their potential, as long as the presumptions of 'school mathematics' prevailed, these boys were unlikely to experience success.

References

Allebone, B. (1998). Providing for able children in the primary classroom, *Education 3–13*, **26**(1), 64–69.

Arnot, M., Gray, J., James, M., Rudduck, J. and Duveen, G. (1998). *Recent Research on Gender and Educational Performance*, The Stationery Office, London.

Bauersfeld, H. (1995). Language games in the mathematics classroom: Their function and their effects. In P. Cobb and H. Bauersfeld (eds) *The Emergence of Mathematical Meaning: Interaction in Classroom Cultures*, Lawrence Erlbaum Associates, Hillsdale, NJ, pp. 271–291.

Brissenden, T. (1988). *Talking about Mathematics: Mathematical Discussions in Primary Classrooms*, Basil Blackwell, Oxford.

Cobb, P. and Yackel, E. (1998). A constructivist perspective on the culture of the mathematics classroom. In F. Seeger, J. Voigt and U. Waschescio (eds) *The Culture of the Mathematics Classroom*, Cambridge University Press, pp 158–190.

Commission on the Future of Multi-ethnic Britain. (2000). *The Future of Multi-ethnic Britain: The Parekh Report*, Runnymede Trust and Profile Books, London.

Houssart, J. (2000a). Get rich quick with the Numeracy Strategy. *Equals*, **6**(1), 9–11.

Houssart, J. (2000b). Nice and easy does it: pupil responses to non-challenging tasks. In B. Jaworski (ed.) *Proceedings of the British Society for Research into Learning Mathematics Day Conference*, May 6th, University of Oxford, pp. 91–96.

Martino, A. and Maher, C. (1999). Teacher questioning to promote justification and generalisation in mathematics: What research practice has taught us. *Journal of Mathematical Behavior*, **18**(1), 53–78.

Pimm, D. (1987). *Speaking Mathematically: Communication in Mathematics Classrooms*, Routledge and Kegan Paul, London.

Richards, J. (1991). Mathematical discussions. In E. von Glasersfeld (ed.) *Radical Constructivism in Mathematics Education*, Kluwer Academic Publishers, Dordrecht, pp. 13–51.

Sinclair, J. and Coulthard, M. (1975). *Towards an Analysis of Discourse*, Oxford University Press, London.

Sukhnandan, L. with Lee, B. (1998). *Streaming, Setting and Grouping by Ability: A Review of the Literature*, National Foundation for Educational Research, Slough.

Voigt, J. (1998). The culture of the mathematics classroom: Negotiating the mathematical meaning of empirical phenomena. In F. Seeger, J. Voigt and U. Waschescio (eds) *The Culture of the Mathematics Classroom*, Cambridge University Press, pp. 191–220.

Watson, A. (1996). Teachers' notions of mathematical ability in their pupils. *Mathematics Education Review*, **8**, 27–35.

Watson, A. and Mason, J. (1998). *Questions and Prompts for Mathematical Thinking*, Association of Teachers of Mathematics, Derby.

10 Steering between skills and creativity

A role for the computer?[1]

Celia Hoyles

Background

Children's and adults' mathematical knowledge frequently appears to be in a state of crisis – a crisis of skills or a crisis of creativity. In the UK and the USA, there are now waves of enthusiasm for basic skills, mental arithmetic and target setting. Studies comparing England's performance in mathematics with other countries have shown England to be performing relatively poorly in comparison with others. For example, evidence from the Third International Mathematics and Science Survey (TIMSS) indicated that our Year 5 pupils (aged 9 and 10) were among the lowest performers in key areas of number out of nine countries with similar social and cultural backgrounds (Harris, Keys and Fernandes, 1997). A huge, multi-million pound National Numeracy Strategy is now underway in the UK and in its first report (DfEE, 1998), the TIMSS studies were cited as one reason for the new focus on numeracy.

At the same time, the news from the Pacific Rim reports rather different pressures for change. For example, Lew (1999) describes Korea, a country which scores very highly on most international comparisons of mathematics attainment, as being in 'total crisis' in mathematics. He illustrates graphically how most students seem quite unable to relate their well-developed manipulative skills to the real world. Lew argues that:

> the direction of the mathematics curriculum in Korea should change from emphasis on computational skills and the 'snapshot' application of fragmentary knowledge to emphasis on problem-solving and thinking abilities.
>
> (p. 221)

Similarly, Lin and Tsao (1999) present a picture of test obsession in Taiwan, where college entrance examinations dominate students' (and parents') lives. Both of these countries are encouraging more 'open' curricula to include opportunities for mathematical creativity: that is, adapting their curricula to be more like those currently being vilified in the UK and the USA.

Other data from TIMSS suggest that English children are comparatively successful at applying mathematical procedures to solve practical problems and are generally positive about mathematics. Is it possible to retain these strengths while at the same time consolidating arithmetic skills and developing the ability to construct deductive arguments? (The latter area is one in which we have shown our students to be surprisingly weak: see Healy and Hoyles, 2000.)

The challenge for the international mathematics education community perhaps appears at first sight to be the design of a globally-effective balanced curriculum. From a UK perspective, this would build on the wealth of informal mathematical knowledge students bring to school, while at the same time drawing attention to mathematical structures and properties and introducing them more systematically to mathematical vocabulary. The mathematical curriculum of the next millennium should harness children's motivation without losing their mathematics – and I envisage that the computer might offer just the context to help do this.

A role for the computer

I was inspired in the early 1980s by Seymour Papert's (1980) radical vision of a mathematics that was playful and accessible, but at the same time rigorous and serious. We[2] dreamed (and still do) of children actively expressing mathematics in different ways. We wanted children to learn by conjecture, reflection on feedback and debugging, as part of their own meaningful projects that required planning, sustained engagement with mathematical ideas represented in diverse ways and the bringing together of a range of skills and competencies. Logo was the vehicle or the catalyst for many of us to try to achieve those dreams. In doing this work and studying the work of others, our eyes were opened to students' strategies and potential – computer interaction was a window onto possibilities, an environment to illuminate pupil meanings and interpretations (Hoyles, 1985; Hoyles and Noss, 1992).

Since that time, we have designed a range of microworlds around different 'open' software and have further developed the notion of technology as a means by which knowledge can become concretised and connected. We have also undertaken more systematic investigation of the nature of the child's activity and how it can be better understood. Inevitably, the boundary of what is and is not mathematics has been explored (Papert, 1996): some say that working experimentally with the computer counts as mathematics, some that it is not, and many are not sure. The software may have changed but the issues have not and the location of this boundary is still a matter of hot dispute.

If we want to design investigative environments with computers that will challenge and motivate children *mathematically,* we need software where children have some freedom to express their own ideas, but constrained in ways so as to focus their attention on the mathematics. Are there lessons to be learned from all the work that has been done with these sorts of environments over several decades? What do we actually know about how children can better learn mathematics with technology?

Mathematics comprises a web of interconnected concepts and representations which must be mastered to achieve proficiency in calculation and comprehension of structures (for elaboration of this theoretical framework, see Noss and Hoyles, 1996). Mathematical meanings derive from connections – *intra-mathematical connections* which link new mathematical knowledge with old, shaping it into a part of the mathematical system and *extra-mathematical meaning* derived from contexts and settings which may include the experiential world. Yet how are these meanings to be constructed? How is the learner to make these connections? To what extent can the software tools encourage this process of meaning-making and connection-making?

A critical weakness of many mathematical learning situations has been the gap between action and expression and the lack of connection between different modes of expression. Over many years, our central research priority has been to find ways to help students build links between seeing, doing and expressing (see, for example, Noss, Healy and Hoyles, 1997). We have shown that technology can change pupils' experience of mathematics, but with several provisos:

- the users of the technology (teachers and students) must appreciate what they wish to accomplish and how the technology might help them;
- the technology itself must be carefully integrated into the curriculum and not simply added on to it (see Healy and Hoyles, 1999);
- most crucially of all, the focus of all the activity must be kept unswervingly on mathematical knowledge and *not* on the hardware or software.

Computers and the curriculum

To date, work with computers in mathematics education has largely been concerned with construction and the potential of software to aid the transition from particular to general cases – specific instances can be easily varied by direct manipulation or text-based commands and the results 'seen' on the computer screen (see, for example, Laborde and Laborde, 1995). Yet, even if students develop a sense of how certain 'inputs' lead to certain results, there remains the question of how to develop a need to explain, a need to prove, as part of (rather than added on to) this constructive process.

In countries like the UK, where proof has all but disappeared from the school curriculum, this issue must be addressed urgently if we are to avoid limiting the mathematical work for most children by the introduction of computers. If we fail, the majority of our students will simply be subjected to even more convincing empirical argument – for example, using powerful dynamic geometry tools simply to measure, spot patterns and generate data.

There is an alternative which we are in the process of investigating. We have designed tasks where, through computer construction, students have to attend to mathematical relationships and in so doing are provided with a rationale for their necessity. Thus, the scenario we envisage is one where students construct mathematical objects for themselves on the computer, make conjectures about the relationships among them and check the validity of their conjectures using the tools available.

This forms part of a teaching sequence which also includes reflection guided by the teacher away from the computer, and the introduction of mathematical proof as a particular way of expressing one's convictions and communicating them to others. It is in this way, we suggest, that constructing and proving can be brought together in ways simply not possible without an appropriate technology: formal proof is simply one facet of a proving culture, revitalised by the 'experimental realism' of the computer work (Balacheff and Kaput, 1996).

Lulu Healy[3] and I have devised algebra and geometry teaching sequences which follow these criteria. Our activities were developed after analysing students' responses to a nationwide paper-and-pencil survey to assess students' conceptions of proving and proof (see, for example, Healy and Hoyles, 2000). This survey was completed by 2459 15-year-old students of above-average mathematical attainment from across England and Wales. Each teaching sequence was designed 'to fit into the curriculum' and to fill at least some of the gaps the survey had revealed in the understandings of students. Overall, 18 students from three schools have worked through the sequences, each of which took nearly five hours of classroom contact supplemented by homework.

I now present snapshots from case studies of two students who engaged in these sequences. The first illustrates the gains that can be made by connecting skills to creative exploration through computer interaction, while the second points to potential pitfalls in planning 'the best' mathematics curriculum incorporating technology.

Tim: making the step to explaining in algebra

Tim was a quiet and diligent student who knew about proof as something that involved verification and explanation, though only recognised it in the context of algebra – a natural consequence of our curriculum with its emphasis on generalising and explaining number patterns (see Figure 10.1).

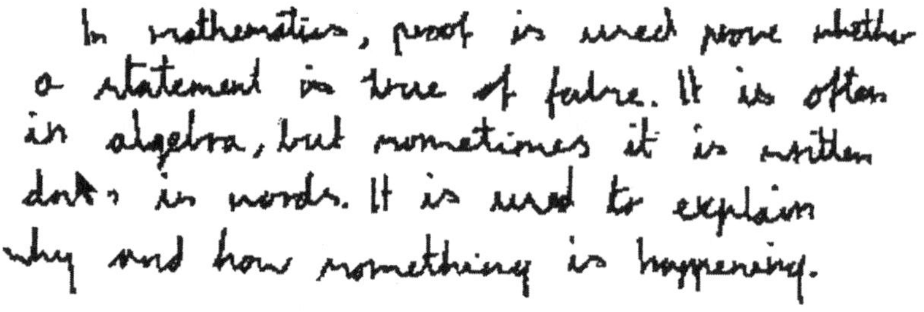
In mathematics, proof is used prove whether a statement is true of false. It is often in algebra, but sometimes it is written dont in words. It is used to explain why and how something is happening.

Figure 10.1 Tim's initial view of proof

It was also clear from Tim's choices in the paper-and-pencil survey that he had a preference for visual argumentation: he evaluated the visual 'proof' by Yvonne in exactly the same way as a 'correct' formal algebra proof; when asked about this, it was clear he 'saw' the general structure *through* this particular visual example (see Figure 10.2).

In the first algebra session of our teaching sequence, students are introduced to our microworld, *Expressor,* in which they build 'matchstick' patterns of number sequences by constructing simple programs. They are encouraged to connect their computer constructions to corresponding mathematical properties and hence find a general formula for the number sequence explaining why any conjecture is true or false, by reference to computer feedback and to the mathematical structures they have constructed. Similar work with more complex number sequences is undertaken in the third session.

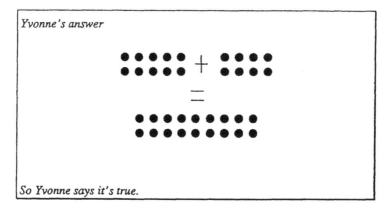

Yvonne's answer:	agree	don't know	disagree
Has a mistake in it	1	2	③
Shows that the statement is always true	①	2	3
Only shows that the statement is true for some even numbers	1	2	③
Shows you why the statement is true	①	2	3
Is an easy way to explain to someone in your class who is unsure	①	2	3

Figure 10.2 Tim's evaluation of a visual proof

Tim found this work of generalising through programming both engaging and challenging – in fact, he described it as the most enjoyable part of our teaching. He also saw a strong connection between proving and his computer work.

> I liked the programming stuff – that helped [to write proofs] because it sort of showed how it was constructed so … It helped prove because it showed you how they were made … how that construction was made step by step.

In the second session, students are introduced to writing formal algebraic proofs and helped to 'translate' their Logo descriptions of the mathematical structures into algebra. They are also taught how to construct deductive chains of argument – systematically starting from properties they had used in their constructions in order to deduce further properties. Both of these tasks are unfamiliar to UK students.

Here is an example. Students are asked to investigate the properties of the sums of different sets of consecutive numbers. They construct by programming a visual representation of numbers as columns of dots (shown in Figure 10.3).[4] Students can, for instance, move the bottom right dot to the bottom left, see that it would 'even up' the three columns, and convince themselves that the conjecture that the sum of three consecutive numbers is divisible by three is always true.

Although these moves can be achieved by, for example, using counters, in *Expressor,* the visual arrangement has a simultaneous 'algebraic' description which is constructed

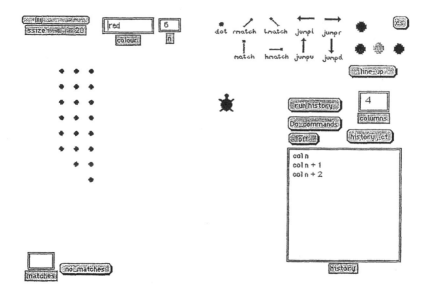

Figure 10.3 A typical *Expressor* screen to explore the sum of three consecutive numbers

by the children. In Figure 10.3, a program *col* has been written to generate 6 (*n*), 7 and 8 columns. The dots can be dragged into columns as with real counters; but as this is done, a recorded 'history' of the actions is stored (see the history box in Figure 10.3) in the form of fragments of computer program.

This code is executable: that is, it can be 'run' to produce the output (or part of the output) which produced it. There is, therefore, a duality between the code and the graphical output of the dots; the *action* (on the dots) to produce a new visual arrangement and the *expression* (in the form of pieces of program) are essentially interchangeable. The code is a rigorous description of the student's action to construct a particular image, and her actions are executable as computer programs. A box *n* is used to store the smallest of the three numbers and our student might see that what is in the box *n* hardly matters, and therefore come to realise that the theorem is independent of the first number.

How did Tim cope with this activity? In his first session, he had been seeking explanations for a general rule in the general symbolic expressions he had constructed (in the form of programs). He built his three columns of dots in *Expressor* and was faced with a screen rather like Figure 10.3. Then he wrote:

$$n + (n + 1) + (n + 2) = 3n + 3$$

But, he obtained this equivalence not as a result of a manipulating algebra but by reference to our microworld: he noted that the three original columns could be changed to three columns of length *n* and a 'tail' of three.

Tim generalised this method to find factors of sums of different numbers of consecutive numbers – always considering columns of dots and a tail, but flexibly using

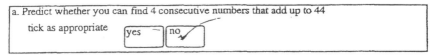

a. Predict whether you can find 4 consecutive numbers that add up to 44

tick as appropriate yes ☐ no ☑

If you think yes, then find these 4 numbers then go to b.

If you think no, go straight to b.

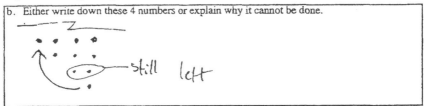

b. Either write down these 4 numbers or explain why it cannot be done.

still left

Figure 10.4 Tim's proof that the sum of four consecutive numbers is not divisible by four

visual manipulation and argumentation. For example, to show that it was impossible for the sum of four consecutive numbers to have a factor of four, and so could never add up to forty-four, he visually moved dots, as he describes in Figure 10.4.

Finally, together with his partner, Tim also came up with a new, visual 'proof' that the sum of five consecutive numbers must have a factor of five. He again focused on the tail of dots, but combined their total using inductive reasoning starting from the case when *n* was 0.

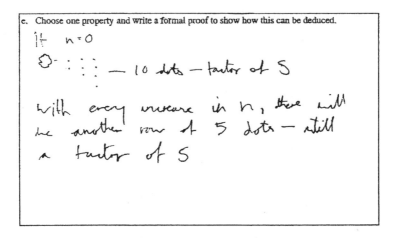

c. Choose one property and write a formal proof to show how this can be deduced.

If n = 0

10 dots — factor of 5

with every increase in n, there will be another row of 5 dots — still a factor of 5

Figure 10.5 Tim's inductive proof that the sum of five consecutive numbers is divisible by five

By this time, it was clear that Tim had found two well-connected ways to explain it: constructing symbolic code and manipulating visual expressions. His explanations came from linking logical and general arguments with visual representations (columns of dots) – and not from algebra, even though he clearly recognised its importance.

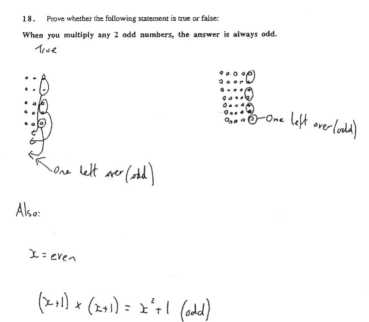

18.   Prove whether the following statement is true or false:

When you multiply any 2 odd numbers, the answer is always odd.

True

One left over (odd)

One left over (odd)

Also:

$x = even$

$$(x+1) \times (x+1) = x^2 + 1 \quad (odd)$$

Figure 10.6 Tim's two explanations

This gap in his repertoire of skills is well illustrated in his final homework (Figure 10.6). Tim creatively generalised 'the dots' microworld into thinking of multiplication as a rectangular array of dots, whose rows could be paired off leaving 'one left over'. But, he was still unable to multiply out brackets correctly.

In contrast to Tim, Susie could say nothing about what proof was and appeared clearly confused about the generality of a mathematical argument. She selected empirical arguments as her own approach in all the multiple-choice 'proofs' in our survey, both in geometry and algebra, and described these as both general and explanatory. She thought mathematics was quite complicated and, in fact, admitted to hating it.

Although Susie offered no description of proof or its purposes, it emerged in interview and by watching her computer work that she did have a view about proof – it was about examples (many examples). It was enough to have shown a statement was true many times. Additionally, for Susie, there was another important aspect of proof, which was a rule or formula. But, its role was to obtain more marks from the teacher rather than to confer generality – the examples were enough for this.

Although Susie could write formal proofs, she did not see them as general and found them no more convincing than empirical evidence: her two 'modes of proving' – examples and formal proofs – were apparently completely disconnected. She believed, for example, that, even after producing a valid proof that the sum of two even numbers is always even, more examples would be needed to check that the statement holds for particular instances.

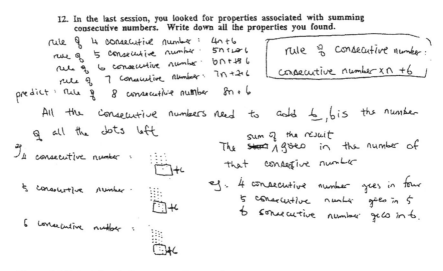

Figure 10.7 Susie's rule for consecutive numbers

In our teaching experiments, both in algebra and geometry, we noticed that Susie followed all the instructions carefully, but rarely if ever experimented with the computer. She found it hard to see the computer as a means to try things out when unsure, hard to learn from feedback.

I will illustrate Susie's work in algebra by reference to the same tasks described earlier. Susie was considering the sum of four consecutive numbers. She constructed the columns of dots and came up with the formula $4n + 6$, ostensibly by making the connection of the '+6' with the 'tail of dots'. For five consecutive numbers, she apparently used the same method to come up with the correct sum of $5n + 10$.

Then she changed her mind. She crossed out the '+10', explaining this by writing that she had checked and 'it was 6'. From this point on, her written work and explanations were disconnected from any generality suggested by the visual display she had constructed in the *microworld,* except she persisted in showing pictures of columns of dots with a six-dot tail, as illustrated in her homework following this session.

The rupture between particular examples and generalisations can be explained by reflecting on what we had discovered as Susie's goal in mathematics – to find examples and then a *rule.* She had achieved this: she had found a rule in which numbers could be substituted and even had pictures to illustrate it, but the pictures did not represent the structure of consecutive numbers.

Susie's story is not completely negative. She did make progress after engaging in these teaching sequences. By constructing matchstick patterns, Susie was beginning to appreciate how an algebraic expression could express generality (and not serve merely as something to be manipulated) and, although proving for Susie remained solidly 'a rule plus examples', she did seem to be beginning to *want to explain* as well.

Some snapshots from the geometry sequence

Briefly, here are some insights gained from the teaching sequence in geometry, simply to illustrate further some points raised in the previous sections. This sequence followed a similar pattern to that in algebra. In the first session, students are encouraged to construct simple geometrical objects on the computer with dynamic geometry software, to describe their constructions, connect each with a corresponding mathematical property and use the computer to explore or reject conjectures.

In the second session, students are encouraged to construct familiar geometrical objects (parallelograms, rectangles) on the computer, identify properties and relations of a figure that had been used in their constructions and distinguish some properties that might be deduced from those given by exploring with the computer. In much the same way as in algebra, students are also taught at this point to construct logical deductive chains of argument and write formal proofs based on their computer constructions.

In the third session, students are faced with more unfamiliar constructions and proofs, which again they can tackle experimentally on the computer.

So how did Tim fare in geometry? Geometry for Tim, as for most of our students, was far more problematic than algebra. He did make some progress in that he learnt to write clear descriptions of his constructions, translate them into given properties and 'see' deduced properties. The computer work helped Tim 'see' relationships and convinced him of their necessity, but the links he could make between constructions and proofs or even explanations were much more tenuous than in algebra.

> T: Well, you could actually see like if they were congruent – you could take however much you were allowed to take and actually make a triangle. If it was congruent then you could … tell it was.
> CH: Tell it how?
> T: Just by seeing.
> CH: And did that help you write your formal proofs?
> T: Not really – not the formal stuff. But, well it made it more enjoyable.

Tim found it hard to appreciate and reproduce 'the game' of proving: that is, systematically separate givens from deduced properties and produce reasons for all his steps. He found the language of formal geometry proofs inhibiting – it stopped him 'seeing it all'.

The construction task in the third session was important in his progress. He had to construct a quadrilateral where adjacent angle bisectors were perpendicular and describe and justify its properties. Tim found this hard, but, after much experimentation and 'measuring' lots of angles, he eventually 'saw' the key relationship – two parallel lines – not by 'just seeing them' but by noticing two numerically equal angles and dragging. The important point is that the measurements for Tim were not simply collecting empirical evidence: they were not only part of the conjecture but also and crucially part of his proof. When he talked about two angles of 44°, it was clear to us that he was seeing *through* the numbers to the general case – just as he had done in *Expressor*. As in algebra, Tim was using his interaction with the computer to help him to find explanations.

Susie again presents us with a different picture. When it came to constructing proofs, Susie's responses were quite unlike the majority of students in our survey. Her proofs in geometry were far better than in algebra and the proof she constructed for the more complex geometry question (a standard Euclidean geometry proof) was much better than almost all the survey students.[5]

Yet despite being able to write these perfectly formal proofs, we found on interview that they were, for Susie, rituals, disconnected from any appreciation of the generality of the mathematical properties and relationships she used. As in algebra, she believed that even after proving a statement, its validity had to be verified in any specific set of cases (see also Chazan, 1993). In her response to the survey, for example, Susie was certain that she needed examples to check that the statement (the sum of the angles of a triangle is always 180°) held for right-angled triangles. These findings point to the complexity of proving in geometry.

So how did Susie manage in our teaching experiment in geometry? In fact, we found rather little evidence that Susie made any progress in geometry as a result of engaging in these tasks. Computer interaction did not seem to help Susie come to appreciate the generality of a proof and the proving process. Also, before she started the sequence, Susie could already construct formal geometry proofs in the context of familiar and fairly routine problems. Faced with more unfamiliar situations such as those described above, she was lost and, unlike Tim, was unable to use the computer to help her.

We can throw light on this lack of progress, by reference to two factors: her interactions with the computer and her interpretation of feedback. First, as I have mentioned, Susie did not exploit the computer to test hypotheses or try things out. But success in our tasks *relied* on experimental interaction – we did not *expect* our students to know immediately what to do. Second, Susie interpreted the feedback from the dynamic geometry software in a way which certainly was unexpected. For her, dragging a Cabri construction was *not* testing a relationship, exploring a property – but merely a way of generating many examples.

Once we had noticed this, we could see it was completely consistent with Susie's view of proof. Susie's reflections on the use of the computer in mathematics are also relevant. When interviewed, it was clear that she thought the computer had given her ideas about 'what it was all about' and had done so quickly: but, rather crucially, it makes examples and checks them.[6]

There were positive outcomes for Susie in relation to her response to mathematics. All through the teaching experiments, Susie picked the most enjoyable aspect of her mathematical work as 'finishing it', 'getting it right', 'writing down the results'. Yet, in algebra, we were beginning to catch glimmers of enjoyment and engagement: Susie began to mention her *activity* rather than simply its end point. In her final interview after the teaching sequences too, she spontaneously offered how much she had enjoyed the work with the computer, although it must be admitted this was only as a contrast with 'normal maths'. Even so, this more positive attitude might be a key to Susie's further development.

Discussion and conclusion

To begin an explanation of the two very different student responses to our teaching sequences and work with computers, we have to consider cultures and curricula – huge issues well beyond the scope of the article, but which simply cannot be ignored. Susie's profile is somewhat less 'odd', if it is known that she had only studied mathematics in an English school for one year – she was, in fact, from Hong Kong and had been educated there, although the language of instruction had been English. Unlike most other students in our survey, Susie had been taught formal geometry proofs as well as algebraic formulae and manipulation and had little experience of 'doing investigations'.

As I have tried to show, Susie's lack of progress might at least partly be explained by the disjuncture between the assumed starting points of our tasks, particularly those with computers – in terms of sense of proving and student–computer interaction – and Susie's world. We had students like Tim in mind when we designed our sequences; students reared in an investigative culture – who wanted to explain but who lacked the tools to do it.

Susie was at odds with this culture in terms of her beliefs about mathematics and about proof. Our activities did not build on *her* existing framework for proof, did not help *her* to connect her informal mathematics to our agenda. Our story of Susie provides compelling evidence that we must take seriously prevailing beliefs about mathematics and computers in our curriculum planning and resist the temptation simply to import 'exemplary tasks' from other cultures.

The comparison of Tim's and Susie's work cautions against any assumption that the computer will lead to a single set of learning outcomes or bring about particular changes. We can only design optimal activities within very limited parameters, given that how children interact with and learn from software depends on their expectations and beliefs. Curricula must seek to build on student strengths – in the case of the UK, on a confidence in conjecturing and arguing – and connect these strengths to new representations. Students like Tim respond positively to the challenge of attempting more rigorous proof alongside their informal argumentation. Susie was less successful as the culture which had shaped our teaching and task design was not shared by her.

Clearly, not all UK students are like Tim or students from Hong Kong like Susie. But the purpose of elaborating their stories is to guard against the stupidity of 'transferring' curricula simplistically across cultures, replacing a curriculum which overemphasises an empirical approach with one in which students are simply 'trained' to write formal proofs. It is all too easy for countries simply to flip between two states of the 'skill and creativity' crisis while attempting to model curriculum innovations which look so alluring to the distant observer. (For an interesting discussion of the cultural implications of traditional Chinese views, see Leung, 1999.)

So, returning to my initial question about the desirability of a globally-effective mathematics curriculum, I can only conclude that this goal is fundamentally misguided. We should not set our sights on the same curricular sequences and targets, because these are not the same in any reality. Incorporating what look like comparable tasks into our curricula will not mean that the meaning derived from them will be comparable.[7] Cultural effects might even be magnified when activities involve technology, which carries its own sets of beliefs and agendas. I have tried to illustrate how the power of microworlds to engage our students with mathematics rests first and foremost on what they believe about curriculum goals and intentions and about what they can learn from computer interactions.

Our aim in mathematics education may be to reach a common goal – a mathematical literacy comprising a better balance between skills and competencies on the one hand and engagement with mathematical thinking on the other. We might even agree that the computer might have a useful role to play. Although it is deeply illuminating and exciting to move beyond the surface features and slogans of international comparisons and focus on what *mathematics* and what *education* we are striving to achieve in our countries, ultimately we have to tease out different routes toward this common goal for ourselves.

Notes

1   This paper is a modified and updated version of a keynote address presented to the ICMI-East Asia Regional Conference on Mathematics Education.

2   'We', in this article, refers to my close colleague in Mathematical Sciences at the Institute of Education, Richard Noss.

3   See the UK ESRC project, *Justifying and Proving in School Mathematics* (Ref. R000236178). I wish to acknowledge the central work of Lulu Healy in all aspects of this project.

4   Noss (1998) borrowed this task in *Expressor*, along with some student work from our pilot study, to illustrate how alternative representations can be used to offer 'a channel of access to the world of formal systems' (p. 10).

5   She produced an almost perfect formal proof – something only achieved by 4.8 per cent of the students in the survey and one which 62 per cent of students did not even start.

6   She also thought that the computer helped her to remember, but there was a disadvantage: 'you can't use the computer in exam'.

7   Similar points have been made in relation to the meaning of test items in TIMSS which are not the same simply because it is the same test (Keitel and Kilpatrick, 1999).

References

Balacheff, N. and Kaput, J. (1996). Computer-based learning environments in mathematics. In A. Bishop, K. Clements, C. Keitel, J. Kilpatrick and C. Laborde (eds) *International Handbook of Mathematics Education: Part 1*, Kluwer, Dordrecht, pp. 469–505.

Chazan, D. (1993). High school geometry students' justification for their views of empirical evidence and mathematical proof. *Educational Studies in Mathematics*, 24(4), 359–387.

DfEE. (1998). *Numeracy Matters: The Preliminary Report of the Numeracy Task Force*, Department for Education and Employment, London.

Harris, S., Keys, W. and Fernandes, C. (1997). *Third International Mathematics and Science Study (TIMSS): Second National Report, part 1*, National Foundation for Educational Research, Slough.

Healy, L. and Hoyles, C. (1999). Visual and symbolic reasoning in mathematics: making connections with computers? *Mathematical Thinking and Learning,* 1(1), 59–84.

Healy, L. and Hoyles, C. (2000). A study of proof conceptions in algebra. *Journal for Research in Mathematics Education,* 31(4), 396–428.

Hoyles, C. (1985). Developing a context for Logo in school mathematics. *Journal of Mathematical Behavior,* 4(3), 237–256.

Hoyles, C. and Noss, R. (eds) (1992). *Learning Mathematics and Logo,* MIT Press, Cambridge, MA.

Keitel, C. and Kilpatrick, J. (1999). The rationality and irrationality of international comparative studies. In G. Kaiser, E. Luna and I. Huntley (eds) *International Comparisons in Mathematics Education,* Falmer Press, London, pp. 241–256.

Laborde, C. and Laborde, J. M. (1995). What about a learning environment where Euclidean concepts are manipulated with a mouse? In A. diSessa, C. Hoyles, R. Noss and L. Edwards (eds) *Computers for Exploratory Learning,* Springer-Verlag, Berlin, pp. 241–262.

Leung, F. (1999). The traditional Chinese views of mathematics and education: implications for mathematics education in the new millennium. In C. Hoyles, C. Morgan and G. Woodhouse (eds) *Rethinking the Mathematics Curriculum,* Falmer Press, London, pp. 240–247.

Lew, H.-C. (1999). New goals and directions for mathematics education in Korea. In C. Hoyles C. Morgan and G. Woodhouse (eds) *Rethinking the Mathematics Curriculum,* Falmer Press, London, pp. 218–227.

Lin, F.-L. and Tsao, L.-C. (1999). Exam Maths re-examined. In C. Hoyles, C. Morgan and G. Woodhouse (eds) *Rethinking the Mathematics Curriculum,* Falmer Press, London, pp. 228–239.

Noss, R. (1998). New numeracies for a technological culture. *For the Learning of Mathematics,* 18(2), 2–12.

Noss, R., Healy, L. and Hoyles, C. (1997). The construction of mathematical meanings: connecting the visual with the symbolic. *Educational Studies in Mathematics,* 33(2), 203–233.

Noss, R. and Hoyles, C. (1996). *Windows on Mathematical Meanings: Learning Cultures and Computers,* Kluwer Academic Publishers, Dordrecht.

Papert, S. (1980). *Mindstorms: Children, Computers, and Powerful Ideas,* Basic Books, New York.

Papert, S. (1996). An exploration in the space of mathematics education. *International Journal of Computers for Mathematical Learning,* 1(1), 95–123.

Section 3

Pupils' and teachers' perceptions

In Section 3 the articles are about pupils' and teachers' perceptions. Over recent years there has been a shift in focus of research from considering the single perspective of the teacher towards listening to the learners. Much of the research with teachers looked at possible changes in classroom practice while the learner's perspective shows how the creation of a collaborative community of practice can impact on the development of mathematical thinking. Although much research has looked at pupils' learning and their opinions (for example, Rudduck, 1996) the focus of this research was not mathematics and the research had a tendency to look at the whole school issues rather than those which pertain specifically to teaching and learning mathematics.

In Chapter 11, Alba Thompson is concerned with the possible link between teachers' views of mathematics and their pedagogic practice. Although this research dates back to the early 1980s it is still relevant today because it shows how a teacher's perception of the nature of mathematics may affect their practice. Thompson presents her research in the form of case studies showing how three teachers behave in different ways depending on their perception of mathematics. She is quick to point out that the way teachers view mathematics and their subsequent classroom practice is not simply down to cause and effect. Not only did she find differences in the classroom practices of the three teachers but also in their view of what evidence of mathematical understanding looked like. There were also differences in the way that teachers planned lessons and this had an impact on the flexibility they displayed in their teaching.

Jo Boaler's research (Chapter 12) was set in two schools that used different approaches to teaching. One school was traditional in its style with pupils in sets while the other was progressive with pupils in mixed ability groups. Boaler found that setting had an impact on pupils' ideas about, and responses to, mathematics as well as their eventual achievement. She found that pupils had four main complaints about setting: the pace of lessons; pressure and anxiety; restricted opportunities; and setting decisions. Boaler also found that a disproportionate number of working-class pupils were placed in the lower sets, which may indicate inequity within the setting system. Some of the students became disillusioned with mathematics due to the pace of lessons and the expectation on them that resulted from their positioning in a particular set. Boaler's findings are significant at a time when setting is becoming increasingly prevalent in UK schools. If the impact of setting is to cause learners to become disillusioned then it may be time to reconsider its use.

Diane Reay and Dylan Wiliam's chapter (Chapter 13) is based on data collected from Year 6 pupils during the term before the National Curriculum tests. They discuss the way that pupil's views of the tests affected their perception of themselves as learners. They were interested in how children are identified and positioned as learners and how this positioning is constructed through the assessment process. They found that pupils have a clear idea about the influence of external assessment in narrowing the curriculum. They also found a shift in the way pupils were working, in that their culture changed from a collaborative environment to one of individualised and competitive working. The regular practice for the National tests also resulted in a change of positioning for some pupils within their peer group. The positioning as an effective learner may become based on the gaining of good marks in tests. The competitive element in lessons leads to a growing polarisation of pupils as learners. There appears to be a need for more research on the way that pupil and teacher identities and practices are changing through the assessment process. What is the impact of the assessment processes on both pupils and teachers?

In Chapter 14, Barbara Allen focuses purely on pupils' perceptions. She was interested in finding out from middle-school pupils how their experiences in mathematics classrooms affected their attitude to the subject and their learning of it. She found that external authority was continually reinforcing a pupil's position in the classroom as a successful or unsuccessful learner of mathematics. The placing of pupils in sets affected their identity and this was supported by the culture of the classroom. By the end of Year 6 many of the pupils were disillusioned with mathematics and the competitive and repetitive nature of the work they faced. She believes that if pupils are to continue with mathematics in school they need to have some control over their learning environment and not be constantly faced with external authority that positions them as successful or unsuccessful learners.

Reference

Rudduck, J. (ed.) (1996). *School Improvement: what can pupils tell us?* David Fulton, London.

Further reading

Askew, M., Brown, M., Rhodes, V., Johnson, D. and Wiliam, D. (1997). *Effective Teachers of Numeracy: Final Report,* King's College, London.
Boaler, J. (2000). *Multiple Perspectives on Mathematics Teaching and Learning,* Ablex Publishing, Westport, CT.
Lerman, S. (1990). Alternative perspectives of the nature of mathematics and their influence on the teaching of mathematics. *British Educational Research Journal,* 16, 15–61.
Morgan, C. and Morris, G. (1999). *Good Teaching and Learning: Pupils and Teachers Speak,* Open University Press, Buckingham.
Slavin, R. E. (1990). Achievement effects of ability grouping in secondary schools: A best evidence synthesis, *Review of Education Research,* 60(3), 471–99.

11 The relationship of teachers' conceptions of mathematics and mathematics teaching to instructional practice[1]

Alba Gonzalez Thompson

14-4-04

Abstract

Case studies were conducted to investigate the conceptions of mathematics and mathematics teaching held by three junior high school teachers. Examination of the relationship between conceptions and practice showed that the teachers' beliefs, views, and preferences about mathematics and its teaching played a significant, albeit subtle, role in shaping their instructional behaviour. Differences among the teachers in their conceptions and practices are explained followed by a discussion of properties of their conceptual systems.

Introduction

Most research on the relationship between the effectiveness of mathematics teachers and their knowledge has focused on the teachers' knowledge of mathematics (Begle, 1972, 1978; Eisenberg, 1977). The questions of how teachers integrate their knowledge of mathematics into instructional practice and what role their conception of mathematics might play in teaching have largely been ignored. With regard to research on teaching in general, Shavelson and Stern (1981) noted:

> Very little attention has been paid to how knowledge of a subject matter is integrated into teachers' instructional planning and the conduct of teaching. Nevertheless, the structure of the subject matter and the manner in which it is taught (e.g., with integrity or improbability, contempt or respect; see Fenstermacher, 1980) is extremely important to what the students learn and their attitudes toward learning and the subject matter.
>
> (p. 491)

Teachers develop patterns of behaviour that are characteristic of their instructional practice. In some cases, these patterns may be manifestations of consciously held notions, beliefs, and preferences that act as 'driving forces' in shaping the teacher's behaviour. In other cases, the driving forces may be unconsciously held beliefs or intuitions that may have evolved out of the teacher's experience.

There is strong reason to believe that in mathematics, teachers' conceptions (their beliefs, views, and preferences) about the subject matter and its teaching play an important role in affecting their effectiveness as the primary mediators between the subject and the learners. Yet, very little is known about the role that these conceptions might play in the formation of instructional practices characteristic of their teaching. Inquiry into this issue calls for an examination of teachers' cognitive and metacognitive processes during instruction. Yet, for various reasons, these processes have been typically slighted by researchers who, instead, have largely concentrated on teacher performance in the classroom (Shulman and Elstein, 1975).

Fenstermacher (1978) suggested two reasons why the study of teaching has focused, for the most part, on teacher behaviour as opposed to teacher cognition. The first reason is the belief of many educational researchers that the teacher's thought 'is not the proper object of empirical inquiry' because 'it is accessible only by inference – a precarious and imprecise way to undertake controlled inquiry' (p. 173). Teacher behaviour, in contrast, 'is directly accessible by observation', thus making it the proper object of study. The second reason has to do with the view of external causation; that is, 'the view that the causative factors which account for a person's behaviour are external to the person'. According to Fenstermacher, 'both reasons are part of the legacy of strong versions of behaviourism' (p. 173).

Recently, however, the need to study the mental processes of teachers to gain understanding of their behaviour has begun to receive increased attention.

> Though it is possible, and even popular, to talk about teacher behaviour, it is obvious that what teachers do is directed in no small measure by what they think.
> (National Institute of Education, 1975, p. 7)

Several researchers who have studied teachers' thoughts and decision-making processes during instruction have questioned the rationality of teachers' behaviour, by pointing to findings that suggest that their behaviour is mostly instinctive and intuitive, as opposed to reflective and rational (Clark and Peterson, 1976; Jackson, 1968; MacKay and Marland, 1978; Morine-Dershimer and Vallance, 1975). Insofar as teachers' behaviour is rational, it is reasonable to assume that their conceptions of the subject matter and its teaching will have some bearing on their actions. However, even if teachers' behaviour is mostly reflexive and spontaneous, it remains worthwhile to examine their conceptions because of the *potential* influence that these might have in the formation of behaviour patterns which may have become habituated.

If teachers' characteristic patterns of behaviour are indeed a function of their views, beliefs, and preferences about the subject matter and its teaching, then any attempt to improve the quality of mathematics teaching must begin with an understanding of the conceptions held by the teachers and how these related to their instructional practice. Failure to recognise the role that the teachers' conceptions might play in shaping their behaviour is likely to result in misguided efforts to improve the quality of mathematics instruction in the schools.

The objectives of the study reported in this paper were to investigate the conceptions of mathematics and mathematics teaching held by three junior high school teachers and to examine the relationship between the teachers' conceptions and their instructional practice.

The investigation sought to answer two questions. One was whether the teachers' professed beliefs, views and preferences about mathematics and mathematics teaching were reflected in their instructional practices. The second question was whether the teachers' behaviour was influenced by their conceptions. In seeking answers to these questions the following more specific questions were investigated:

1   Are there incongruities between the teachers' characteristic instructional behaviour and their professed conceptions of mathematics and mathematics teaching?
2   How can incongruities between the teachers' professed conceptions and their instructional practices be explained?
3   Are differences among the teachers in their characteristic instructional practices related to differences in their beliefs and views about mathematics and mathematics teaching?

In addition to investigating these questions, a cross-sectional analysis sought to identify the formal properties of conceptual systems that could best be used to describe differences among the teachers in their conceptions of mathematics and mathematics teaching.

Method

The method of inquiry used was the case study method (Stake, 1978). Three junior high school mathematics teachers participated in the study. Each teacher was observed daily teaching a mathematics class over a period of four weeks. During the first two weeks the investigation was limited to observations. During the last two weeks, daily interviews were conducted following the observed lesson. There was no time overlap among the case studies – no two were conducted simultaneously.

There were several reasons for limiting the initial phase to observations. One reason was to become better acquainted with the social context before starting the more direct inquiry in the interviews. Another reason was to generate conjectures about what the teacher's conceptions might be, and thus gain a better sense of direction for later probing. The first phase allowed for inferences that led to a tentative characterisation of the teacher's conceptions based only on her instruction, without direct input concerning her professed beliefs and views. This procedure was intended to avoid the potential influence that the teacher's professed views might have on the investigator's sensitivity to the different events observed. The interviews provided the opportunity to test the accuracy of the inferences made by eliciting relevant information. The inferred and the professed conceptions were examined for consistency.

The lessons were audio-recorded for two purposes: to secure a record of the lesson for later analysis and to be used during the interviews as an aid in stimulating the teachers' recall of the lesson's events. The interview sessions were also audio-recorded for later analysis. The interviews typically lasted 45 minutes, although occasionally they took longer.

The interview questions were, for the most part, related to specific events of the day's lesson. However, other questions were used to fill in missing information or to test conjectures generated from the accumulated data.

Each teacher was also asked to respond in writing to six tasks administered at different times throughout the case study. Five tasks were intended to get at the teachers' views about various aspects of mathematics teaching. The information sought in each task dealt with the teachers' views about: the relative importance of various goals of mathematics instruction; the relative emphasis that should be given to several instructional objectives; the relative importance of several pedagogical practices; the more common reasons for students not making satisfactory progress in mathematics; and, the more valuable types of information in judging their own teaching effectiveness. The other task came from an instrument developed by Confrey (1978) for assessing students' conceptions of mathematics. This task consisted of six bipolar dimensions that one might use to describe mathematics. It was used to obtain a succinct description of the teachers' view of mathematics in terms of general characteristic qualities of the subject.

At the end of each day, the data obtained that day were reviewed. The new data were examined in light of data obtained on previous days. Tentative hypotheses and inferences were made from them. As each case study proceeded, the analysis of the accumulated observational and theoretical notes provided new focuses for subsequent observations and interviews (see Schatzman and Strauss, 1974, for a detailed description of the methodology).

The teachers

The teachers who participated in this study were three of a group of 13 teachers who had cooperated in a pilot study that the author conducted during the 1979–1980 school year. There were no specific criteria used in the selection of the three teachers other than the fact that they were qualified junior high school mathematics teachers with more than three years of experience teaching mathematics at that level, and that they had expressed an interest and willingness to participate in the study.

The three teachers were Jeanne, Kay, and Lynn. Jeanne had been teaching junior high school mathematics for ten consecutive years and was the mathematics coordinator for the middle school. Kay had taught for five years and was in charge of the mathematics component of a programme for 'gifted' students at her school. Lynn had been teaching junior high mathematics for three and one-half years and was also mathematics coordinator for her middle school.

Jeanne and Lynn were observed teaching an eighth grade general mathematics class. Jeanne's class was fairly homogeneous, consisting mostly of what she described as slightly above-average students. Lynn described her class as heterogeneous, showing a very wide range in mathematical preparation and achievement. Kay's class was a seventh grade general mathematics class made up of 'gifted' students. (See Thompson, 1982, for a thorough description of the teachers and their classes.)

The case studies

What follows is a summary of each teacher's conceptions of mathematics and mathematics teaching with a discussion of the relationship between the teacher's professed views and her instructional behaviour. Following this is a cross-sectional analysis of the teachers' conceptions which is then used as a basis to explain key differences among the teachers with respect to their conceptions of mathematics and its teaching.

Jeanne

Jeanne's teaching reflected a view of mathematics as a coherent collection of interrelated concepts and procedures. Although she did not explicitly refer to her views of mathematics during instruction, several teaching episodes seemed to indicate that she regarded mathematics as a consistent subject, free of ambiguity and arbitrariness. This view could be inferred from her marked tendency to stress the meaning of the concepts taught in terms of their relationship to other mathematics concepts and to emphasise the reasons or logic underlying the mathematical procedures used in class. A view of mathematical activity as some sort of game of symbols played according to rules whose justification is an essential part of the game seemed implicit in the way she dealt with the content. Although not rigorous, her approach to the content was formal. She typically relied on mathematical symbols in her explanations and frequently referred to the structural properties of mathematics. She seldom appealed to intuition, hers or the students', and did not allude to the practical significance of the topics studied.

Consistently, Jeanne's remarks in the interviews indicated that she regarded mathematics as the mathematics of the school curriculum. She admitted that she rarely thought about mathematics as a scientific discipline.

> In my world now, I haven't thought about how I fit in the picture of mathematics as a ... as a ... as a science. I don't see how I fit in that picture at all. I see fractions and decimals, those little things. My scope is very narrow.

She clearly held two separate, unrelated views of mathematics that seemed to be the result of two distinct experiences in her study of the subject. One was a positive view that seemed to have been influenced by a favourable experience with school mathematics. The other view was related to an unpleasant experience with college mathematics – specifically with calculus and linear algebra.

She commented:

> For the first time in my whole life I sat in a classroom and heard the teacher explain something and had no idea of what she was talking about ...

This experience appeared to have caused Jeanne to question her mathematical ability, which she conceded was not very strong.

Jeanne's professed views of mathematics are summarised in the following statements:

- Mathematics is an organised and logical system of symbols and procedures that explain ideas present in the physical world.

- Mathematics is a human creation, but mathematical ideas exist independently of human ability to discover them. Because of this, mathematics is more than just a system of symbols, it is the idea as well.
- Mathematics is mysterious – its broad scope and the abstractness of some of its concepts make it impossible for a person to understand it fully.
- Mathematics is accurate, precise, and logical.
- Mathematics is consistent, certain, and free of contradictions and ambiguities.
- Mathematical content is fixed and predetermined, as it is dictated by ideas present in the physical world.
- Mathematical content is coherent. Its topics are interrelated and logically connected within an organisational structure or 'skeleton'.
- Changes in the content of mathematics occur only at the extreme as it continues to expand.

The appeal that mathematics held for Jeanne lay in the logical interrelatedness of its topics and the organisation inherent in its underlying structure. Although she was aware of its practical utility, this, she admitted, was not a characteristic that contributed to her liking mathematics or that she alluded to in teaching. Aside from teaching, mathematics held little relevance in Jeanne's life.

Once, while discussing percentages smaller than one per cent, a student indicated that such percentages frequently appeared in interest rates and the stock market reports. In response to the student's remark, Jeanne indicated: 'I don't know very much about that because my husband takes care of those things at home'.

Jeanne's conceptions of mathematics teaching can be characterised in terms of her view of her role in teaching the subject and the students' role in learning it. A precise analysis reveals that:

- The teacher must establish and maintain an atmosphere of order, respect, and courtesy in the classroom.
- The role of the teacher is to present the content in a clear, logical, and precise manner. To accomplish this she must stress the reasons and logic underlying mathematical rules and procedures and emphasise the logical relations among concepts (to establish their mathematical meaning).
- It is the responsibility of the teacher to direct and control all instructional activities, including the classroom discourse. To this end, she must have a clear plan for the development of the lesson.
- The teacher has a task to accomplish – to present the lesson planned – and must see that it is accomplished without digressions from, or inefficient changes, in the plan.
- The role of the students is to assimilate the content. 'Assimilate' means that the students 'see' the relationships between the new topic and those already studied as explained by the teacher.
- Students learn best by attending to the teacher's explanations and responding to her questions.
- Students should not be satisfied with just knowing how to carry out mathematical procedures; they should seek to understand the logic behind such procedures.

Most of the views inferred from Jeanne's instructional behaviour were manifested either in her remarks during our conversations or in her responses to the written tasks. For example, she expressed a strong belief in the importance of establishing and maintaining positive teacher–student relationships. This belief was consonant with the atmosphere of courtesy and respect that prevailed in her classroom, although her relationship with the students was not one of open friendliness and warmth.

Some of Jeanne's professed beliefs and views about mathematics teaching, although not incongruous with her teaching, were not apparent in her instructional practices. However, the most striking contrast between Jeanne's professed views and her teaching was posed by her indication that it is important for the teacher to encourage student participation in class and to be alert to clues from the students to adjust the lesson to their needs. Although Jeanne conducted class in a question-and-answer fashion, there were no observable signs that she was making an effort to encourage discussions among the students or between them and herself. The students' participation typically was limited to responding to her questions which, for the most part, were intended to elicit short, simple answers, and she had a tendency to disregard the students' suggestions and not to follow through with their ideas. Although she frequently seemed to disregard the difficulties of individual students in responding to her questions in class, the difficulties and needs she inferred from their written work appeared to be her primary source of data for adjusting future lessons.

Besides lack of attention and poor motivation, Jeanne attributed the students' poor performance on tests to their failure to retain the material taught earlier in the year and to their insufficient preparation in previous grades. Although she did not seem to relate the students' difficulties in learning mathematics to difficulties inherent in the subject matter or to her teaching, she did indicate that their successful performance in examinations was a valuable sign of her own effectiveness in teaching.

Kay

An enthusiasm for mathematics was apparent in Kay's teaching. Her enjoyment of mathematics was most clearly manifested during the frequent problem-solving sessions she conducted in her classes. On several occasions she remarked to the students about the excitement and satisfaction to be derived from dealing with a challenging problem and being able to solve it. Whenever the students made insightful comments about the topic at hand or succeeded in making a discovery, Kay shared in their excitement and encouraged them in this type of activity.

Kay's teaching reflected more of a process-oriented approach than a content-oriented approach. A view of mathematics as a subject that allows for the discovery of properties and relationships through personal inquiry seemed to underlie her instructional approach. Her instructional practices suggested that: mathematics is more a subject of ideas and mental processes than a subject of facts; mathematics can be best understood by rediscovering its ideas; discovery and verification are the essential processes of mathematics; the main objective of the study of mathematics is to develop reasoning skills that are necessary for solving problems; mathematical notational schemes are not verifiable, they are more or less arbitrarily determined and conventionally adopted; the nature of mathematical proof is such that conclusions must be derived only from given or logically (not empirically) substantiated information; mathematics is a useful tool for the study of science; and mathematical knowledge is necessary and useful in many professions.

Kay's view of mathematics, as revealed in her comments during the interviews, were as follows:

- The primary purpose of mathematics is to serve as a tool for the sciences and other fields of human endeavour.
- Mathematical content originates from two sources: from the needs of the sciences and other practical needs, and from mathematics itself.
- Mathematics is a challenging, rigorous, and abstract discipline whose study provides the opportunity for a wide spectrum of high-level mental activity.
- The study of mathematics sharpens one's ability to reason logically and rigorously.
- Except in statistics, conclusions and results in other branches of mathematics are certain.
- The validity of mathematical propositions and conclusions is established by the axiomatic method.
- Mathematics is continuously expanding its content and undergoing changes to accommodate new developments.

Kay held an 'action' view of mathematics. She regarded mathematics primarily as a stimulating subject that provides the opportunity for high-level mental work. It was not its practical value that made mathematics appealing to her. Rather, its appeal lay in the challenge of its problems, the aesthetic quality of its theory, and the disciplinary effects of its study. Her enjoyment of mathematics was derived from the many opportunities its study provides to exercise one's inventiveness and reasoning skills and from the self-satisfaction ensuing from succeeding in tasks considered difficult by many.

Kay's professed views of mathematics were consistent with her teaching. Furthermore, they appeared to have a strong influence on the instructional decisions she made. The heuristic approach that she often used in presenting the content and the frequent problem-solving sessions that she conducted in class were consistent with her view of mathematics as a stimulating and challenging subject. She frequently encouraged the students, in a rather persuasive tone, to guess, conjecture, and reason on their own, explaining to them the importance of these processes in the acquisition of mathematical knowledge.

Kay's view of mathematics as a formal discipline was manifested in discussions of geometric proofs involving congruent triangles. She insisted on the importance of deriving conclusions only from the stated information and not from what appeared to be true about the drawing. In other contexts, however, her instructional approach was more empirical and intuitive than formal. She explained that, because of the grade-level of the class, she often needed to compromise rigour in favour of intuition in order to make the material more meaningful.

Kay was confident about her knowledge of mathematics and her ability to teach it. This confidence was apparent in her remarks as well as in her instructional behaviour.

Her confidence seemed to result from her successful experience in studying mathematics, which she attributed in part to a natural inclination toward analytical thinking and logical reasoning.

Several basic aspects of Kay's conceptions of mathematics teaching could be inferred from her characteristic instructional practices. The conception of her own role as the teacher that was reflected in her teaching is summarised in the following views:

- The teacher must create and maintain an open and informal classroom atmosphere to ensure the students' freedom to ask questions and express their ideas.
- The teacher must be receptive to the students' suggestions and ideas and should capitalise on them.
- The teacher' should encourage the students to guess and conjecture and should allow them to reason things on their own rather than show them how to reach a solution or an answer. The teacher must act in a supporting role.
- The teacher should appeal to the students' intuition and experiences when presenting the material in order to make it meaningful.
- The teacher should probe for potential misconceptions in the students by using carefully chosen examples and non-examples.

The practices that Kay identified as essential in teaching mathematics were: using a variety of approaches to stimulate the students' interest and to suit the different topics; asking questions frequently; encouraging the students to ask questions, guess, theorise, and be wrong; using appropriate examples and non-examples; providing a variety of justifications; showing applications of the topics taught, either practical or mathematical applications; and using games and puzzles as motivational devices.

In addition, Kay expressed a strong belief in the teacher's knowledge of, and enthusiasm for, mathematics as necessary qualities of a good teacher. She expressed a concern for positive student attitudes toward mathematics and a belief in the importance of the teacher's ability to transmit her enthusiasm for the subject to the students, her ability 'to sell' mathematics.

Kay often reflected on methodological issues. Although in theory she favoured the use of discovery methods and frequently used them in teaching, she was aware of the potential shortcomings in their implementation. Her comments in this regard revealed a view of teaching as a non-prescriptive task in which the teacher frequently has to make difficult methodological decisions. In her view, there was no single most effective method to teach mathematics. Her judgement was that the appropriateness of a method was highly circumstantial and generally unpredictable. She explained that the difficulties experienced at times by some of the students caused her to compromise her belief in the benefits of discovery. Despite these remarks, she seemed uncompromising in her view of the importance of allowing the students the opportunity to reason for themselves.

The questions that Kay asked the students in class, her test items, and some of her interview remarks indicated that in her view mathematical understanding was evidenced in the students' ability to identify the relevant attributes of mathematical concepts; in the meaning and logic of rules, formulas, and procedures; and in their ability to integrate these into more general processes used in the solution of problems.

When discussing the students' difficulties, Kay generally attributed them to difficulties inherent in the content or to an oversight on her part in presenting it. She believed that the most common reasons for insufficient progress by the students were their weak backgrounds, misbehaviour, and inattention or lack of motivation. As an aside, Kay expressed the view that, in general, girls were less motivated than boys in taking up and persevering in challenging mathematical tasks, such as puzzles and problems. On the other hand, she believed that girls tended to be more conscientious about their school work and, consequently, in overall school performance tended to do better than boys.

An aspect of Kay's personality that seemed to contribute to the consistency between her professed conceptions and her teaching was her tendency to reflect upon her instructional actions vis-à-vis her students' apparent progress. By reflecting on her own actions and their effect on the students, she had developed her own views about the effectiveness of different instructional approaches and practices. Likewise, she had gained insights into the sources of students' difficulties in learning the content that helped her to anticipate their potential problems and to plan her lessons accordingly.

There was only one inconsistency between Kay's expressed beliefs and her teaching: her view concerning the practical value of mathematics – the instrumental role it plays in the study of science and in other fields of human endeavour – was not reflected in her teaching. Although on several occasions she referred to this in class, she did so in general and not in reference to practical applications of a specific mathematical topic.

Lynn

Lynn's teaching reflected a view of mathematics as prescriptive in nature and consisting of a static collection of facts, methods and rules necessary for finding answers to specific tasks. Her comments and responses during the interview sessions were, for, the most part, consonant with such a view. Her professed views of mathematics are summarised as follows:

- Mathematics is an exact discipline – free of ambiguity and conflicting interpretations.
- Certainty is an inherent quality of mathematical activity. The procedures and methods used in mathematics guarantee right answers.
- The content of mathematics is 'cut and dried'. Mathematics offers few opportunities for creative work.
- Mathematics came about as a result of basic needs that arise in everyday situations.
- Mathematics is predictable, absolute, and fixed. The content of mathematics has not changed much in the recent past.
- Mathematics is logical and free of emotions. Its study trains the mind to reason logically. Mathematical activity is like 'mental callisthenics'.

A view of mathematics as exact and certain prevailed in Lynn's comments. She indicated that, as a student, her enjoyment of mathematics was derived from the fact that there were right answers that provided immediate feedback on the correctness of her work. Although she repeatedly indicated that mathematics appealed to her for its exactness and certainty, she noted that it was not the mechanical application of rules and procedures that she enjoyed about mathematics. She expressed a preference for mathematical activities of the type that call for logical reasoning over others that are performed mechanically without requiring much thought – specifically computations and drill activities. Yet her teaching was characterised by a prescriptive approach in which the objective was clearly to get the students to memorise specific procedures.

Consistent with that approach was her remark that mathematics provided few opportunities for creative work. She noted that: 'Mathematics is cut and dried. This is the answer. Follow this procedure and this is the answer." These comments accurately describe the manner in which she presented the content. Although Lynn's teaching was in sharp contrast with her expressed preference for activities involving mental work, it was, nevertheless, consistent with her views of mathematics as 'cut and dried' and allowing few opportunities for creative work.

That Lynn did not teach in a manner that encouraged the students to reason and enquire may be explained by her view of the curricular content as not suitable for such activities. However, her instructional behaviour appeared to be most influenced by her low expectations of the students and her pervasive concern to get through the day's lesson in a manner that would minimise the potential for student disruptive behaviour.

Lynn's comments about mathematics during the interview sessions were brief, simplistic, and somewhat vague, reflecting a rather narrow view of the scope of mathematics and mathematical activity. In none of her comments and responses did she refer to a particular branch of mathematics or provide examples from its content to clarify and expand her remarks. The views about mathematics teaching that seemed to underlie Lynn's instructional behaviour may be summarised as follows:

- Mathematics instruction is the means for transferring information from teacher to student.
- Students learn mainly by attentively watching the teacher demonstrate procedures and methods for performing mathematical tasks and by practising those procedures.
- Students' skills in solving problems are determined by the extent to which they can: identify the type of problem, or the appropriate operation for solving it by focusing on key words; recall the appropriate method or procedure for solving it; correctly apply the method or procedure and obtain the right answer.
- The main goal of mathematics instruction is to produce students who can perform the mathematical tasks specified in the curriculum, using standard procedures or methods.

A concern with the managerial aspects of teaching appeared to influence much of Lynn's characteristic instructional behaviour. This concern appeared to take precedence over any others. As a result, she conducted class in a way that allowed as little interaction as possible. Her explanations were brief and aimed at demonstrating the procedures that the students were to use in working out the day's assignment. The bulk of the remaining class time was given to independent seatwork during which the students practised the procedures taught. Implicit in her attitude was a belief that little could be accomplished in terms of teaching and learning given the poor disposition of the students and the wide diversity in their background knowledge.

Lynn's conception of mathematical understanding, as revealed in her remarks, was akin to Mellin-Olsen's notion of 'instrumental understanding' (see also Skemp, 1978). She regarded mathematical understanding as tantamount to one's ability to follow and verbalise a specified procedure to obtain the correct answer or solution to a given task. The students' knowledge of the content was evidenced in their possession of 'fixed plans' to carry out specific tasks, and their understanding was evidenced in their ability to carry out those plans.

Lynn indicated a belief in the importance of encouraging the students to ask questions in class and in providing quick feedback on their work. The provision of quick feedback was consistent with her usual practice of having the students correct their work at the end of the class period or at the beginning of the next day's class. However, her view of the importance of encouraging the students' participation was in sharp contrast with her use of a lecture method that allowed very little interaction.

With respect to pedagogical practices that were specific to the teaching of mathematics, Lynn expressed a belief in the importance of relating the mathematical topics studied to real life situations and of providing sufficient practice to develop the students' mathematical skills. However, the first of these was not reflected in her instruction. She explained that she had once made an attempt to relate the content to a real life situation, but that it had failed because of the students' poor reading skills.

Lynn's failure to implement the majority of the practices that she identified as important or desirable in teaching mathematics may be explained by: the little time that she devoted to preparing for instruction as a result of her multiple commitments and her almost complete disillusionment with teaching; her low expectations of the students; and her fear that any departure from the daily routine would increase the potential for disruptive behaviour.

Lynn expressed a strong belief in the importance of positive teacher–student relationships. She indicated that the students' decision to do their work and their general attitude towards learning were largely dependent on the rapport between the teacher and the students. She attributed the students' difficulties in learning mathematics to their lack of attention and motivation which, for most students, she viewed as the result of their lack of maturity and their weak background in mathematics.

Lynn admitted that she seldom reflected on her actions in teaching. She described her behaviour as analogous to a tape recorder whose 'play' key is pressed and plays automatically. Her analogy accurately described her teaching behaviour.

Cross-sectional analysis

The discussion in this section looks across the teachers, examining those aspects of their conceptions and behaviour on which they differed most markedly. Three perspectives or dimensions are used to examine the differences among them:

1   Differences in the specific elements of the teachers' conceptions of mathematics and mathematics teaching.
2   Differences in the 'integratedness' of the teachers' conceptions.
3   Differences in the teachers' reflectiveness on their instructional actions, the subject matter, and their beliefs.

Each of these perspectives is treated separately, with a discussion of how such differences were manifested in teaching.

Differences in elements of the teachers' conceptions

The case studies show evidence of differences among the teachers in the specific beliefs, views, and preferences that they held regarding mathematics and its teaching. Although the complexity of the relationship between conceptions and practice defies the simplicity of cause and effect, much of the contrast in the teachers' instructional emphases may be explained by differences in their views of mathematics. For example, Jeanne viewed mathematics as a coherent subject consisting of logically interrelated topics and, accordingly, emphasised the mathematical meaning of concepts and the logic of mathematical procedures. Kay regarded mathematics primarily as a challenging subject whose essential processes were discovery and verification. Although Lynn expressed views that were somewhat contradictory, most of her remarks indicated a view of mathematics as essentially prescriptive and deterministic in nature.

Jeanne and Lynn conceived of mathematics as a rather static body of knowledge. In teaching, both teachers presented the content as a finished product. However, Jeanne used a more conceptual approach that conveyed a view of mathematics as a set of integrated and interrelated topics, whereas Lynn used a more computational approach that portrayed mathematics as a collection of more or less arbitrary rules and procedures for finding answers to specific questions. Kay, in contrast, held a more dynamic view of mathematics and believed that the best way for the students to learn it was to engage in its creative generative processes. In teaching, only Kay referred to the heuristic processes of mathematics, discussing them independently of the content being studied.

Related to the teachers' prevailing views of mathematics were their beliefs about the appropriate locus of control in the teaching process. For example, Kay's belief that students learn best by doing and reasoning about mathematics on their own was consistent with her dynamic view of mathematics. Jeanne, in contrast, believed that it was her responsibility to direct and control all classroom activities. She attempted to present the lessons in an orderly and logical sequence, avoiding digressions to discuss the students' difficulties and ideas. Lynn's view of her role in teaching was to demonstrate the procedures that the students were to use in performing the tasks in the daily assignments and to allow time for the students to work independently on them.

There was a sharp contrast among the teachers with respect to their views about what constituted evidence of mathematical understanding in the students. Jeanne was not satisfied with evidence of the students' ability to carry out procedures and obtain correct answers. In her view, it was also necessary for them to know the reasons or logic underlying the procedures and to be able to recognise relationships among the topics studied. Kay took as evidence of the students' understanding their ability to integrate their knowledge of facts, concepts, and procedures so as to find solutions to a variety of related mathematical tasks. To Lynn, mathematical understanding was tantamount to the students' ability to follow and verbalise the procedures taught to obtain correct answers. In short, each teacher's view of what constituted evidence of the students' understanding reflected her underlying conception of mathematics.

Likewise, the teachers' views about planning and preparing for instruction were related to their conception of mathematics. Because, in her view, learning mathematics was essentially learning a collection of procedures, Lynn saw little benefit in planning her lessons. Jeanne and Kay, on the other hand, regarded the careful and thorough preparation of their lessons as an essential first step towards ensuring the quality of instruction. However, Jeanne's purpose in planning was different from Kay's. Jeanne sought to delineate a logical sequential path for her explanation of the material, and she used this plan as a 'mental script' in teaching. Kay, in contrast, sought to organise the lesson's activities and to strengthen her knowledge of the topic in order to be prepared to handle the students' questions and potential difficulties. In preparing her lesson, Kay resorted to a variety of sources, including a notebook where she entered teaching notes. She acknowledged the limitations of the textbook in providing her with adequate mathematical information. Jeanne, on the other hand, generally followed the textbook closely and used no other reference materials. Lynn's planning was limited to identifying an objective from a published list of objectives and selecting worksheets that matched it.

The teachers' views and practices regarding the planning of instruction seemed to contribute in part to the flexibility they showed in teaching. Jeanne showed a marked tendency to adhere to her plan and a resistance to depart from it, whereas Kay's planning was intended to afford her greater flexibility in teaching. Lynn held a view that having lesson plans would somehow hinder her flexibility, and she offered this as one reason for not putting more effort into planning. In her case, however, flexibility seemed to take on the meaning of freedom to make whimsical decisions about the topics she would discuss, how she would discuss them, and what assignments she would count towards a grade.

Of the three teachers, only Kay showed signs of acute perceptiveness of the students' needs and difficulties during the lessons. Only she showed a tendency to capitalise on the students' unexpected remarks, incorporating them into the mainstream of the lesson or shifting the discussion to clarify the students' difficulties. In sharp contrast with Kay, Jeanne behaved as if compelled to adhere to her preconceived plan in order to ensure the thoroughness and clarity of her presentation.

A final difference was in the teachers' views about the overall cognitive goals and objectives of mathematics instruction. Jeanne regarded practical outcomes as more important than disciplinary or cultural outcomes, whereas Kay and Lynn saw the disciplinary outcomes of studying mathematics as more important than the other two. Kay's view was consistent with her instructional mode. Furthermore, it seemed to play a significant role in affecting her instructional decisions. This was not the case with Jeanne or Lynn.

Jeanne and Kay shared a concern for the development of the students' interest in mathematics and of their positive attitude toward the subject. However, Jeanne saw such affective outcomes as somehow beyond her control and as more likely to result from the students' appreciation of the qualities of mathematics than from pedagogical approaches intended to enhance their enjoyment of the lessons. Kay, on the other hand, sought to make her lessons lively and to involve the students in activities that would improve their disposition toward learning mathematics. Although Lynn, too, was concerned with the affective side of teaching, her concern was with her personal relationship with the students and their attitudes toward learning in general, and not specifically with their attitude towards mathematics.

The discussion in this section has looked at the most salient differences among the teachers in the specific views and beliefs that they held and at how such differences seemed to be related to differences in their characteristic behaviour. In the section that follows, the discussion takes on a broader perspective by focusing on differences in two general characteristic qualities of the teachers' conceptions and behaviour.

Integratedness

A criterion for inferring the integratedness of someone's beliefs and views in a given domain – the extent to which these form a coherent conceptual system, as opposed to each belief existing in isolation from the others – is the extent to which they interrelate and interact to modify each other. By this measure, if someone holds incongruous or contradictory beliefs, then it is legitimate to infer that those beliefs exist in isolation with respect to each other; inversely, if it appears that someone modifies his or her beliefs so as to resolve or avoid inconsistencies, either in thought or deed, then it is legitimate to infer that he or she is holding these beliefs in relation to one another, and hence has integrated them into a more or less coherent system. Integratedness, as it is used here, refers to a property of conceptual systems that may be thought of as the opposite of what Rokeach (1960) defined as 'isolation'. This, according to Rokeach, is manifested in a failure or even reluctance to see beliefs that are intrinsically related as interrelated. Isolation is manifested in the coexistence of logically contradictory beliefs within the belief system.

By the above criterion, Lynn did not have an integrated conceptual system with regard to mathematics. Her views of mathematics as 'cut and dried' and essentially prescriptive in nature, allowing little opportunity for creativity, appeared to be in sharp contrast with her remarks about the mental disciplinary effects of its study. Although it is conceivable to think of mathematics as having disciplinary effects on the mind regardless of whether it is learned prescriptively or otherwise, it was clear from Lynn's comments that she was referring to mathematical activities that call into play creativity and inventiveness as well as activities involving formal, logical reasoning (Rokeach, 1960, p. 199).

Though Lynn's creative-and-uncreative view was the only apparent incongruity in her beliefs about mathematics, it was a major one. The two beliefs existing in isolation allowed her to mould her teaching to administrative and displinary pressures without any felt conflict between thought and deed. Had she attempted to relate the two, either in thinking about her beliefs or in reflecting on her actions, she would have had to either modify her belief in 'creative' mathematics or change her instructional practice so as to acknowledge the constructive aspect of doing mathematics.

The bulk of the inconsistencies in Lynn's case lay in the relationship between her expressed views about mathematics teaching and her practice. The fact that so many of her views in this regard were discrepant with her instructional practice suggests the absence of an integrated conceptual system operating to modify her actions. Had she an integrated conceptual system, one would expect to have seen some evidence that she experienced conflict between, say, her attempt to individualise instruction and the fact that she consistently gave every student identical worksheets.

It is not possible to infer the extent to which Jeanne's beliefs about mathematics were integrated into a coherent system. They were certainly consistent, as was noted in the summary of her case study. However, there was no evidence that she juxtaposed beliefs in order to relate them or modified one in relation to another. The fact that they were consistent and narrow in scope, and that her teaching behaviour was largely consistent with her beliefs about mathematics, suggests that she had few occasions to feel conflict between beliefs, and hence few occasions to relate them.

Kay seemed to have a more integrated system of beliefs about mathematics and mathematics teaching than either Lynn or Jeanne. Kay often qualified her beliefs in light of her teaching experience and other views she had expressed, pointing to relationships among them and acknowledging limitations to their generalisability. Indeed, on several occasions she provided unsolicited explanations for what, on the surface, appeared to be inconsistencies between her expressed views and her teaching practice. That Kay's conceptual system, as suggested in her remarks, is more integrated than Lynn's or Jeanne's may be a result of her greater reflectiveness upon her actions, her beliefs, and the subject matter.

Reflectiveness

The case studies show that, besides differences in the integratedness of the teachers' conceptions of mathematics, they differed in their awareness of the relationships between their beliefs and their practice, the effect of their actions on the students, and the difficulties and subtleties of the subject matter. These differences seemed to be related directly to differences in the teachers' reflectiveness – in their tendency to think about their actions in relation to their beliefs, their students, and the subject matter. Lynn, for example, described her behaviour in teaching as resembling a tape recorder, admitting her lack of reflectiveness upon her actions and their effects. Jeanne's comments typically were based on general impressions of the ease or difficulty she had experienced in following her lesson plan or in eliciting correct answers from the students. Kay, on the other hand, showed a marked tendency to reflect on her actions and their effects on the students. Through reflection she had gained insights into possible sources of her students' difficulties and misconceptions, thus becoming aware of the subtleties inherent in the content.

Given that neither Jeanne nor Lynn appeared to have formed their beliefs through reflection, it is legitimate to ask from whence they came. In both cases many of their beliefs seemed to be manifestations of unconsciously held views or expressions of verbal commitment to abstract ideas that may be thought of as part of a general ideology of teaching (A case in point was both teachers' indication of a belief in the importance of encouraging student participation.) As a result of their failure to reflect on their actions in relation to their beliefs and in the face of other needs and pressures, this belief seemed to have little, if any, effect on their teaching. The same can be said about the their belief in the desirability of using a variety of approaches in presenting mathematical content.

Kay's remarks, in contrast, revealed more personalised beliefs about mathematics teaching. She seemed to have formed and modified them by reflecting on her actions and their effects. Not only was Kay more discriminating in remarks than the other teachers, but in discussing her beliefs and views she occasionally justified them in the light of her experience in teaching. Occasionally, she related a view expressed in one context to other views expressed in other contexts or to her instructional actions – something that was not observed in the other teachers. Her reflectiveness in teaching seemed to account for the integratedness of her conceptions which, in turn, seemed to contribute to the consistency between her professed views and her instructional practice.

Conclusions

This study was a first step in a line of research whose ultimate goal is to identify key factors that, because of their influence on teachers' instructional practice, may play an important role in their teaching effectiveness. By focusing on the conceptions of mathematics and mathematics teaching held by three teachers and their instructional practice, the study examined the content of the teachers' conceptions and their relationship to the teachers' instructional practice.

Consistent with the findings of Shirk (1973) and Bawden, Burke and Duffy (1979) (the study found that the teachers' conceptions are not related in a simple way to their instructional decisions and behaviour. Instead, the relationship is a complex one. Many factors appear to interact with the teachers' conceptions of mathematics and its teaching in affecting their decisions and behaviour, including beliefs about teaching that are not specific to mathematics.)

Although the complexity of the relationship between teachers' conceptions of mathematics and mathematics teaching cautions against making conclusive statements, the findings supported the original assumption that led to this investigation. (That is, teachers' beliefs, views, and preferences about mathematics and its teaching, regardless of whether they are consciously or unconsciously held, play a significant, albeit subtle, role in shaping the teachers' characteristic patterns of instructional behaviour. In particular, the observed consistency between the teachers' professed conceptions of mathematics and the manner in which they typically presented the content strongly suggests that the teachers' views, beliefs, and preferences about mathematics do influence their instructional practice.)

Teachers possess conceptions about teaching that are general and not specific to the teaching of mathematics. They also have conceptions about their students and the social and emotional make-up of their class. These conceptions appear to play a significant role in affecting instructional decisions and behaviour. For some teachers, these conceptions are likely to take precedence over other views and beliefs specific to the teaching of mathematics.

Recommendations for future research

In order to gain a better understanding of the role that teachers' conceptions of mathematics and mathematics teaching play in their instructional behaviour, much more remains to be learned about their conceptions and how these relate to their instructional practices. The present study was limited in its potential for finding answers to a number of important questions. In each case study the observations were conducted in a single class, although on a few occasion other classes were visited. Consequently, it was not possible to examine in depth whether differences in the composition of the class or the content bore any relationship to differences in the teachers' professed conceptions and in their characteristic instructional patterns. Studies are needed to examine the stability of teachers' conceptions of mathematics and mathematics teaching, specifically whether or not teachers' conceptions are likely to change with changes in grade level, the students' academic aptitude, and the mathematical content taught. Such studies may identify stable patterns of views, beliefs, and preferences held by the teachers as well as those beliefs that are most susceptible to contextual factors. In the quest to understand better how teachers' conceptions mediate and interact with contextual factors, there is a need to examine the continuing development of stable patterns of beliefs over time and under different conditions.

Another important question in need of investigation is whether or not differences in teachers' conceptions have an effect on the conceptions of mathematics of their students. Do teachers communicate their views about mathematics to their students? Are the teachers' views communicated explicitly or implicitly? If teachers can effectively communicate their views to their students, do differences in the teachers' conceptions have any effect on their students' performance and attitude?

Other issues for investigation are suggested by the following observations, which are based on the findings of the present study: some teachers apparently have more comprehensive conceptions of mathematics and mathematics teaching than others; some teachers apparently have more integrated conceptions than others, and some teachers appear to adhere to their beliefs and views with greater consistency than others. A key factor that appeared to account for the consistency between conceptions and their instructional practice was the teachers' reflectiveness. Further studies are needed to examine the relationship between teacher reflectiveness and consistency in their beliefs and views as well as between these and teaching practice.

As more is learned about teacher conceptions of mathematics and mathematics teaching, it becomes important to understand how these conceptions are formed and modified. Only then will the findings be of use to those involved in the professional preparation of teachers, attempting to improve the quality of mathematics education in the classroom.

In order to investigate the research questions listed above, in-depth studies of an anthropological, clinical, or case study nature are needed. Traditional experimental or large-scale correlational studies are not appropriate for dealing with the kinds of questions that have been posed above. Studies employing intensive audio-visual records and documentation of teachers' instructional behaviour, followed by systematic analysis and stimulated recall in informal interview settings, are necessary in order to gain access to the thoughts and mental processes that accompany the teachers' actions.

Note

1 This paper is based on the author's doctoral dissertation which was directed by Professor Thomas J. Cooney of the University of Georgia and was partly supported by a grant from San Diego State University. I wish to express my appreciation to the teachers who participated in the study and their administrators.

References

Bawden, R., Burke, S. and Duffy, G. (1979). *Teacher Conceptions of Reading and Their Influence on Instruction (Research Series No. 47)*, Institute for Research on Teaching, East Lansing, Michigan.

Begle, E. G. (1972). *Teacher Knowledge and Student Achievement in Algebra (SMSG Reports, No. 9)*, School Mathematics Study Group, Palo Alto, California.

Begle, E. G. (1978). *Critical Variables in Research in Mathematics Education*, National Council of Teachers of Mathematics, Reston, Virginia.

Clark, C. and Peterson, P. (1976). Teacher stimulated recall of interactive decisions. Paper presented at the *Annual Meeting of the American Educational Research Association*, San Francisco.

Confrey, J. (1978). Conception of mathematics survey. Unpublished manuscript, Mount Holy Oak College, South Hadley, Massachusetts.

Eisenberg, T. A. (1977). Begle revisited: Teacher knowledge and student achievement in algebra. *Journal for Research in Mathematics Education*, 8, 216–222.

Fenstermacher, G. D. (1978). A philosophical consideration of recent research on teacher effectiveness. *Review of Research in Education*, 6, 157–185.

Fenstermacher, G. D. (1980). The value of research on teaching for teaching skill and teaching manner. Paper presented at the *Annual Meeting of the American Educational Research Association*, Boston.

Jackson, P. W. (1968). *Life in Classrooms*, Holt Rinehart and Winston, New York.

MacKay, D. A. and Marland, P. (1978). Thought processes of teachers. Paper presented at the *Annual Meeting of the American Educational Research Association*, Toronto.

Morine-Dershimer, G. and Vallance, E. (1975). A *Study of Teacher and Pupil Perceptions of Classroom Interaction (Technical Report No. 75-11-6)*. Beginning Teacher Evaluation Study, Far West Laboratory, San Francisco.

National Institute of Education. (1975). *Teaching as Clinical Information Processing (Report of Panel 6)*. National Conference on Studies in Teaching, Washington, DC.

Rokeach, M. (1960). *The Open and Closed Mind*, Basic Books, New York.

Schatzman, A. and Strauss, A. (1974). *Field Research: Strategies for a Natural Sociology*, Prentice Hall, Englewood Cliffs, New Jersey.

Shavelson, R. J. and Stern, P. (1981). Research on teachers' pedagogical thoughts, judgements, decisions, and behaviour. *Review of Educational Research*, 51, 455–498.

Shirk, G. B. (1973). An examination of conceptual frameworks of beginning mathematics teachers. Unpublished doctoral dissertation, University of Illinois, Urbana-Champaign.

Shulman, L. S. and Elstein, A. S. (1975). Studies of problem solving, judgement, and decision making. In F. N. Kerlinger (ed.) *Review of Research in Education (Vol. 3)*, F. E. Peacock, Itasca, Illinois.

Skemp, R. R. (1978). Relational understanding and instrumental understanding. *Arithmetic Teacher*, **26**, 9–15.

Stake R. E. (1978). The case study method in social inquiry. *Educational Research*, 7, 5–8.

Thompson, A. G. (1982). Teachers' conceptions of mathematics and mathematics teaching: Three case studies. Unpublished doctoral dissertation, University of Georgia, Athens.

12 Setting, social class and survival of the quickest

Jo Boaler

Abstract

The question of whether students should be grouped and taught in classes according to their perceived 'ability' during their school careers is one of the most controversial issues in education. This is partly because the issues that surround setting, streaming and mixed ability teaching are relative, both to ideology and personal values. Decisions about student grouping are also of immense importance to the education of students and this importance extends beyond the development of subject understanding. In the UK moves from streaming to setting to mixed ability teaching and back again to setting can be related directly to developments in research, educational theory and the political agenda of the time. In this chapter I will present a brief overview of the theoretical and historical developments which surround student grouping. I will then aim to extend theoretical positions further by examining the way in which setting and mixed-ability teaching influenced the motivations, perceptions and eventual attainment of students in two schools.

Historical and political developments

In the 1950s almost all of the schools in the UK were streamed and students were differentiated within, as well as between, schools. Jackson (1964) conducted a survey of junior schools and found that 96 per cent were streamed and 74 per cent of the schools had placed children into ability groups by the time they were 7 years old. Jackson's study also identified some of the negative effects of streaming, including the tendency of teachers to underestimate the potential of working-class children, and the likelihood that low-stream groups would be given less experienced and less qualified teachers. This report contributed towards an increasing public awareness of the inadequacies of streamed systems. In 1967 the Plowden report recommended the abolition of all forms of ability grouping in primary schools (Bourne and Moon, 1994).

The 1970s and early 1980s witnessed a growing support for mixed-ability teaching in the UK. The extent to which this support was influenced by the results of educational research conducted at that time is salutary to reflect upon in the 1990s. Studies by Hargreaves (1967) and Lacey (1970) both explored and highlighted the ways in which setting and streaming created and maintained inequalities, particularly for working-class students. Ball (1981) also conducted a highly influential study of a school moving from setting to mixed-ability teaching that served to establish the link between setting and working-class underachievement. Schools appeared to be receptive to the results of these research studies, which fitted with the more pervasive concern for educational equality at that time. However, the 1990s have witnessed an apparent reversal of this thinking, manifested by large numbers of schools returning to policies of setting (OFSTED, 1993). This turn around does not seem to have occurred because schools have forgotten about the reported consequences of setting, or because they have ceased to be concerned about educational equality. Rather, schools appear to be responding to a set of policies, emanating directly and indirectly from the Education Reform Act (ERA), 1988, that have forced them to turn their primary attention away from equality and towards academic success, particularly for the most able.

The ERA required schools to adopt a National Curriculum and research has shown that a number of teachers regard this curriculum as incompatible with mixed ability teaching (Gewirtz *et al.*, 1993). This is partly because of its levelled nature and, related to this, the introduction of a tiered examination system. The creation of an educational 'market place', which forces schools to compete with each other for students, also means that schools have become concerned to create images that are popular with the parents of 'valued' students (Ball *et al.*, 1994). Both setting and streaming appear to be regarded as positive school attributes, particularly amongst the middle-class parents that schools generally want to attract. The establishment of league tables which position schools in order of their General Certificate of Secondary Education (GCSE) results, also forces schools to pay more attention to potential high achievers than other students. This has impacted upon setting policies via a widespread belief that setting enhances achievement for high ability students (Dar and Resh, 1986). In addition to all of these indirect pressures upon schools, primary schools received a set of government directives to group their students according to ability. In 1993 all primary schools were sent reports from both the National Curriculum Council (1993) and the Department for Education (1993) which explicitly encouraged schools to introduce or reintroduce setting. More recently Tony Blair has put on public record his intention to promote setting and actively discourage mixed ability teaching under the new Labour government (Blair, 1996).

The direct and indirect influences of political pressures have had a clear impact upon student grouping policies in schools. Unfortunately, the thinking behind such pressures does not seem to have been informed by research but by memories of times-gone-by in which setting played a predominant part in traditionalist school policies. The 'back to basics' policies of the Conservative Government and the anti-mixed-ability stance of the New Labour party derive from a widely-held opinion that setting advances achievement, particularly for high ability students. But this notion flies in the face of evidence collected from a wide variety of research studies. Indeed there is little, if any, research, anywhere in the world, that supports this notion. Slavin (1990) produced a review of all of the research that contrasted setted or streamed ability grouping with mixed ability grouping and that fulfilled certain methodological criteria. His review included the results of six randomised experiments, nine matched experiments and 14 correlational studies that compared 'homogeneous' and 'heterogeneous' ability groupings. Across the 29 studies reported, Slavin found the effects of ability grouping on achievement to be essentially zero for students of all levels and all subjects. The median effect size was +0.01 for high achievers, −0.08 for average achievers and −0.02 for low achievers; effects of this size are indistinguishable from zero. Four British studies were included in Slavin's analysis and these found no differences in achievement between students taught in mixed ability and setted classes.

A recent piece of research conducted in Israel consisted of four longitudinal studies that considered mathematical attainment and student grouping (Linchevski, 1995a, 1995b). In one of the studies Linchevski compared the eventual attainment of students in 12 setted schools with their expected attainment, based upon entry scores. This showed that ability grouping had no effect on attainment in 10 of the schools and a small *negative* effect in the other two. A second study examined the thinking and performance of similar ability students who were at the border of different ability bands and assigned to different groups. This showed that the students of similar ability assigned to different groups varied in attainment, with the students assigned to higher groups attaining more than students of a similar ability assigned to lower groups. Linchevski concluded from this that 'the achievements of students close to the cut off points are largely dependent on their being arbitrarily assigned to a lower or higher group level' (Linchevski, 1995a, p. 11). Ball (1981) also noted the arbitrary nature of success in a setted system for those students who were at or near the border of different ability bands. Another of Linchevski's studies compared the achievements of two groups of students at the same school assigned either to setted or mixed ability groups. This showed that the average scores of the most able students placed in setted groups were slightly, but not significantly, higher than the able students placed in mixed ability groups. However, the scores of students in the two lower setted groups were *significantly* lower than similar ability students in mixed ability classes. Linchevski found that low ability students in mixed ability classes coped well with tests because they were used to high demands and expectations. Other studies which have found differences in achievement between homogeneous and heterogeneous groupings have tended to replicate Linchevski's finding with some small, statistically insignificant increases for students in high sets gained at the expense of large, statistically *significant* losses, for students in low sets (Hoffer, 1992; Kerckhoff, 1986).

Consideration of the research, policies and practices that have surrounded student grouping decisions over the last 25 years reveals two clear trends that are worth remarking upon. First of all, patterns in the 1960s, 1970s and 1980s have indicated that research into ability grouping has a potentially important and formative role to play in shaping policy decisions in UK schools. Second, the number of schools that are returning to policies of setting in attempts to raise achievement reveal the extent and strength of belief in the setting process as a panacea to underachievement. It is clear from this that schools are generally unaware, or unconcerned, that research has failed to demonstrate any links between setting and high achievement. Both of these phenomena, taken alongside the achievement-based priority shift in schools, suggest that there is an urgent need for the results of setting research to reach schools and policy-makers. A review of the research that has been conducted in this field also reveals the need for new forms of research that will increase our understanding of the impact of student grouping policies upon student attainment.

Research into the effects of setting and streaming in the UK and 'tracking' in the USA has been polarised by virtue of its concerns, its methodology and its geography, and this polarisation has left important gaps in our understanding of the setting process. Research in the UK has concentrated, almost exclusively, upon the inequities of the setting or streaming system for those students who are allocated to low sets or streams. These are predominantly students who are also disadvantaged by the school system because of their race, class or gender (Hargreaves, 1967; Lacey, 1970; Ball, 1981; Tomlinson, 1987; Abraham, 1995). These research studies have used mainly qualitative, case study accounts of the experiences of students in high and low sets and streams to illustrate the ways in which curricular differentiation results in the polaris- ation of students into 'pro'- and 'anti'-school factions. Such studies, by virtue of their value-based concerns about inequality (Abraham, 1994), have paid relatively little attention to the effects of setting or streaming upon the students' development of subject understandings. In the USA on the other hand, there has been a wealth of research studies that have compared the average scores of students taught in homoge- neous and heterogeneous groups. However, these studies have tended to compare average group scores rather than consider the responses of individual students to setting. The quantitative nature of these studies has also meant that they have not considered the ways in which setting influences achievement or the processes by which it takes effect. In the following report of a three-year research study I hope to bridge these gaps, both by combining qualitative and quantitative methods to consider the responses of students to setted and mixed-ability teaching, as well as by consid- ering the differential ways in which setted and mixed-ability teaching impacted upon the achievement of individual students.

The research study

Research methods

The issues reported in this chapter emerged as part of wider, ethnographic (Eisenhart, 1988) case studies of two schools. The aim of the studies was to monitor the learning of students who experienced 'traditional' and 'progressive' approaches to the teaching of mathematics. Particular attention was paid to the influence of the students' teaching approach upon the degree to which students could use mathematics in new, unusual or out-of-school situations (see Boaler, 1996, 1997a, 1997b, 1988). The research involved a longitudinal study of a year group of students in each of two schools as they moved from Year 9 to Year 11. In one of the schools there were approx- imately 200 students in the year group, in the other school there were approximately 110. A variety of qualitative and quantitative methods were employed in the study. In order to learn about the students' day-to-day experiences of mathematics I observed approximately 100 lessons in each school, interviewed approximately 40 students in each school, and gave questionnaires to all of the case study students each year. I also performed a number of secondary analyses such as recording time-on-task and elic- iting constructs (Fransella, 1978) from teachers. To learn about the students' devel- oping understanding of mathematics I performed a wide range of assessments of the students and analysed their school-based assessments and their GCSE performance. All of the qualitative and quantitative methods were used to inform each other in a continual process of comparison and re-analysis. Interviews and field notes were analysed using open coding (Strauss, 1987) and observation data were collected and analysed using a grounded theory approach (Glaser and Strauss, 1967). Extensive use of triangulated data was made in the formation of emergent theories. As the study developed I used progressive focusing to form and shape new research ideas, in response to events occurring in the field. Setting was not an initial focus of the research study but it quickly emerged as a major and significant factor for the students; one that influenced their ideas, their responses to mathematics and their eventual achievement.

In Year 11, 24 students from each school were interviewed about mathematics lessons, and the qualitative analysis that forms the first part of this chapter draws heavily upon the students' perceptions about setting, which were reported in these interviews. The students were not specifically interviewed about setting and the 24 students were chosen because they held a range of positive and negative views about mathematics lessons.

The two schools

Amber Hill

Amber Hill is a mixed, 11–18 comprehensive school located in an area of social disadvantage. The students who attend the school are mainly white and working class. In my case study year group there were approximately 200 students; 68 per cent of these were classified as working class, using the Office of Population Censuses and Surveys (OPCS) classification of fathers' occupations; 20 per cent were from single-parent families; 47 per cent were girls and 17 per cent were from ethnic minorities. When the students entered the school they took National Foundation for Educational Research (NFER) tests; the results of these tests showed that 75 per cent of the students were below the national average for the examination. Amber Hill is located on the edge of a large city and recently became grant-maintained, largely due to the wishes and campaigns of the headteacher. The school is run by an 'authoritarian' (Ball, 1987) headteacher whose commitment to traditionalism is evident throughout the school. In the classrooms students can generally be seen sitting quietly in rows watching the blackboard, whilst the corridors display icons of traditionalism.

Amber Hill uses setting as a grouping policy to greater or lesser extents within different subject departments. The mathematics department used to operate a fairly loose system of setting whereby they would divide students into three or four bands at the beginning of Year 9. One year prior to the beginning of my research they were forced to change this policy at the direction of the head; they now place students into one of eight or nine sets at the beginning of Year 9. The teachers decide upon the set students go into based upon their NFER test scores and their work in Years 7 and 8. The school reviews the performance of students in different sets annually, with the aim of moving students who are inappropriately placed. However, it is rare for more than two or three students to move sets in any one year. There are eight mathematics teachers at Amber Hill and they are all in favour of some form of setting. Most of the teachers in the department had never experienced mixed-ability mathematics teaching beyond Years 7 and 8. This is fairly typical for a department of mathematics; a recent OFSTED survey showed that 94 per cent of schools use setting in the upper secondary years for mathematics *(The Guardian,* 8 June 1996).

The Amber Hill mathematics department was an interesting place to consider the impact of setting because the students experienced both mixed-ability and setted approaches within the same school for mathematics, at different times. This gave the students important insights into the advantages and disadvantages of the two approaches. At Amber Hill mathematics was taught using the SMP scheme. As part of this scheme the students worked through individualised booklets, at their own pace, in Years 7 and 8, in mixed ability groups. In Year 9 they changed to a setted textbook system. There was no departmental policy that dictated the way that teachers should operate in Years 9 to 11, but all of the teachers used the same approach. They stood at the front of the class and explained methods and procedures from the blackboard for 10–20 minutes; they then set the students questions to work through in their textbooks. At periodic intervals they would stop the students and check answers, then move them on to the next exercise. This process ensured that the students all moved at a similar pace through their textbooks. Despite reports in the press, there is evidence that this traditional, textbook model of teaching is still predominant in secondary mathematics departments in the UK (OFSTED, 1993).

In the qualitative analysis that forms the first part of this chapter, 20 out of the 24 students interviewed were taken from the top four out of eight sets (because of the wider aims of the case studies). Their views about setting may not therefore be considered as representative of students from across the setting spectrum. The other four students were taken from set seven.

Phoenix Park

Phoenix Park school was chosen as a contrast to Amber Hill because the students who attended the two schools were very similar but the schools offered different and, in many respects, opposing approaches. Phoenix Park is also located in an area of social disadvantage and most of the students who attend the school are white and working class. Comparisons of the case study students attending the two schools showed there to be no significant differences between the cohorts in terms of social class, ability (measured on NFER tests), ethnicity or gender. At Phoenix Park 79 per cent of the students were classified as working class, 23 per cent were from single-parent families, 42 per cent were girls and 11 per cent were from ethnic minorities. In NFER tests, which the students took on entry to their school, 76 per cent of the students were below the national average for the examination. Phoenix Park is a 13–18 upper school. Prior to joining Phoenix Park all of the students had attended middle schools that used the SMP scheme. This meant that like the Amber Hill students, they had all learned mathematics through SMP booklets for the two years prior to the beginning of my three-year research period. At this point the Amber Hill students changed to setted groups and textbook teaching, the Phoenix Park students changed to mixed ability groups and a project-based teaching approach. There were approximately 110 students in the case study year group at Phoenix Park.

In stark contrast to Amber Hill, Phoenix Park is an extremely 'progressive' school. The staff believe in giving the students freedom, independence, and choice. The mathematics teachers allow the students to work unsupervised in separate rooms if they want to, because students are meant to be responsible for their own learning. In mathematics lessons the students work in mixed ability groups from the beginning of Year 9, when they start the school, to halfway through Year 11. At this point the students are moved into one of three 'examination' groups according to the level of examination they have been entered for. In mathematics lessons at Phoenix Park the students work on open-ended projects at all times – the department does not use any textbooks or published materials. The teachers generally give the students open starting points, such as 'what is the maximum sized fence that can be built out of 36 gates?' The students are then encouraged to go away and work on this information, develop questions of their own, extend the problem and use mathematics to answer their questions, for approximately three weeks. At the end of this time they complete a description of the activities they have worked on and their results. Discipline is very low key in Phoenix Park and the teachers show little overt concern to keep the students 'on task'. Lessons are extremely relaxed and it is fairly typical for at least one-third of the students to be off-task at any one point in time during lessons.

In the analysis that follows I will mainly concentrate upon the students at Amber Hill and their responses to setting. At times I will refer to the differences between the students at the two schools in relation to their grouping arrangements, but there is not enough space to analyse Phoenix Park in the same depth as Amber Hill in this chapter. (For further information on Phoenix Park and the students' overall responses to a 'progressive' approach, see Boaler, 1997a.)

Research results

The students' responses to setting

At an early stage of my case study at Amber Hill I became aware that certain features of the students' mathematical experiences were causing some students to become disaffected about mathematics and, subsequently, to underachieve. A number of these features were intrinsically linked to the setted nature of their learning environments. I have grouped the complaints of the students which relate to setting into four main areas which, inevitably, overlap in places. I will now discuss each of these areas in turn, starting with the one that seemed to have the most impact upon the largest number of students.

Working at a fixed pace

Probably the main reason that teachers place students into sets in mathematics is so that they can reduce the spread of 'ability' within the class, enabling them to teach mathematical methods and procedures to the entire group, as a unit. Mathematics departments that use class teaching tend, therefore, to put students into setted groups, whilst mathematics departments that use individualised schemes generally teach to mixed ability groups. This link between classroom pedagogy and classroom grouping is not inevitable, but it is the prevalent model in the UK. Hence, OFSTED data showing that 94 per cent of secondary schools use setting for mathematics in the upper years fit with their reports that the majority of these lessons involve students listening to the teacher and then working through exercises. In this analysis I have therefore linked working at a fixed pace with setting, because these two features tend to go hand-in-hand in the majority of UK mathematics classrooms:

> It's good [setting] because you're putting similar abilities together. I mean it's easier to pitch your lesson, to pitch the work at them, to teach them all together, you know, from the front, as a class.
>
> (Edward Losely, mathematics teacher, Amber Hill)

There is evidence that the way in which teachers proceed in setted lessons is by teaching towards a reference group of students (Dahllöff, 1971). Teachers generally pitch their lessons at the middle of the group, on the basis that faster or slower students will be able to adjust to the speed at which lessons are delivered. At Amber Hill many of the students were unable to make this adjustment and when they changed in Year 9 from working at their own pace, to working at a fixed pace, many students became disaffected and started to underachieve. In interviews conducted in Years 9, 10 and 11, working at the pace of the class was a major complaint for almost all of the students and one that they variously related to disaffection, boredom, anxiety and underachievement. Many of the students were unhappy because they felt that the pace of lessons was too fast, which often caused them to become anxious about work and to fall behind; this then caused them to become more anxious. This response was particularly prevalent amongst the top set girls and I have written elsewhere about the marked underachievement of many of these students in response to setting arrangements (Boaler, 1997a, 1997b). However, the anxiety caused by fixed paced lessons did not only prevail amongst the top set students. In the following extracts the students all relate the fixed pace of lessons to a loss of understanding:

> A: I preferred the booklets.
> S: Yeah 'cos you just get on with it don't you?
> A: Yeah, work at your own pace. You don't have to keep up with the others.
> JB: Do you feel that now?
> A: In a way because if you don't do all the work, then you get left behind and you don't understand it.
>
> (Suzy and Anna, Amber Hill, Year 11, set 2)

Well in the first two years you worked at your own pace, this last year or two you got to do it all, with everyone else at the same time, at the same speed, and if we're too slow or something, you've got to be able to do it, *quickly,* even if you've got it wrong, just to catch up with everyone else, which is bad, 'cos you don't learn if you're just rushing and trying to make sure you get it done just so you don't get in trouble and you can catch up with everyone else.

(Lindsey, Amber Hill, Year 11, set 3)

The majority of students interviewed related their reservations about setting and class teaching to what they perceived as a resultant loss of understanding. However, whilst some students, who were generally girls, complained about the fast pace of lessons, other students in the same groups linked their lack of understanding to the fact that lessons were too slow. These were usually boys:

Yeah, if the work's easier, like the pace, it's normally quite fast and the teacher will set us questions we have to get up to ... we'll do that and if it's hard it will take longer, but if we find it easy we'll get it done quicker but there will still be people that are struggling behind, which means you have to go back ... and go over it again. It's a waste of time.

(Colin, Amber Hill, Year 11, set 1)

M: It's silly now, it's just, most of the people slow the class down, it gets more boring.
C: You don't learn as much.
M: Like people laze around, when they've completed the work ... say we've completed the work and we can go further up the book, we have to do that piece of work and then stop, and wait for the others to catch up and then people laze around.

(Chris and Marco, Amber Hill, Year 11, set 4)

The fact that some students complained about the pace of lessons being too fast, whilst other students in the same classes complained about lessons being too slow seems to reveal an important limitation of a class-taught approach. For the teacher it shows how difficult it is to teach a group at the same pace, even when they are supposed to be of 'homogeneous' ability. Amber Hill divided the students into eight sets which should produce relatively little variation amongst students in the same set. The complaints of the different students at Amber Hill may also reflect the fact that the ability of a student does not necessarily indicate the pace they feel comfortable working at, although this is an assumption that class teaching to setted groups is predicated upon.

Despite the variation amongst girls and boys in their preferences for the pace of lessons, they were clearly united in their view that a fixed pace of lessons decreased their opportunities for learning. None of the girls or boys interviewed expressed a preference for mixed ability lessons because they allowed them to do less work; the students were clear that they preferred mixed ability groups because working at their own pace gave them a greater access to understanding:

JB: What did you think about the booklets you used in the first two years here?
S: I thought they were good.
L: I dunno if the booklets were good – or if it was working at your own pace.

JB: Do you like going at your own pace?

S: Yes, definitely.

L: Yes, but it's not like we go slow if we go at our own pace, it's not that we go slow, we don't think, oh going at our own pace, let's do one sum a lesson type of thing.

S: It's good, because you know if you understand something you can move on.

L: And if you don't you can spend more time on it. You spend more time on it, but she wants to move on, so you just leave that bit and go on to the next bit even though you don't know the bit before and you don't understand the chapter.

(Sara and Lola, Amber Hill, Year 11, set 3)

The view that working at a pace which was determined by the teacher diminished understanding was prevalent both amongst students who found lessons too fast and students who found lessons too slow. But this did not only affect unusual students; almost all of the students seemed to find some lessons, or some parts of lessons, either too fast or too slow:

C: I felt like I was learning – you feel you was learning more, 'cause the teacher would help you – if you went up to him and showed him the book he would help you and I felt I learned more in the first and second year, but in the fourth and fifth year it's more slow and like if you finish first you have to wait for the others, or if you're behind you have to work fast because everyone else is finished.

M: And that's why I don't like maths any more 'cause I can't go at my own pace.

(Chris and Marco, Amber Hill, Year 11, set 4)

The pace that students felt comfortable working at seemed to be determined by a wide range of factors. These included the difficulty of individual topics, the students' own prior experience, individual preferences and, of course, their feelings on that day.

The fact that Amber Hill used setting did not mean that the teachers had to teach students as a group at a fixed pace, but for many teachers the only reason for establishing setted groups is to enable teaching from the front to whole classes. There would be very little point in setting students, given the known disadvantages this confers upon low set students, if the students then worked at their own pace, which they could do in mixed ability groups. At Amber Hill the main purpose of setted groups was also the main source of disaffection for the students, as well as the factor that almost all students linked with diminished learning opportunities and underachievement.

The students' second major complaint about setting was also related to class teaching, but it extended beyond this. A major concern of significant numbers of students interviewed was the pressure that they felt was created by the existence and form of their setted environments.

Pressure and anxiety

Various research studies have shown that the presence or absence of mathematical anxiety is an important determining factor in a student's response to mathematics (see, for example, Buxton, 1981). Women and girls, in particular, have been shown to be prone to mathematical anxiety (Dweck, 1986; Fennema and Leder, 1990) and this has been shown to have serious negative consequences for their achievement (Fennema and Sherman, 1977, 1978; Hart, 1989). At Amber Hill mathematical anxiety was commonplace, particularly amongst girls. In a questionnaire given to the students in Year 9, significantly more boys than girls thought that they were good at mathematics ($\chi2$ = 18.04, 2 df, $p < 0.001$, n = 163), whereas at Phoenix Park there were no significant differences between the attitudes of girls and boys. These patterns continued throughout Years 9, 10 and 11 at the two schools. In interviews, the girls at Amber Hill linked their anxiety not to the intrinsic nature of mathematics, but to the pressure created by setted classes. Some of this pressure derived from the need to work at a pace set by the teacher:

> I don't mind maths but when he goes ahead and you're left behind, that's when I start dreading going to maths lessons.
>
> (Helen, Amber Hill, Year 11, set 1)

> I mean she's rushing through and she's going 'we've got to finish this chapter by today' but I'm still on C4 and I don't know what the hell she's chatting about and I haven't done any of it, 'cause I don't know it, she hasn't explained it properly she just says 'take this off, take that off' and she puts the answers up and like – what? I don't know what she's doing.
>
> (Karen, Amber Hill, Year 11, set 3)

Another aspect of the students' anxiety related to a more reflective pressure. This concerned the competitive standard that students believed they had to live up to within their setted groups:

> H: You're expected to know more.
> M: They expect too much, yeah … you should know this.
> H: You should know that …
> M: You're the top set.
>
> (Helen and Maria, Amber Hill, Year 11, set 1)

The creation of groups intended to be homogeneous in ability caused many students to feel that they were constantly being judged alongside their peers:

> L: I preferred it when we were in our tutor groups.
> JB: Why?
> L: 'Cause you don't worry so much and feel under so much pressure then, 'cause now you've got people of the same standard as you and they can do the same stuff and sometimes they can do it and you can't and you think oh I should do that and then you can't … but if you're in your tutor group you're all a different status … it's different.
>
> (Lindsey, Amber Hill, Year 11, set 3)

One of the reasons commonly given for the formation of setted groups is that the competition created by setted classes helps to raise achievement. For some students this was probably true:

> You have to keep up and it actually, in a way it motivates you, you think if I don't do this then I'll get behind in the class and get dropped down a set.
>
> (Gary, Amber Hill, Year 11, set 3)

However, of the 24 students interviewed in Year 11, only one student, Gary, gave any indication that the competition and pressure created by their setted environments enhanced motivation or learning. At Amber Hill setting was a high profile concept and the students were frequently reminded of the set they were in. This served as a constant standard against which they were judged. The students gave many indications that this continual pressure was not conducive to their learning. Undoubtedly the most intense pressure was experienced by top set students and at Amber Hill placement in the top set appeared to have serious negative consequences for the learning and achievement of students (Boaler, 1997a, 1997b). What I am attempting to show here is not that the pressure of setting is bad for all students, but that individual students respond differently to setted situations. This individual variation in response is frequently overlooked within setting debates. Some students, even those placed in high sets, are disadvantaged because of setting and at Amber Hill there was much evidence that the students who were negatively affected were not the least able in the setted groups. In set 1 for example, the students who experienced the most difficulties in response to setting were originally the highest attainers in the group. At the end of Year 8, immediately before the students were setted, Carly and Lorna attained the highest and second highest NFER scores in the school. At the end of Year 11 these two students attained the lowest GCSE grades in set 1 (grade E).

> JB: Can you think of some good and bad things about being in set 1?
> L: I can think of the bad things.
> C: I agree.
> JB: OK, what are the bad things?
> L: You're expected to know everything, even if you're not sure about things.
> C: You're pushed hard.
> L: He expects you to work all the time at a high level.
> C: It makes me do less work, they expect too much of me and I can't give it, so I just give up.
>
> (Carly and Lorna, Amber Hill, Year 11, set 1)

It appeared from a variety of data sources in the two case studies that a student's success in their set had relatively little to do with their ability, but a great deal to do with their personal preferences for learning pace and style. These preferences, in turn, seemed to relate to the sex of students. The vast majority of students who reported in interviews that they were disaffected by a fixed pace of lessons were girls. Other data sources, that I shall discuss later, show that social class also had a significant impact upon the students' responses to setting.

The third major complaint of the students was particularly prevalent amongst students outside of set 1, and this related to the way in which setting limited their potential opportunities and achievements.

Restricted opportunities

In interviews, many of the students at Amber Hill expressed clear feelings of anger and disappointment about what they felt to be unfair restrictions upon their potential mathematical achievement. The students, from a variety of sets and ability ranges, cared about their achievement, they wanted to do well and they were prepared to put effort into their work, but many felt that they had been cheated by the setting system:

> L: The thing I don't like about maths is ... I know because we're in set 4 you can only get a D.
> S: Yeah, you can't get any higher than a D.
> L: So you don't do as much.
> S: Yes you could work really hard and all you can get is a D and you think, well what's the point of working for a D?
>
> (Lindsey and Sacha, Amber Hill, Year 11, set 4)

> I'm in set 3 and the highest grade I can get is a C ... it's silly because you can't, maybe I wanted to do A level, 'cause maths is so useful as an A level, but I can't because ... I can get a C if I really push it, but what's the point?
>
> (Alan, Amber Hill, Year 11, set 3)

A number of the students explicitly linked the restrictions imposed by the set they were in to their own disaffection and underachievement. They reported that they simply could not see any point in working in mathematics for the grades that were available to them:

> JB: How would you change maths lessons? If you could do it any way you wanted what would you do?
> C: Well, work at your own pace and different books.
> JB: How would working at your own pace help?
> M: Well it would encourage people more wouldn't it? They'd know they're going for an A wouldn't they? Like what's the point of me and Chris working for a D? Why are we gonna work for a D?
> C: I'm not saying it's not good a D, but ...
> M: It's *not* good, it's crap, they said to us if we get 100 per cent in our maths we're gonna get a D, well what's the point?
>
> (Chris and Marco, Amber Hill, Year 11, set 4)

These extracts raise questions about the accuracy of the students' assessments of their own potential but, in many ways, the degree of realism in the students' statements is irrelevant. For what the students clearly highlight is the disaffection they felt because of their setting arrangements. The students may have been unrealistic, but the disaffection they experienced because of their restricted attainment was real:

> S: We're more to the bottom set so we're not expected to enjoy it.
>
> JB: Why not?
>
> S: I'm not putting, I'm not saying 'cause we're in the lower set we're not expected to enjoy it … it's just … you're looking at a grade E and then you put work in towards that … you're gonna get an E and there's nothing you can do about it and you feel like … what's the point in trying, you know? What's the difference between an E and a U?
>
> JB: How did you feel about maths before you were put into sets?
>
> K and S: Better.
>
> (Keith and Simon, Amber Hill, Year 11, set 7)

These feelings of despondency were reported from students in set 2 downwards and many of the students suggested that the limits placed upon their attainment had caused them to give up on mathematics. The students believed that they had been restricted, unfairly and harmfully, by their placement into sets.

The fourth and final response that prevailed amongst students primarily affected the students in low sets and this related to the way in which the sets were chosen.

Setting decisions

Many of the students interviewed did not feel that the set that they had been put into was a fair reflection of their ability:

> I was alright in the first year, but like me and my teacher had a few problems, we didn't get on, that's why I think it's really better to work really hard in the first years, 'cause that's when you've got a chance to prove a point, you know, that you're good and then in the second year you'll end up in a good set and from then on you can work. But me in the first year, I got dumped straight into the bottom set. And I was like huh? what's going on? you know? and they didn't teach me anything there and I was trying hard to get myself up, but I couldn't, 'cause once you're in the bottom it's hard to get up in maths. That's another bad thing about it, and other people now, there's people now in like higher sets man and they just know nothing, they know nothing.
>
> (Simon, Amber Hill, Year 11, set 7)

Some of the students, particularly the boys, felt the set they were in reflected their behaviour more than their ability:

> Yes, but they're knocking us down on our behaviour, like I got knocked down from second set to bottom set and now, because they've knocked me down, they've thrown me out of my exams and I know for a fact that I could've got in the top A, B or C.
>
> (Michael, Amber Hill, Year 11, set 7)

Tomlinson (1987) provides evidence that the behaviour of students can influence the examination groups which they are put into and some of the Amber Hill students were convinced that their behaviour, rather than their ability, had determined their mathematics set, which in turn had partly determined their examination grade.

The impact of setting

The students at Amber Hill were coherent in their views about setting. The 24 students interviewed in Year 11 were in general agreement about the disadvantages they perceived and all but one of the students interviewed expressed strong preferences for mixed-ability teaching. This was because setting, for many of the students, meant one or more of:

- a lack of understanding when the pace of lessons was too fast;
- boredom when the pace of lessons was too slow;
- anxiety, created by the competition and pressure of setted environments;
- disaffection related to the restricted opportunities they faced;
- and perceived discrimination in setting decisions.

Twenty-four students represents only 12 per cent of the year group at the school, but these students were chosen because they varied in their views towards mathematics lessons. The remarkable consistency in their views about setting and class teaching seems unlikely, therefore, to be a product of the particular group chosen. It was also clear from the students that setting did not have a single influence that affected all students in the same way. Some students were probably advantaged by setted lessons, but others had been negatively affected by processes of setting. In almost all cases the disadvantages students reported concerned their learning of mathematics and their subsequent achievement. Nevertheless, some students also experienced other negative repercussions:

> K: You walk around the school and you get people in the top set and you get people in our set and if you walk round the school and you're talking about maths, they put you down because you're not in that set, it's like …
> S: They're dissing you and that.
> K: They're saying you haven't got the ability they've got.
> (Keith and Simon, Amber Hill, Year 11, set 7)

Despite the labelling associated with setting, the major concern for the majority of students interviewed was the consequences setting might have for their achievement. In the next section I shall present various forms of data that give some indication of the way in which the students' achievement was affected by their placement in sets.

Setting and achievement

The students' different responses to setting, given in interviews, indicate that the success or failure of a student in a setted group related to their preferred learning style and their responses to competition, pressure and opportunity (or lack of it). Various quantitative indicators add support to the idea that success was strongly related to factors other than ability. For example, at Amber Hill, there was a large disparity between the attainment of students when they entered setted lessons and their success in GCSE examinations at the end. This may be demonstrated through a consideration of the students' scores on their mathematics NFER tests at the end of Year 8 and the number of correct marks they attained on their GCSE mathematics examinations at the end of Year 11[1]. This information is provided for both of the schools, giving an insight into the different implications of setted and mixed-ability teaching for students' achievement.

At Amber Hill a high correlation would be expected between NFER results at the end of Year 8 and eventual achievement, because the students were setted largely on the basis of their NFER results and, once inside their sets, the range of their attainment would be severely restricted. At Phoenix Park a smaller correlation would be expected, because prior to their NFER tests the students had attended fairly traditional middle schools. At Phoenix Park they experienced considerable freedom to work if and when they wanted to in lessons which, combined with the openness of the school's teaching approach, may have meant that some students would not perform at

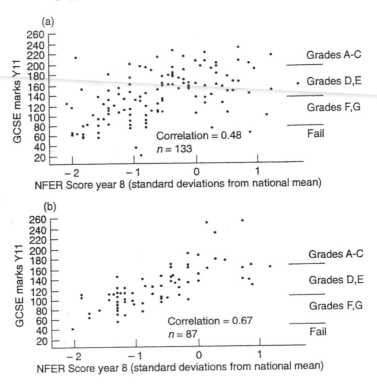

Figure 12.1 Relationship between mathematics GCSE marks and NFER entry scores at (a) Amber Hill and (b) Phoenix Park

Note
The actual GCSE *marks* at the two schools are not directly comparable because the schools used different examination boards, but GCSE grades are.

Table 12.1 Means and standard deviations (SD) of GCSE marks and NFER scores

	GCSE		NEFR	
	Amber Hill	Phoenix Park	Amber Hill	Phoenix Park
Mean	130.8	132.9	−0.56	−0.41
SD	47.9	42.4	0.83	0.74

the end of Year 11 as would be expected from their performance at the end of Year 8. However, a comparison of performance, before and after setting and mixed-ability teaching at the two schools is shown in Figure 12.1 and in Table 12.1.

The figure displays an interesting phenomenon. It shows that at Amber Hill there was a relatively small relationship between the students' attainment in Year 8 and their eventual success, after three years of working in setted lessons, demonstrated by a correlation of 0.48. This meant that some students did well, even though indications in Year 8 were that they were not particularly able and some students did badly, despite being high achievers at the end of Year 8. At Phoenix Park, where students were taught in mixed ability groups and given considerably more freedom, there was a correlation of 0.67 between initial and eventual attainment. This correlation is significantly larger than the correlation at Amber Hill ($r_1 = 0.67$, $n_1 = 87$, $r_2 = 0.48$, $n_2 = 133$, $p < 0.05$). These results support the idea that once inside a setted group a number of factors, that are relatively independent of initial attainment, influence a student's success.

A second interesting phenomenon was revealed at Amber Hill through a consideration of the relationship between social class and the set students were placed into. This relationship could be examined at both schools because the students were put into setted examination groups at Phoenix Park in the middle of Year 11. Partial correlations from the two schools enable the impact of 'ability' (measured via NFER tests) and social class upon the sets students were given, to be considered. These showed that at Amber Hill the correlation between the social class of students and the set they were placed into was 0.25, after ability was controlled for, with students of a 'low' social class being more likely to appear in a low set. A similar analysis of partial correlations at Phoenix Park showed that there was a small, negative correlation of −0.15 between social class and examination group, after the effect of ability was taken out. This showed that at the end of their mixed ability teaching experiences there was a small tendency for students of a 'lower' social class to be placed into a higher examination group at Phoenix Park. At Amber Hill there was a significant tendency for students of a 'lower' social class to be placed into a lower set, irrespective of their mathematical 'ability', as measured on the NFER tests that were used as indicators of the set students should be placed within.

Further insight into the possibility of class bias at Amber Hill is demonstrated by locating individuals at the two schools who 'under' or 'over' achieved, in relation to their initial ability scores. At both schools I located the most extreme 20 per cent of students, represented by the outliers on the graph. At Amber Hill this amounted to 22 students,

Table 12.2 Amber Hill overachievers

	Social class					
	Middle class			Working class		
	1	*2*	*3*	*4*	*5*	*6*
Girls			1			1
Boys		4	1	1		

Table 12.3 Amber Hill underachievers

	Social class					
	Middle class			Working class		
	1	*2*	*3*	*4*	*5*	*6*
Girls			2	4	1	2
Boys	1			5		

who were made up of seven 'over' achievers and 15 'under' achievers. Closer examination of these students gives the sex and class profiles shown in Tables 12.2 and 12.3.

Tables 12.2 and 12.3 show that amongst the overachievers there was a ratio of 3:1 of middle-class to working-class students, who were mainly boys. Amongst the underachievers there was a ratio of 1:4 of middle-class to working-class students, made up of roughly even numbers of girls and boys. These outliers represent only a small proportion of the students at Amber Hill but they show quite clearly that those students who did better than would be expected from their initial ability scores tended to be middle-class boys, whereas those who did worse tended to be working-class students (of either sex). It is interesting to contrast this with the most extreme 20 per cent of Phoenix Park students ($n = 18$). These students did not 'under' or 'over' achieve to the same extent as the Amber Hill students, as can be seen from Figures 12.1a and 12.1b.

Table 12.4 Phoenix Park overachievers

	Social class					
	Middle class			Working class		
	1	*2*	*3*	*4*	*5*	*6*
Girls					1	
Boys		1	1	4		

Table 12.5 Phoenix Park underachievers

	Social class					
	Middle class			Working class		
	1	2	3	4	5	6
Girls	1	2		1		
Boys	1	1		2	1	2

However, the students who were nearest to the edges of the graph did not reveal any class polarisation in achievement at Phoenix Park, as shown in Tables 12.4 and 12.5.

Tables 12.4 and 12.5 show that amongst the overachievers at Phoenix Park there was a ratio of 2:5 of middle-class to working-class students. Amongst the underachievers there was a ratio of 5:6 of middle-class to working-class students. The overachievers at Phoenix Park were generally working-class boys, whereas the underachievers were roughly equal numbers of middle-class and working-class girls and boys.

What these results indicate is that at Amber Hill the disparity between initial mathematical capability and eventual achievement shown in Figure 12.1 is partly created by a small number of mainly middle-class students who achieved more than would be expected and a relatively large number of mainly working-class students who achieved less than would be expected. Similar evidence of class polarisation is not apparent at Phoenix Park. This quantitative analysis enables social class to be added to the list of factors that appeared to influence achievement in setted lessons. It also re-establishes the notion that success in a setted environment had little to do with 'ability'. The influence of class bias over setting decisions is well documented (Ball, 1981; Tomlinson, 1987) and some of the students gave some indications, in interviews, about the way that this process may have taken effect. In the following extract Simon, a working-class student, talked about the way in which he opted out of the 'game' of impressing the mathematics teacher:

> Yes and in a way right, when I came to the school, I was scared to ask questions man, so I just thought, no forget it man.
>
> (Simon, Amber Hill, Year 11, set 7)

This withdrawal because of Simon's fear probably served to disadvantage him when setting decisions were made. The disproportionate allocation of working-class students to low sets shown by the correlations at Amber Hill would certainly have restricted the achievement of working-class students. However, it seems likely that the social class of students may also have affected the way in which individuals responded to the experiences of setted lessons. In the next section I will attempt to draw together the various results that have been reported so far, in order to illuminate the different factors that influence a student's achievement in setted and mixed ability groups. Before doing so I would like to consider the overall achievement of the students at the two schools.

Table 12.6 GCSE mathematics results shown as percentages of students in each year group

	A*	A	B	C	D	E	F	G	Fail	Non-entry	n
Phoenix Park (mixed ability)	1	2	1	8	11	24	24	17	7	5	115
Amber Hill (setted)	0	1	2	9	11	18	17	12	13	16	217

In any debate about setted and mixed ability teaching it is important to consider the achievement of students. The approaches of Amber Hill and Phoenix Park schools differed in many important ways but it is important to note that the setted classes at Amber Hill did not achieve better results than the students in the mixed ability classes at Phoenix Park, despite the increased time spent 'working' by the Amber Hill students (see Boaler, 1997a, 1998). The students who learned mathematics in an open approach in mixed ability classes achieved significantly more A–G grades ($\chi^2 = 12.5$, 1 df, $p < 0.001$), despite the comparability of the two cohorts of students on entry to their schools. It is also important to note that this did not reflect simple differences in teacher effectiveness. There is not the space to expand upon this here, but there were clear forms of evidence, reported in Boaler (1997a), that the general enhanced success of the students at Phoenix Park related to their open, 'progressive' models of teaching, combined with the increased 'opportunity to learn' (Burstein, 1993, p. 304) that was provided by mixed ability classes.

The superior performance of the Phoenix Park students was due partly to the effectiveness of the school's open teaching approach, but the negative responses to setting reported by students in low and high sets at Amber Hill also contributed to the differences in achievement at the two schools. Indeed, part of the reason that significantly more Amber Hill students failed the GCSE examination could be related directly back to the fact that the students were placed in low sets and this had caused them to give up on their mathematics education (see Table 12.6).

Discussion and conclusion

At Phoenix Park school the students experienced a great deal of freedom to work when they wanted to work and talk or wander about when they did not. The students were grouped in mixed ability classes; the high ability students were not placed in high sets that would 'push' them, the low ability students were not placed in sets in which teachers could 'concentrate upon their individual needs'. At the end of three years of this relaxed and open approach the students who did well were those of a high ability. Students who did exceptionally well, compared with their entry scores, were mainly working-class students. Those who did exceptionally badly were both working-class and middle-class students.

In all of these respects Amber Hill differed from Phoenix Park and although ability grouping was not the main focus of my research study, there were a number of clear indications from various forms of data, that at Amber Hill:

- social class had influenced setting decisions, resulting in disproportionate numbers of working-class students being allocated to low sets;
- significant numbers of students experienced difficulties working at the pace of the class, resulting in disaffection and reported underachievement;
- students became disillusioned and demotivated by the limits placed upon their achievement within their sets; and
- some students responded badly to the pressure and competition of setted lessons, particularly girls and students in top sets (Boaler, 1997a, 1997b).

The two schools reported in this study differed in a number of ways that all contributed, to greater or lesser extents, towards the students' achievement (see Boaler, 1997a).

However, the complexity that is inherent in the learning process should not detract from the clarity of the sentiments offered by the students about their setting experiences, or the clear patterns relating class polarisation and setting decisions at Amber Hill. It could be argued that the setting system at Amber Hill would have been more effective with greater flexibility between sets, but I am not convinced that this is true. This is because there will always be students who are located at the extremes of sets, no matter how much movement between sets takes place, and the results of this study indicate that these students will always be disadvantaged by systems that are based upon assumptions of homogeneity.

For a student, being able and hard working at Amber Hill was not a guarantee of success within their setted classrooms. Indeed, the students indicated that success depended more upon working quickly, adapting to the norms for the class and thriving upon competition than anything else. A number of different results from this study cast doubt upon some widespread beliefs about setted teaching. For example, there was no qualitative or quantitative evidence that setting raised achievement, but there was evidence that setting diminished achievement for some students. A comparison of the most able students at the two schools showed that the students achieved more in the mixed ability classes of Phoenix Park than the high sets of Amber Hill (at Phoenix Park 3 per cent of the year group attained A*/A grades, compared with 0.5 per cent of the Amber Hill year group). This may be related to a number of features of the two schools' approaches, but there were many indications from the top set students at Amber Hill that features of their top set learning had diminished their achievement (reported in Boaler, 1997a, 1997b).

The various forms of data also seem to expose an important fallacy upon which many setting decisions are based. Students of a similar 'ability', assessed via some test of performance, will not necessarily work at the same pace, respond in the same way to pressure or have similar preferences for ways of working. Grouping students according to ability and then teaching towards an imaginary model student who works in a certain way at a certain pace, will almost certainly disadvantage students who deviate from the ideal model. The stress and anxiety reported by the students in interviews at Amber Hill is probably an indication of this phenomenon. There was much evidence that the students who were disadvantaged by this system were predominantly working class, female or very able. The class polarisation that existed within the setted system of Amber Hill and that was completely absent at Phoenix Park is consistent with the results of other research studies that have considered the links between setting and class bias (Hargreaves, 1967; Lacey, 1970; Ball, 1981; Tomlinson, 1987; Abraham, 1995). A common feature that links all of the findings of this study concerns the individual nature of students' responses to setting. Students at Amber Hill responded to setting in a variety of different ways, indicating that it is too simplistic to regard the effects of setting as universally good or bad for all students, even students in the same set. The various quantitative studies that have compared the group scores of setted and mixed ability classes overlook this fact and, in doing so, overlook the complexity of the learning process for different individuals.

The results reported in this chapter are based upon a case study of two schools and the reports given in the first part come from a sample of only 24 students in one of the schools. It would not be sensible, therefore, to make hard and fast claims about the generalisability of the data. However, the students interviewed at Amber Hill were clear that their achievement had been diminished because of factors that related to setting and class teaching and it would seem unwise to dismiss the students' reported experiences or to assume that they were unique to Amber Hill school. If future research studies are to investigate the prevalence of negative responses to setted teaching, it seems likely that conversations with students will be the most informative means of communication, particularly as these have been lacking in existing research studies that have considered the effectiveness of different student groupings.

To conclude, 'survival of the quickest' is probably not the most accurate way to describe the experiences of setted students, for this research has indicated that it was the students who were most able to adapt to the demands of their set who were most advantaged, or least disadvantaged by setting. In predicting who those students may be, it seems fair to assume that if a student is middle class, confident, thrives on competition and pressure and is motivated, regardless of limits on achievement, they will do well in a setted system. For the rest of the students success will probably depend upon their ability to adapt to a model of learning and a pace of working which is not the most appropriate for their development of understanding.

The consequences of setting and streaming decisions are great. Indeed, the set or stream that students are placed into, at a very young age, will almost certainly dictate the opportunities they receive for the rest of their lives. It is now widely acknowledged in educational and psychological research that students do not have a fixed 'ability' that it is determinable at an early age. However, the placing of students in academic groups often results in the fixing of their potential achievement. Slavin (1990) makes an important point in his analysis of research in this area. He notes that as mixed-ability teaching is known to reduce the chances of discrimination, the burden of proof that ability grouping is preferable must lie with those who claim that it raises achievement. Despite the wide range of research studies in this area, this proof has not been forthcoming.

Acknowledgements

I would like to thank Paul Black and Mike Askew for the support and guidance they provided me with throughout my three-year research study and the Economic and Social Research Council who funded the research. I am also grateful to Stephen Ball and Dylan William who gave me valuable feedback on earlier drafts of this article.

Note

1 This information was provided to me by the examination boards of the two schools.

References

Abraham, J. (1994). Positivism, structurationism and the differentiation–polarisation theory: A reconsideration of Shilling's novelty and primacy thesis, *British Journal of Sociology of Education*, **15**, pp. 231–241.

Abraham, J. (1995). *Divide and School: Gender and Class Dynamics in Comprehensive Education*, Falmer Press, London.

Ball, S. J. (1981). *Beachside Comprehensive*, Cambridge University Press.

Ball, S. J. (1987). *The Micro-politics of the School*, Methuen, London.

Ball, S., Bowe, R. and Gewirtz, S. (1994). Competitive schooling: Values, ethics, and cultural engineering. *Journal of Curriculum and Supervision, 9*, pp. 350–367.

Blair, T. (1996). Comprehensive schools: A new vision. *Speech by Rt Hon. Tony Blair, MP, Leader of the Labour Party, at Didcot Girls' School, Oxfordshire*, Friday 7 June (Labour Party press release).

Boaler, J. (1996). Learning to lose in the mathematics classroom: A critique of traditional schooling practices in the UK. *Qualitative Studies in Education, 9*, pp. 17–33.

Boaler, J. (1997a). *Experiencing School Mathematics: Teaching Styles, Sex and Setting*, Open University Press, Buckingham.

Boaler, J. (1997b). When even the winners are losers: evaluating the experiences of 'top set' students. *Journal of Curriculum Studies, 29*, pp. 165–182.

Boaler, J. (1998). Open and closed mathematics approaches: Student experiences and understandings. *Journal of Mathematics Education, 29*(1), pp. 41–62.

Bourne, J. and Moon, B. (1994). A question of ability? In B. Moon and A. Mayes (eds) *Teaching and Learning in the Secondary School*, Routledge, London, pp. 25–37.

Burstein, L. (ed.) (1993). *The IEA Study of Mathematics III: Student Growth and Classroom Processes*, Pergamon Press, Oxford.

Buxton, L. (1981). *Do You Panic about Maths?: Coping with Maths Anxiety*, Heinemann Educational Books, London.

Dahllöf, U. (1971). *Ability Grouping, Content Validity and Curriculum Process Analysis*, Teachers College Press, New York.

Dar, Y. and Resh, N. (1986). *Classroom Composition and Pupil Achievement*, Gordon and Breach, New York.

Department for Education (1993). *DFE News 16/93. Improving Primary Education-Pattern*, DfE, London.

Dweck, C. S. (1986). Motivational processes affecting learning. *American Psychologist (Special Issue: Psychological Science and Education), 41*, pp. 1040–1048.

Eisenhart, M. (1988). The ethnographic research tradition and mathematics education research. *Journal for Research in Mathematics Education, 19*, pp. 99–114.

Fennema, E. and Leder, G. (eds) (1990). *Mathematics and Gender*, Teachers College Press, New York.

Fennema, E. and Sherman, J. (1977). Sex-related differences in mathematics achievement: Spatial visualisation and affective factors. *American Educational Research Journal, 14*, pp. 51–71.

Fennema, E. and Sherman, J. (1978). Sex-related differences in mathematics achievement and related factors: A further study. *Journal for Research in Mathematics Education, 9*, pp. 189–203.

Fransella, E. (ed.) (1978). *Personal Construct Psychology 1977*, Academic Press, London.

Guardian, The (1996). Blair rejects mixed ability teaching, 8 June, p. 7.

Gewirtz, S., Ball, S. and Bowe, R. (1993). Values and ethics in the education market place: The case of Northwark Park. *International Studies in Sociology of Education,* 3, pp. 233–254.

Glaser, B. G. and Strauss, A. L. (1967). *The Discovery of Grounded Theory: Strategies for Qualitative Research,* Aldine, New York.

Hargreaves, D. (1967). *Social Relations in a Secondary School,* Routledge and Kegan Paul, London.

Hart, L. E. (1989). Classroom processes, sex of student, and confidence in learning mathematics. *Journal for Research in Mathematics Education,* 20, pp. 242–260.

Hoffer, T. B. (1992). Middle school ability grouping and student achievement in science and mathematics. *Educational Evaluation and Policy Analysis,* 14, pp. 205–227.

Jackson, B. (1964). *Streaming: An Education System in Miniature,* Routledge and Kegan Paul, London.

Kerchhoff, A. C. (1986). Effects of ability grouping in British secondary schools. *American Sociological Review,* 51, pp. 842–858.

Lacey, C. (1970). *Hightown Grammar,* Manchester University Press, Manchester.

Linchevski, L. (1995a). Tell me who your classmates are and I'll tell you what you are learning: Mixed ability versus ability-grouping in mathematics classes. Paper presented at *Mathematics Education* seminar held at King's College, London.

Linchevski, L. (1995b). Tell me who your classmates are and I'll tell you what you learn. *PME XIX,* 3, pp. 240–247 (Recife, Brazil, PME).

National Curriculum Council (1993). *The National Curriculum at Key Stages 1 and 2: Advice to the Secretary of State for Education,* NCC, York.

OFSTED (1993). *Mathematics Key Stages 1, 2, 3 and 4, Fourth year 1992–93,* Office for Standards in Education, HMSO, London.

Slavin, R. E. (1990). Achievement effects of ability grouping in secondary schools: A best evidence synthesis. *Review of Educational Research,* 60, pp. 471–499.

Strauss, A. L. (1987). *Qualitative Analysis for Social Scientists,* Cambridge University Press.

Tomlinson, S. (1987). Curriculum option choices in multi-ethnic schools. In B. Tryona (ed.) *Racial Inequality in Education,* Tavistock, London, pp. 92–108.

13 'I'll be a nothing'

Structure, agency and the construction of identity through assessment[1]

Diane Reay and Dylan Wiliam

Abstract

Drawing on data from focus group and individual interviews with Year 6 pupils in the term leading up to Key Stage 2 National Curriculum tests, this article explores the extent to which children's perceptions of the tests contribute to their understandings of themselves as learners. The tension between agency and structure becomes apparent in children's differential dispositions to view the testing process as a definitive statement about the sort of learner they are. Although children's responses are varied, what most share is a sense of an event which reveals something intrinsic about them as individuals. The article also explores the emotions, in particular the anxiety and fear, which permeate such understandings of the National Curriculum assessment process.

Introduction and background

The primary purpose of the 1988 Education Reform Act was to create an educational 'market' that it was assumed by its proponents, would increase standards of performance in schools. Freeing schools from the homogenising effects that local education authorities were believed to exert would create a diversity of provision, allowing parents, who were generally viewed as the 'consumers' of education (rather than, say, students, or the wider community), to choose schools that reflected their aspirations and wishes.

Popular schools would expand, and those that were not, would have to improve, or, if they could not, would close. However, in order to allow the market to function 'efficiently', it was necessary to create an index of performance. The national school-leaving examination (the General Certificate of Secondary Education) provided such an index for students at age 16, but of course would provide no information about the performance of students in primary schools. The solution enacted in the Education Reform Act was the creation of a National Curriculum for all students of compulsory school age in England and Wales, with national assessments for all 7-, 11- and 14-year-olds, the results of which, at least for 11- and 14-year-olds, were to be published for each school.

Although it was claimed that these results would also be useful for informing parents of the academic progress of their children, the information on the attainment of 7-, 11- and 14-year-olds is not available until June or July, and is therefore far too late to influence choices of junior or secondary schools, or of subject options in upper secondary school. The primary purpose of National Curriculum assessment is to provide information on the performance of schools, rather than individuals, in order to inform parental choice (Daugherty, 1995).

Over the 10 years since the development and implementation of the National Curriculum, however, it has become clear that parents and students have not relied exclusively, or even primarily, on aggregate measures of the academic achievement of students in selecting schools, as might have been hoped for by the proponents of the Education Reform Act (see, for example, Gewirtz *et al.*, 1995). A range of other factors, such as the appropriateness of the school for the individual child, are also taken into account.

More recently, however, the pressure on schools to improve their students' performance on National Curriculum tests and in national examinations has been increased by the use of aggregate measures of student performance in the national system of school inspections. The original report of the National Curriculum Task Group on Assessment and Testing (1988) proposed a system of reporting National Curriculum assessment results that would allow the *increase* in students' attainment over a period of schooling (the so-called 'value added') to be reported alongside any absolute measures of achievement. Despite the considerable technical difficulties in agreeing an operational definition of 'value added' (Wiliam, 1992; Jesson, 1996), it is government policy that such value-added measures of achievement should be published alongside absolute measures of students' academic performance.

In view of this, the insistence of Her Majesty's Chief Inspector of Schools (OFSTED, 1997) that inspections of schools take into account absolute levels of achievement in schools, irrespective of the students' prior attainment, seems rather perverse. While it cannot be denied that there are considerable variations in the academic success of schools drawing students from similar cultural and socio-economic backgrounds, to subject a school to 'special measures' (the preliminary stage of a process that can result in the school being closed) because its students arrive at the school with lower attainment than might be expected for their age is clearly unjust. More importantly for the purpose of the present study, it creates a situation in which schools, particularly those in socio-economically disadvantaged areas, are under pressure to increase the *indices* of performance (e.g. the proportion of students achieving a given level in the National Curriculum tests) at almost any price.

The effects of such 'top-down' attempts to improve educational provision on teachers and on school communities have been the subject of extensive studies (see, for example, Corbett and Wilson, 1991), but apart from the work of Rudduck *et al.* (1995) with secondary school students and that of Andrew Pollard and his colleagues with primary pupils (Pollard with Filer, 1996; Pollard *et al.*, 1997), there is virtually no literature which engages with students' perspectives. Rather, it is in the silences in relation to children's perspectives that it is assumed either that National Curriculum assessments have minimal impact on children's subjectivities or that children's concerns and attitudes are merely a backdrop to the assessment process; simply part of the social context. On the one hand the interplay between the assessment process and children's identities and identifications is not considered an important area for research and theoretical consideration, while on the other hand children are subsumed as a means to an end within a process which is primarily an exercise in evaluating schools and teachers. However, despite the former assumption that

their agency is unaffected by the assessments and the latter assumption that
caught up in a process where the main focus is teachers and the instit
simultaneously active in the assessment process and profoundly affected by it.

The research study

Patricia Broadfoot describes the assessment arrangements for National Curriculum
assessment as an example of the ways in which apparently benign and rational techniques of assessment are currently being used to impose norms by reducing value
debates to technical questions (Broadfoot, 1996). However, the consequences of the
new assessment system for pupils have been overlooked in much of the research which
examines changes in assessment. This small-scale study attempts to highlight the importance of considering children's perspectives on assessment if we are to glimpse the extent
to which new subjectivities are being constructed in the primary classroom. Although
the research project extended over the full school year from September 1997 until July
1998, this article draws on empirical data gathered over the Easter term 1998 to provide
some preliminary indications of the impact of National Curriculum assessment on Year
6 (age 10–11) students' self-definitions as learners.

The focus of this article is a class of 20 students in Windermere School – a south
London primary school serving a predominantly working-class, ethnically mixed commu-
nity, and whose students typically achieve levels slightly below the national average.
Initially, all the students were interviewed in focus groups and half the class were then
interviewed individually about their attitudes towards, and feelings about, impending
National Curriculum tests.[2] Additionally, both the children and their class teacher were
observed over the term as increasing amounts of time were devoted to test preparation.
The themes generated through focus group discussions were strongly supported both in
individual interviews and by the data collected through participant observation.

The SATs: shifting identifications as learners

> HANNAH: I'm really really scared about the SATs [standard assessment tasks].
> Mrs O'Brien [a teacher at the school] came and talked to us about our
> spelling and I'm no good at spelling and David [the class teacher] is giving us
> times tables tests every morning and I'm hopeless at times tables so I'm
> frightened I'll do the SATs and I'll be a nothing.
>
> DIANE: I don't understand Hannah. You can't be a nothing.
>
> HANNAH: Yes, you can 'cause you have to get a level like a level 4 or a level 5 and
> if you're no good at spellings and times tables you don't get those levels and
> so you're a nothing.
>
> DIANE: I'm sure that's not right.
>
> HANNAH: Yes it is 'cause that's what Mrs O'Brien was saying.

This is a particularly stark example but it exemplifies some of the ways in which children's identifications as learners (Skeggs, 1997) are constructed through the assessment process. For Hannah what constitutes academic success is correct spelling and

knowing your times tables. She is an accomplished writer, a gifted dancer and artist and good at problem-solving yet none of those skills make her somebody in her own eyes. Instead she constructs herself as a failure, an academic non-person, by a metonymic shift in which she comes to see herself entirely in terms of the level to which her performance in the SATs is ascribed. Although Windermere School had a general policy of playing down the importance of SATs, Hannah's teacher, in his second year of teaching, was still feeling under intense external pressure to ensure his pupils did well. As is apparent in the following quotation, the fever pitch in the classroom surrounding the impending SATs is generated in no small part by his anxieties:

> I was appalled by how most of you did on the science test. You don't know anything. I want to say that you are judged at the end of the day by what you get in the SATs and some of you won't even get level 2.

Some children resist and challenge such all-embracing assignments; for example, Terry was outraged by his teacher's comment and shouted out, 'Hold on, we're not that bad'. However, others, like Hannah, appear to accept and internalise its strictures.

Hannah's account underscores the extent to which SATs have set in motion a new set of tensions with which Year 6 students are expected to cope. As the quotations presented later indicate, all the children, apart from Terry, expressed varying degrees of anxiety about failure. While there is a gender dimension to this anxiety in that girls expressed higher degrees of anxiety than boys (see also Shaw, 1995), the overall impression from the Year 6 interviews was that most pupils of both sexes took the SATs very seriously. They wanted to do well. At the same time, children expressed a great deal of concern about the narrow focus of the SATs and not being able to produce their best under strict (and unfamiliar) test conditions. Their concerns seem to be borne out by research into the validity of the Key Stage 2 English SATs:

> Nicely rounded handwriting and reasonable spelling of fairly simple words seemed to impress some markers favourably. In contrast, idiosyncratic or jerky handwriting with insecure spellings seemed to prejudice some markers against the content.
>
> (Close *et al.*, 1997, p. 430)

The students also seemed very aware of the (not-so-) hidden agenda surrounding SATs:

> MARY: SATs are about how good the teachers have been teaching you and if everybody gets really low marks they think the teachers haven't been teaching you properly.

and

> DIANE: So what are the SATs for?
> JACKIE: To see if the teachers have taught us anything.
> TERRY: If we don't know nothing then the teacher will get all the blame.
> JACKIE: Yeah. It's the teacher's fault.
> TUNDE: Yeah. They get blamed.

Yet, despite frequent rationalisations that SATs were primarily judgements of teaching, nearly all the children indicated a sense of unease and feelings of discomfort about what SATs might reveal about themselves as learners. Some of the children seemed to be indicating far-reaching consequences in which good SATs results were linked to positive life prospects and, concomitantly, poor results meant future failures and hardships:

> SHARON: I think I'll get a two, only Stuart will get a six.
> DIANE: So if Stuart gets a six what will that say about him?
> SHARON: He's heading for a good job and a good life and it shows he's not gonna be living on the streets and stuff like that.
> DIANE: And if you get a level two what will that say about you?
> SHARON: Um, I might not have a good life in front of me and I might grow up and do something naughty or something like that.

In three of the focus group sessions the children drew on an apocalyptic tale of 'the boy who ruined his chances'. There follows an excerpt from the girls' focus group, but both the boys' and the mixed group referred to the same example in order to exemplify how things can go terribly wrong in the SATs if you don't make the right choices:

> NORMA: There was someone so good at writing stories …
> MARY: Yeah, and he wrote a leaflet …
> NORMA: He picked to write a leaflet and then when he wrote the leaflet he blew it.
> LILY: He just ruined his whole SAT. He ruined it. If he'd written the story he would have got a really good mark. He was the best at writing stories. And he thought he wanted to try it out … and he just ruined it for himself.
> NORMA: Mrs O'Brien said that he was … what was the word, kind of scared thing … ?
> DIANE: Got in a panic.
> NORMA: Yeah, and he didn't do the story because he thought he would get that wrong.
> MARY: So he did the leaflet and he just ruined his chances, totally ruined his chances.

In this excerpt and the others, performance in SATs is about more than simply getting a test right or wrong, it is conflated in the children's minds with future prospects. To perform badly is 'to ruin one's chances'. At other times there was far more disputation and contention about the importance of SATs for future prospects:

> DIANE: So are they important, SATs?
> LILY: Depends.
> TUNDE: Yes.
> TERRY: No, definitely not.
> LEWIS: It does affect your life.
> AYSE: Yeah, it does affect your life.

TERRY: No, as if it means you know I do badly then that means I'm gonna be a road sweeper.

However, while Terry is clear that SATs have no impact on future prospects, other students lack his certainty:

DIANE: You mean, you think that if you do badly in SATs then you won't be able to do well or get good jobs?

JACKIE: Yeah, 'cause that's what David's saying.

DIANE: What is he saying?

JACKIE: He's saying if we don't like, get good things, in our SATS, when we grow up we are not gonna get good jobs and …

TERRY: Be plumbers and road sweepers …

TUNDE: But what if you wanted to do that?

DIANE: Instead of what?

TERRY: Footballers, singers, vets, archaeologists. We ain't gonna be nothing like that if we don't get high levels.

DIANE: And does that worry you about your future?

JACKIE: Yeah.

LEWIS: Yeah.

AYSE: Yeah, it worries me a lot.

TERRY: No, because he's telling fibs.

Assessment in English schooling in the late 1990s is surrounded by controversy and disputation (Black, 1998). It has become a political football. Yet, despite heavily contested changes there are enduring continuities. Students have always informally assessed their own academic performance and that of their peers. Class 6S is no different. There is unanimous agreement among the children that Stuart is the cleverest child in the class and almost unanimous agreement that Peter is the second cleverest:

NORMA: Stuart is the cleverest child in the whole school. He'll get level 6 for everything.

In this short excerpt cleverness is very clearly conflated with doing well in the SATs. There is an assumption of causation; being clever automatically leads to good SAT results. Yet, later on Norma talks about her own nervousness and how that might affect her own performance in the same tests:

NORMA: I'm no good at tests. I get too nervous so I know I won't do very well.

Patricia Broadfoot writes of the elements of panoptic surveillance embedded in assessment processes whereby pupils learn to judge themselves 'as if some external eye was constantly monitoring their performance' (Broadfoot, 1996, p. 68), encouraging the internalisation of the evaluative criteria of those in power.

Because the commitment to technical efficiency is increasingly being incorpo-
rated at the level of meaning and volition, as well as that of practice, this provides
pressure for the non-bureaucratic, potentially contradictory languages of profes-
sionalism and democratic participation to define their own criteria of value and,
hence, personal accountability in the same terms.

(Broadfoot, 1996, pp. 239–240)

One result is a strong pressure on both pupils and teachers to assume that value can be
quantified.

Belief systems concerning the individual should not be construed as inhabiting a
diffuse field of 'culture', but as embodied in institutional and technical practices
– through which forms of individuality are specified and governed. The history of
the self should be written at this 'technological' level, in terms of the techniques
and evaluations for developing, evaluating, perfecting, managing the self, the way
it is rendered into words, made visible, inspected, judged and reformed.

(Rose, 1989, p. 218)

The battle over assessment and the triumph of publishable, measurement-based,
competitive, pencil-and-paper tests over diagnostic, open-ended, process-oriented
assessments has resulted in the establishment of assessment procedures which operate
primarily 'as performance indicators of teacher effectivity' (Ball, 1994, p. 41). At the
macro-level SATs can be seen as regulatory mechanisms that link the conduct of individuals and organisations to political objectives; the assumption being that they will
impact powerfully on teachers' subjectivities and practices. However, as the children's
discussions quoted earlier illustrate, at the micro-level of the classroom there are
regular glimpses of the normalising and regulatory function of the SATs on children.

Perhaps Tracey provides the best example of 'the governance of the soul' (Rose, 1989):

TRACEY: I think even now, at night times I think about it and I think I'm going
to get them.
DIANE: You think about your SATs at night time?
TRACEY: Yeah, lots. When I'm in bed, because I've got stars on my ceiling, I'm
hoping and I look up and I go, 'I know I'm gonna get there'. And my mum
goes, 'Who's talking in there?' And I goes, 'Nothing mum'.
DIANE: So what are you hoping?
TRACEY: Um, I think about a three. I dunno. I don't think I'll get a five. I'm
hoping to get a five. When I look at the stars I hope I'll get a five.

Allan Hanson writes about the increasing disposition of American students to define
themselves in terms of test scores, citing an example of college students who displayed
their scores on the Scholastic Aptitude Test on their T-shirts (Hanson, 1993). While
we are not suggesting that processes of quantifying academic ability were anything like
as extreme as Hanson found in some American colleges, there were disturbing shifts in
how children viewed themselves and others, which could be attributed to the assessment

process and the ways in which the classroom pedagogy transformed in response to the imminence of the SATs.

Assessment procedures are implicated in technologies of the self and the struggle to gain 'intimate and secure' social relations – intimate because they feed into the ordering of subjectivity, and secure because of the apparent naturalness of the categories they generate (Donald, 1985). As the term progressed children increasingly referred to the levels they expected themselves and others to achieve. Their talk raises concerns about the crudeness of the assessments to which pupils have access. The SATs levels constitute very simplistic judgements purged of any subtlety and complexity about the sort of learners pupils are judged to be.

Children's emotional responses to assessment

As is evident throughout the children's texts cited earlier, there are strong currents of fear and anxiety permeating children's relationships to the SATs process:

> TUNDE: Because if you get too scared or something, or paranoid, or something it kind of stops you from doing it, because you just think you are going to get everything wrong and it's easy to get paranoid about the SATs.

and

> DIANE: Norma, why are you worried about SATs now?
>
> NORMA: Well, it seems like I'll get no points or I won't be able to do it, too hard or something.
>
> DIANE: What would it mean to get no points?
>
> NORMA: Well instead of being level three I'll be a nothing and do badly – very badly.
>
> DIANE: What makes you think that? Have you been practising?
>
> NORMA: No, like I analyse … I know I worry about loads of things.
>
> DIANE: Like what?
>
> NORMA: I don't know, I just worry about things and my mum is going to take me to a special aromatherapy lady, or something like that. I don't know, but she said something about that because I am always panicking and I've been worrying about when it's SATs.
>
> DIANE: But no one was mentioning SATs last term, were they? What's made everybody start worrying about it now?
>
> NORMA: Mrs O'Brien came in today and she was doing language and she said loads of things, well not language, but dictionaries and she said loads of things about SATs.
>
> DIANE: And you got in a panic.
>
> NORMA: [Laughing] Well, not in a big panic, it was just like, what if I get stuck here and I don't finish the story and I don't get any points or things like that?

and

> STUART: What if I get level one?

DIANE: You won't get level one. Honestly, I'm quite positive you won't get level one.

STUART: I might in English, since Mrs O'Brien told us about that boy messing up his chances I've been worried about it 'cause it's the sort of thing I could do.

After children have marked each others' practice mathematics SATs there is the ritual recounting of marks. Nadia, Mary, Jessica, Terry, Peter and Lewis have all got 20 but a big commotion breaks out when the others realise Stuart has only got 16. Peter says, 'God did you really only get 16?' Simon tells him, 'Your brain must have stopped working', while Lewis comments, 'He's lost his genius man'. Stuart rather forlornly comments, 'At this rate I'm only going to get level one for maths'. As these excerpts indicate, the negative emotions generated by the impending SATs and a changing classroom curriculum affected all the children, regardless of ability levels.

Impact on pedagogy and the curriculum on offer

Many studies have examined the consequences of high-stakes assessment systems on the breadth of curriculum that students experience (see, for example, Kellaghan *et al.,* 1982*)*. However, almost all of these studies have taken an 'outsider's' perspective on curricular changes. Even where studies have attempted to work from an 'insider's' perspective, it has been assumed that the students themselves have little to contribute on this aspect of the social consequences of test use (Messick, 1980). However, the evidence from the current study is that students as young as 11 have very clear perceptions about the influence of external assessment on the curriculum:

JACKIE: We've already had SATs. We've been doing them for so long, all the old papers we must have done, we must have done three SATs already.

A narrowing of the curriculum was very evident in 6S over the spring term and was a cause of both complaint and regret among the children:

LEWIS: I wish we did technology.

JACKIE: Yeah, that would be good.

TUNDE: We should do more dance. We should have dance in the SATs.

TERRY: And they never teach you anything about cavemen either.

AYSE: And we don't do history any more.

TERRY: All I know is because I've read about it on my own.

AYSE: And we don't do geography. Only science, language and maths. Just over and over again.

DIANE: So is the curriculum very different this term to what it was last term?

TERRY: Yeah.

JACKIE: Last year we done music and dance, interesting things.

TERRY: The best thing we did is PE. And last week was the best session we've had in ages 'cause it was something different. And I hate football and it was football but it was the best session we done in ages.

But it was the emphasis on more individualised, competitive ways of working, which were increasingly displacing the mutually supportive, collaborative group work to which the children were accustomed – a shift from a 'communitarian climate' to 'academic press' (Phillips, 1997) – that caused the most disquiet:

> TUNDE: Peter helped me, Peter and Lewis.
> TERRY: But we're not allowed to help, to help anyone, they're all on your own.
> JACKIE: Yeah, but we're used to helping each other.
> LEWIS: I still help people.
> JACKIE: So do I.
> AYSE: I didn't get no help.
> TERRY: We're not allowed to help any more. It's cheating.

Progressive primary schools like Windermere have not traditionally been subject to processes of overt differentiation and polarisation (Lacey, 1970). Such processes have normally been found in selective secondary schools where streaming and setting are common practice. However, there were indications of both increasing differentiation and polarisation in the class under study (6S), with negative repercussions for both teacher–pupil and pupil–pupil interaction. Webb (1993) suggests that the Key Stage 2 teachers in her study appeared to be altering both their curriculum and pedagogic strategies as a result of the pressures exerted by OFSTED and the new assessment regimes and this also seemed to be the case in 6S.

Over the course of the spring term 1998 the researcher spent 60 hours observing teaching and learning processes in the classroom and also amassed extensive field notes, documenting both changing pedagogic approaches and the children's responses to them. During this period there were innumerable mundane examples of overt academic differentiation as a direct consequence of the teacher's increasing preoccupation with SATs. Concomitantly, there were many examples within the peer group of the deepening of existing divisions, as well as the opening up of new divisions based on academic rather than social criteria as a direct result of SATs and SATs practice, of which the two examples described next are only the most stark.

In March 1998 the children were working their way individually through an old science SATs paper. Fumi had protested at the beginning of the session when told the children were expected to work on their own, telling the teacher, 'But we're used to working together'. Every few minutes she would sigh audibly until eventually the teacher came across to where she was sitting and proceeded to put lines through a number of the SATs questions, commenting, 'Don't try and do these. They'll be too difficult for you. Answer the easy ones'. Fumi struggled on for a few more minutes. It was clear to the researcher and the children sitting near her that she was crying. After a few more minutes she got to her feet, pushing her chair out of the way and stormed out the classroom, sobbing. Out in the corridor she kept on repeating over and over again, 'He thinks I'm thick. He thinks I'm thick. He wants all the others to think I'm thick'. As we have discussed earlier, children did engage in informal assessments of each others' academic ability, but prior to the SATs such processes had a benign air and had never resulted in confrontations between either the teacher and a student or between students.

Even when Fumi was eventually coaxed back into the classroom she was openly rebellious, scribbling all over the SATs paper and muttering 'I hate you' under her breath at the teacher – behaviour which resulted in her missing her playtime.

Equally worrying was the consequence of regular SATs practice for Stuart's positioning within the peer group. In earlier interview sessions, carried out over the autumn term, children often compared themselves academically to Stuart, citing him as the cleverest child in the class. Such comments were presented simply as statements of fact and there was no malice or ill-feeling expressed. However, towards the end of the Easter term, with a programme of daily mathematics tests and regular science and English SATs practice, Stuart's situation among the peer group, particularly with the other boys, was becoming increasingly vulnerable. On one occasion, after the teacher had pointed out that Stuart was the only child to get 20 out of 20 for the mathematics test and that everybody else must try to do better, Terry leaned over and thumped him hard in the back. Twice Stuart came back from playtime with scratches either to his cheek or the back of his neck. He was not sure 'exactly who was responsible' but complained that the other boys had started to 'gang up' on him. The language other children used to describe him shifted discernibly. Before he had simply been recognised as clever; now he was increasingly labelled as 'a swot' by both girls and boys. There are frequent entries in the field notes which testify to a growing climate of hostility towards Stuart. For example:

JOLENE: I hate Stuart, he's just a teacher's pet – a spotty swotty …

and

ALICE: Stuart's such a clever clogs that's why no one likes him.
DIANE: But you said you liked him.
ALICE: That's before he started showing off.

But Stuart had not started to show off. Rather, the classroom practices in 6S over the spring term had dramatically increased processes of differentiation, which in turn had led to a growing polarisation among the peer group. In particular, the relationship between Stuart and the rest of 6S noticeably worsened.

Conclusion

While we make no claims that the shifts in both the children's self-perceptions and the teaching regime in 6S over the course of the term are representative of all Year 6 classrooms, we would argue that what our evidence does indicate is a need for further investigation to map out the extent to which both pupil and teacher identities and practices are being modified through new assessment processes. We believe that the data that we have presented here provide convincing evidence that students as young as 10 or 11 are well aware of the effects of National Curriculum assessments, and their voices are an important part of any picture of the social consequences of the use of test results as measures of educational effectiveness.

The threat to the continued existence of a school posed by poor SATs results creates a situation in which individual teachers are under increasing pressure to improve the scores achieved by the students, *irrespective of the consequence for students' achievement in wider terms.* For some, this may be exactly what was intended. By asserting that National Curriculum assessments embody all that is valid, the narrowing of the experiences of students to just those aspects that can be assessed in a one-hour written test represents a return to the certainties of the 'curriculum of the dead' (Ball, 1993). However, it seems to us far more likely that for most observers, this narrowing of the focus of assessment, together with an emphasis on achieving the highest scores possible, produces a situation in which unjustifiable educational practices are not only possible, but encouraged. Whether 'teaching to the test' in this way is regarded as cheating or not is open to question (Smith, 1991), but there is no doubt that such activities rob National Curriculum assessments of the power to say anything useful about what the students have learnt. The more specific the Government is about what it is that schools are to achieve, the more likely it is to get it, but the less likely it is to mean anything.

The teacher of the class we have been describing is relatively inexperienced, and therefore, perhaps, less able to resist the pressure to concentrate on the narrow range of achievements assessed in the SATs. However, as the Government's new requirements on schools to set targets for aggregate school and individual achievement increases pressure on schools to improve measured performance, it seems more than likely that students will be inscribed into school practices entirely in terms of their ability to contribute to the school's target for the proportion of students achieving specified levels in the National Curriculum assessments.

Notes

1   This article was originally presented as a paper at the British Educational Research Association conference at Queen's University, Belfast in August 1998.

2   National Curriculum assessment at the ages of 7, 11 and 14 (the end of each of the first three 'key stages' of compulsory education) consists of two components – a series of judgements made by the school about a student's performance over the key stage, generally called 'teacher assessment' and an externally set standardised assessment. When the first National Curriculum assessments for 7-year-olds were introduced in 1991, the external assessments were called 'standard assessment tasks' or SATs, following the recommendation of the TGAT report (National Curriculum Task Group on Assessment and Testing, 1988). However, following representations from Educational Testing Services, the New Jersey-based developers of the American Scholastic Aptitude Test, which is known by the same acronym, the term Standard Assessment Task was changed to Standard Tasks. Furthermore, when the format for the first assessments at Key Stage 3, held in 1992, was changed from that originally prescribed by Kenneth Clark, then Secretary of State for Education, the name of the external component of Key Stage 3 National Curriculum assessment was changed to 'National Curriculum tests', as was that for the first Key Stage 2 assessments when they were introduced two years later. The external components of Key Stage 2 National Curriculum assessment have therefore never been called 'SATs', but teachers, students and parents continue to refer to them in this way, and so for simplicity of presentation, we have followed this usage.

References

Ball, S. J. (1993). Education, Majorism and the 'curriculum of the dead'. *Curriculum Studies, 1,* pp. 195–214.

Ball, S. J. (1994). *Education Reform: A Critical and Post-structural Approach,* Open University Press, Buckingham..

Black, P. J. (1998). *Testing: Friend or Foe? The Theory and Practice of Assessment and tTsting,* Falmer Press, London.

Broadfoot, P. M. (1996). *Education, Assessment and Society: a Sociological analysis,* Open University Press, Buckingham.

Close, G. S., Furlong, T. and Simon, S. A. (1997). *The Validity of the 1996 Key Stage 2 Tests in English, Mathematics and Science.* Report prepared for Association of Teachers and Lecturers, King's College London School of Education, London.

Corbett, H. D. and Wilson, B. L. (1991). *Testing, Reform and Rebellion,* Ablex, Hillsdale, NJ.

Daugherty, R. (1995). *National Curriculum Assessment: a review of policy 1987–1994,* Falmer Press, London.

Donald, J. (1985). Beacons of the future: Schooling, subjection and subjectification. In V. Beechey and J. Donald (eds) *Subjectivity and Social Relations,* Open University Press, Buckingham.

Gewirtz, S., Ball, S. J. and Bowe, R. (1995). *Markets, Choice and Equity in Education,* Open University Press, Buckingham.

Hanson, F. A. (1993). *Testing Testing: social consequences of the examined life,* University of California Press, Berkeley, CA.

Jesson, D. (1996). *Value Added Measures of School Performance,* Department for Education and Employment, London.

Kellaghan, T., Madaus, G. F. and Airasian, P. W. (1982). *The Effects of Standardised Testing,* Kluwer, Boston, MA.

Lacey, C. (1970). *Hightown Grammar: the school as a social system,* Manchester University Press, Manchester.

Messick, S. (1980). Test validity and the ethics of assessment, *American Psychologist, 35,* pp. 1012–1027.

National Curriculum Task Group on Assessment and Testing (1988). *A Report,* Department of Education and Science, London.

OFSTED (1997). *Annual Report of Her Majesty's Chief Inspector of Schools,* Office for Standards in Education, HMSO, London.

Phillips, M. (1997). What makes a school effective? A comparison of the relationships of communitarian climate and academic climate to mathematics achievement and attendance during middle school, *American Educational Research Journal, 34,* pp. 633–662.

Pollard. A. and Filer, A. (1996). *The Social World of Children's Learning: case studies of pupils from four to seven,* Cassell, London.

Pollard, A., Thiessen, D. and Filer, A. (eds) (1997). *Children and their Curriculum: the perspectives of primary and elementary school pupils,* Falmer Press, London.

Rose, N. (1989). *Governing the Soul: the shaping of the private self,* Routledge, London.

Rudduck, J., Chaplain, R. and Wallance, G. (1995). *School Improvement – what can pupils tell us?* David Fulton, London.

Shaw, J. (1995). *Education, Gender and Anxiety,* Taylor and Francis, London.

Skeggs, B. (1997). *Formations of Class and Gender: becoming respectable,* Sage, London.

Smith, M. L. (1991). Meanings of test preparation, *American Educational Research Journal, 28,* pp. 521–542.

Webb, R. (1993). *Eating the Elephant Bit by Bit: the National Curriculum at Key Stage 2.* Final report of research commissioned by the Association of Teachers and Lecturers (ATL), ATL Publishers, London.

Wiliam, D. (1992). Value-added attacks? Technical issues in publishing National Curriculum assessments, *British Educational Research Journal,* **18**, pp. 329–341.

14 Pupils' perspectives on learning mathematics

Barbara Allen

Introduction

There have been numerous changes in UK schools over recent years. These changes include the introduction of statutory testing, the system of inspecting schools under the auspices of the Office for Standards in Education (OFSTED) and the Framework for Teaching Mathematics. However, despite being a time of immense change in schools, there has been relatively little consideration of pupils' experiences.

In this chapter I attempt to redress that balance by reporting on pupil perspectives on their own learning experiences, and the impact this has on the way pupils view themselves as learners. Significant learner experiences are found to relate to three aspects of schooling: setting, assessment and rewards. Implications of these findings for learning mathematics are discussed.

In any social situation people tend to behave in ways that are appropriate for that culture. In the culture of the classroom the type of behaviour that is generally valued is that which conforms with learning expectations and discourages disruption. How pupils' behaviour and achievement are perceived by their teachers and peers in the classroom has an impact on the way they view themselves as learners of mathematics.

The way that pupils are perceived within a classroom depends on their positional identity. Positional identity is a term coined by anthropologists Holland *et al.* (2001) and refers to the way people understand and act out their position within a community. Pupils' positional identities are formed in response to how they participate in classroom activities and how that participation is seen by themselves and others.

But how do pupils become positioned as successful or unsuccessful learners? What are the issues that have value within the classroom that have an impact on their positional identity?

The study

The research reported here was part of a larger study that was concerned with exploring pupils' perspectives on their mathematics classrooms. Although I used a variety of qualitative and quantitative methods of data collection, each meeting with the pupils included a semi-structured interview. These interviews were carried out with small groups of pupils, usually in twos or threes. Over five terms I interviewed 18 pupils in a rural middle school in the UK. The interviews started when the pupils were in Year 6 and ended in Year 7. Nine girls and nine boys self-selected into the project and were in each of three mathematics sets. I named the school Marsden Middle School and all pupil names are pseudonyms that they chose.

During the interviews I used a number of prompts and probes to encourage the pupils to talk about their experiences. These either involved specific questions, drawing or sorting tasks. One series of interviews was based on questions about how the pupils felt in their mathematics lessons and included the prompts: 'Tell me about a time when you felt happy in a maths lesson'; and 'Tell me about a time when you felt anxious in a maths lesson'.

Another set of interviews was designed to find out the classroom changes that occurred prior to the pupils sitting the statutory tests (referred to by the pupils as SATs). These interviews were based on two questions: 'Have you noticed any changes in your classrooms in the last few weeks?' and 'Why do you think those changes have happened?'

All the interviews were tape-recorded and were analysed using a grounded theory approach (Glaser and Strauss, 1967). A number of issues emerged from the pupils' comments but here I consider the pupils' perceptions of themselves as learners of mathematics and how they became positioned as successful or unsuccessful.

Findings

The experiences that impacted on the pupils' positional identity related to the school's systems of setting, assessment and rewards. I deal with each of these in turn.

Positioning in a set

The pupils at Marsden Middle School were placed in years and classes. In Year 6 they were placed in sets for Mathematics and English. Historically the pupils were allocated to sets based on teacher assessment and sometimes an internally written and administered test. Once they were allocated to a set, over the two years of data collection none of them moved set. A lack of movement was found by Troyna (1992) to be common in schools that set pupils. The organisation of the Marsden pupils into sets was entirely in the hands of the teachers and it had a direct impact on the pupils' perceived mathematical competence. If the pupils were placed in a set in which they felt comfortable then it confirmed their feelings about themselves and helped to create a positional identity as a successful learner.

> GUY: Well if we're put in sets then that's the set for us. We can't be stupid if we are in top set. (Set 1)
> ABBIE: I always felt quite good about myself when I went into top set. I didn't sort of boast about it but at home I was really proud of myself. (Set 1)
> ALAN: I was cheerful when I found out I was in top set maths. (Set 1)
> CONNOR: I reckon they should have a set which you feel comfortable in ... And ... the right set for me would be middle, which I'm in now. (Set 2)

However, if they were placed in a set that they deemed inappropriate then they started to question their perceived identity.

> GUS: I wasn't stupid when I was a fifth-year; they put me in bottom set. (Set 3)
> CAROLINE: I'm absolutely rubbish at maths even though I'm in top set. (Set 1)

The pupils were initially positioned as successful (or unsuccessful) learners of mathematics by their set allocation. They appeared to be constantly making judgements about their performance but did not perceive these judgements as lying within their personal authority. Instead, they relied on the authority of the teacher who placed them in the set and then marked and commented on their work.

The girls in Set 1 perceived an additional pressure on them to maintain or improve their position within the set. Since they were already in the top set, the only way to improve their position was by competing to perform better within the set. They appeared constantly to be comparing themselves to others in the set in order to verify and sustain their position. The induced competition was, consequently, an inherent part of the classroom culture.

> SARAH: I try and do my best so that I don't go down a set because I know I can't go up a set ... Instead of getting into the next set up you're getting into the top of the year really, aren't you? ... It's nice to feel that you are better than some people below you. It's nicer to feel that you are not the bottom person. (Set 1)
> CAROLINE: Say you forget about the other sets and there's just your set you wanna be somewhere near the top, don't you? ... You feel you've achieved something as long as you are not at the bottom. (Set 1)
> NATALIA: I mean we're split into groups because we're all at different standards but I think in each set there is another different standard. There's the boffins and there's the lower ones. (Set 1)
> ABBIE: I know we're meant to be in top set and we're meant to keep the standard up but I sometimes think we get just as confused as other people do and sometimes she takes it for granted we know what we're doing and we don't always know what we're doing. (Set 1)

Simply being in Set 1 did not mean the pupils were necessarily viewed as successful learners of mathematics. This depended on whether their performance and behaviour were valued within the classroom by both teacher and pupils. Also if a pupil's view of what constituted successful work was in conflict with that of others then they could be viewed as unsuccessful. Natalia drew attention to how these judgements of one pupil were made by others.

> NATALIA: Lydia is like really good at maths but she writes it down really, really slowly and everything and so people class her as like quite bottom 'cos she never gets to finish the work and she likes everything to be perfect and pristine and everything. (Set 1)

In summary, a pupil's position in a set was not constant; it seemed that it was necessary for them constantly to review their position and continue to demonstrate success in their classroom.

But it was their performance in formal and informal assessments that dictated whether or not pupils maintained their position. This ensured that assessment assumed a central important position for them in their classroom life. I address this next.

Positioning by assessment

The types of assessment the pupils talked about were both formal and informal, all being summative rather than formative, and an assessment *of* learning rather than an assessment *for* learning (Wiliam, 2000). The responsible evaluator was always either the teacher, or an examining authority, thereby ensuring that, again, they were dependent upon the judgements of others.

The pupils' positioning as successful learners, therefore, was in competition with their peers and was a consequence of them achieving high marks, rather than demonstrating understanding or competent mathematical behaviour.

> DAVID: [Felt successful] When I got a high score in a test. That's when I felt successful. A good amount of a per cent, 80 or 90 per cent out of a hundred. (Set 1)
>
> TIM: The best memory for me in maths was when ... I got the best marks in the class in a maths test. (Set 2)
>
> JANE: [Felt happy] When we were doing the maths test I got 81 and that was the top out of the whole set. (Set 2)
>
> EMMA: [Felt cheerful] When we had a test and I got quite a lot right and I felt cheerful then. (Set 2)

Getting low marks on a test had a negative effect on their perceived positioning and they reported feelings of failure and anger.

> DAVID: [Felt sad] It's like the tests when I get a low result, feel a bit of a failure, and all my friends have got high ones ... you feel sad, you feel angry with yourself, you feel a failure and you've embarrassed all your friends. (Set 1)
>
> ABBIE: [Felt embarrassed] We did the practice SAT test in maths, and I think I got 68 and even Viki beat me by one point. So I was the lowest, I think there was one lower and that was Kim who got 54 and I got 68 and I was like, 'Arrgghh! I just felt a bit embarrassed because everyone goes, 'You only got 68.' I was a bit embarrassed about the result ... and then I was embarrassed about everyone knowing. (Set 1)
>
> CONNOR: [Felt angry] Like this person was sitting next to me and when I had my maths test ... and he got 20 out of 20 and he goes, 'Look who's got 19 then,' and I'm really angry and it's like I want to hit him really hard because he's getting on my nerves. (Set 2)
>
> IAN: [Felt sad] I actually felt sad when I had a test and I only got 2 [out of 10] and

felt a bit down … we had another test and you had to get 10 points and I actually didn't get none. [I felt] a bit sad. (Set 3)

Sometimes, as with the earlier description of Lydia, the position of a pupil was questioned when their performance was not what was normally expected.

> NATALIA: We had these fake SATs tests and Mrs Boyle came up to me and she said, 'I didn't know you were that good in maths. Why didn't you show it before?' (Set 1)

The pupils' positioning as successful or unsuccessful appeared to be dominated by external authority. In this situation authority is seen as 'external to the self' (Povey, 1995) and being in the hands of experts. The Marsden pupils did not appear to be able to assess their own capabilities; instead they relied on the teacher to do so (Povey, 1995). When such circumstances persist it is likely that the pupils will start to question the position of external authority as did the pupils in Boaler's study (1997). She found that this questioning of external authority emerged at Years 10 and 11 and could result in disaffection.

Duffield *et al.* (2000) also found pupils were dependent on assessment as a gauge to their achievement and used results to compare their performance with others or with past experiences. These pupils saw themselves as disengaged from the learning process and believed that schoolwork:

> consisted of a fixed content of information or techniques for which they had to learn right answers and correct performance.
>
> (Duffield *et al.*, 2000, p. 271)

The lack of personal authority (see Chapter 3, Povey *et al.*, 1999) meant the pupils had little influence over the discursive practices in their classrooms because the qualities valued were accuracy and speed, working individually, avoiding collaboration and consequent negotiation of meaning.

In summary, the pupils' approach to learning was competency based with performance goals rather than learning goals (Middleton and Spanias, 1999). They were working in classrooms where good test results and getting the work correct were valued. The resultant classroom culture induced competition.

> GUS: Work is just getting down, get your work finished and just getting a good mark. (Set 3)

Often the school assessment system is related to the reward system. This is the final way that the pupils felt themselves to be positioned as learners.

Positioning by rewards

Marsden Middle School had a system of external rewards based on merits and commendations. The awarding of commendations (equivalent to two merits) was a public event that took place weekly at a whole school assembly. A pupil could build up their merits to constitute a certificate, the first being obtained on collection of 20 merits.

Although this was a whole-school policy, the pupils reported that teachers awarded merits and commendations in different ways. The teacher of the Set 3 pupils appeared to use a more complex system of rewards, where points built to make merits.

> GUS: And we've got these points, you've got to sit up straight and all good work and then you get a point. (Set 3)
> TIFFANY: It's 6 points a merit. (Set 3)
> JO: She doesn't really give you much merits. (Set 3)

The pupils' perception was that they did not get many merits or commendations. No pupil suggested that the awarding of merits or commendations was in the hands of anyone other than the teachers. They did not, for example, describe a situation where they could request a merit or commendation for themselves or a peer, or that the rewards were open to negotiation. They did, however, deny the value of the reward system at the same time as they competed to gain the rewards.

> DAVID: All merits are is a piece of writing and paper. (Set 1)
> GUS: Because merits just put a tick up on your chart. You only get a bit of card that says, 'Gus has got 25 merits.' It's not an achievement really is it? Not really. (Set 3)

A successful learner appeared to be viewed as one that finished the sheets and got the correct answer. The pupils did not seem to question the validity of viewing a successful learner in this particular way.

The pupils were reliant on extrinsic rewards as a form of motivation. One of the complications of the reliance on extrinsic rewards in this way is that:

> when rewards are used to get someone to engage in some activity, the probability of subsequent disillusionment with the activity increases significantly.
>
> (Middleton and Spanias, 1999, p. 69)

Whilst the Marsden pupils were focused on performance goals and extrinsic motivation, in the USA, the National Council of Teachers of Mathematics (NCTM) has recommended motivation goals alongside learning goals in an attempt to change the nature of pupil experience of school mathematics (Middleton and Spanias, 1999). In their research, Middleton and Spanias (1999) found that intrinsically motivated pupils tend to:

- be more persistent when they find work challenging;
- spend more time on tasks;
- use more complex processing and monitor their comprehension;
- select more challenging tasks;

- employ greater creativity; and
- take risks.

Stipek *et al.* (1998) found that if pupils are offered tasks with which they could persist they gained greater enjoyment. This enjoyment was associated with:

> longer persistence on tasks, greater use of active problem-solving strategies, more intense and greater creativity, and cognitive flexibility.
>
> (Stipek *et al.*, 1998, p. 467)

Duffield, Allan, Turner and Morris (2000) believe that the concentration on raising standards is leading teachers and educators away from the vital issue of learning and argue that the assumptions about improvements in schools take little account of how pupils view their experiences or how they construct their identities as learners. Their research on groups of 13–14 years olds in Scottish secondary schools found that pupils in their study, like the Marsden pupils, gave accounts of being extrinsically motivated and having instrumental goals.

Pollard *et al.* (2000) found that primary school pupils were unlikely to be intrinsically motivated and had an instrumental view of learning. They suggested that:

> the structured pursuit of higher standards in English and Mathematics may be reducing the ability of many children to see themselves as self-motivating, independent problem solvers taking an intrinsic pleasure in learning and capable of reflecting on how and why they learn.
>
> (Pollard *et al.*, 2000, p. xiii)

Any system of rewards, such as the one used at Marsden, requires that pupils have performance goals rather than learning goals, external motivation rather than internal motivation and that they accept external authority over internal authority. If the pupils accepted this system, which the Marsden pupils appeared to do, then the system itself was constantly reinforcing the importance of external forms of power over internal forms of power by the teacher being the only recognised judge of pupil success.

Implications

In order to be positioned as a successful learner of mathematics the pupils at Marsden Middle School only had to demonstrate that they could do the mathematics work correctly. It is easy to see how tenuous this position might be for their learning. If on one day a pupil got all their work correct they might be viewed as successful whilst on the next they could get the work wrong. Are they then immediately an unsuccessful learner? What do they perceive their position to be?

Performance goals and extrinsic motivation influenced the positional identities of the Marsden pupils with the support of the results of summative assessment. In order for pupils to develop both learning goals and intrinsic motivation it seems necessary to use a form of assessment other than summative. Indeed there has been some interest in the UK in different forms of formative assessment that could be used by teachers. A study reported by Lee (2001) showed that teachers who used formative assessment and focused on learning in the classroom rather than results, found the pupils 'were much better prepared to take the statutory tests in their stride' (Lee, 2001, p. 41). Formative assessment as described by Lee tends to be of a much more informal nature and becomes part of everyday life. The pupils are encouraged to discuss their answers and the processes they have used. All comments are open to discussion but are not labelled right or wrong.

If pupils are to be encouraged to think mathematically and to develop learning goals rather than performance goals then these findings suggest that the type of summative assessment experienced by the Marsden pupils is not appropriate. Indeed Pollard *et al.* (2000) go further and suggest that if this type of assessment persists then pupils will become not more but less interested in doing mathematics.

Some readers may think this situation does not occur in their classrooms. Without listening to pupils one cannot be sure how they perceive what is going on in the classroom or how they view their positioning as a learner of mathematics.

Cullingford (1991) warned that adult egotism leads to 'an unexamined assumption that children do not really know what they think' (ibid., p. 6) and that 'what children say is the clearest and most revealing insight into their minds' (op. cit. p. 8).

Rudduck (1996) held a similar opinion and felt that what pupils tell us:

> provides an important – perhaps the most important – foundation for thinking about ways of improving schools.
>
> (Rudduck, 1996, p. 1)

It is important that teachers of mathematics consider what they are trying to achieve for the learners with whom they work. Do they want learners simply to be capable of reproducing techniques and developing skills that will enable them to get correct answers? Or do they want independent thinkers who can solve problems and see a variety of ways of reaching a solution? It seems that many pupils may be in the position of the Marsden pupils, being required to produce the right answers to particular questions.

It is time for teachers and policy makers to start **listening to pupils** and working with them to support their learning of mathematics and improve the environment in which they learn. Connor summed up the situation of the Marsden pupils when he said:

> Maths lessons is all sums and hard stuff isn't it. It's not something you'd enjoy.
> (Set 2)

References

Boaler, J. (1997). *Experiencing School Mathematics Teaching Styles, Sex and Setting*, Open University Press, Buckingham.

Cullingford, C. (1991). *The Inner World of the School: Children's Ideas about School*, Cassell, London.

Duffield, J., Allan, J., Turner, E. and Morris, B. (2000). Pupils' voices on achievement: An alternative to the standards agenda. *Cambridge Journal of Education*, **30**(2), pp. 263–274.

Glaser, B. and Strauss, A. (1967). *The Discovery of Grounded Theory*, Aldine, New York.

Holland, D., Lachicotte, W., Skinner, D. and Cain, C. (2001). *Identity and Agency in Cultural Worlds*, Harvard University Press, Cambridge, MA.

Lee, C. (2001). Using assessment for effective learning. *Mathematics Teaching*, 175, pp. 40–43.

Middleton, J. A. and Spanias, P. A. (1999). Motivation for achievement in mathematics: Findings, generalisations, and criticisms of the research. *Journal for Research in Mathematics Education*, January, pp. 65–88.

Pollard, A. and Triggs, P. with Broadfoot, P., McNess, E. and Osborn, M. (2000). *Changing Policy and Practice in Primary Education*, Continuum, London.

Povey, H. (1995). Ways of knowing of student and beginning mathematics teachers and their relevance to becoming a teacher working for change. Ph.D. thesis, University of Birmingham, School of Education.

Povey, H. and Burton, L. with Angier, C. and Boylan, M. (1999). Learners as authors in mathematics classrooms. In L. Burton (ed.) *Learning Mathematics: From Hierarchies to Networks*, Falmer Press, London.

Rudduck, J. (ed.) (1996). *School Improvement: What Can Pupils Tell Us?* David Fulton, London.

Stipek, D., Salmon, J. M., Givvin, K. B., Kazemi, E., Saxe, G. and MacGyvers, V. L. (1998). The value (and convergence) of practices suggested by motivation research and promoted by mathematics education reformers. *Journal for Research in Mathematics Education*, July, pp. 465–488.

Troyna, B. (1992). Ethnicity and the organisation of learning groups: A case study. *Educational Research*, **34**(1), pp. 45–55.

Wiliam, D. (2000). *Integrating Summative and Formative Functions of Assessment*. Keynote address to the European Association for Educational Assessment, Prague, November 2000.

Index